How to Use the Internet to Advertise, Promote, and Market Your Business or Website

With Little or No Money

Revised 2nd Edition
By Bru ___ C. Brown

How to Use the Internet to Advertise, Promote, and Market Your Business or Website — With Little or No Money REVISED 2nd Edition By Bruce C. Brown

Copyright © 2011 Atlantic Publishing Group, Inc.
1405 SW 6th Avenue • Ocala, Florida 34471 • Phone 800-814-1132 • Fax 352-622-1875
Web site: www.atlantic-pub.com • E-mail: sales@atlantic-pub.com
SAN Number: 268-1250

Brown, Bruce C. (Bruce Cameron), 1965-
  How to use the Internet to advertise, promote, and market your business or website-- with little or no money / by Bruce C. Brown. -- Rev. 2nd ed.
     p. cm.
  Includes bibliographical references and index.
  ISBN-13: 978-1-60138-440-9 (alk. paper)
  ISBN-10: 1-60138-440-8 (alk. paper)
  1. Internet marketing--Handbooks, manuals, etc. 2. Internet advertising--Handbooks, manuals, etc. 3. Web sites--Design--Handbooks, manuals, etc. 4. Electronic commerce--Handbooks, manuals, etc. I. Title.
  HF5415.1265.B765 2010
  658.8'72--dc22

                              2010051634

PROJECT MANAGERS: Erin Everhart & Shannon McCarthy
INTERIOR DESIGN: James Ryan Hamilton
PROOFREADER: Hayley Love • hloveunlimited@gmail.com
BACK/FRONT COVER DESIGN • Jackie Miller • millerjackiej@gmail.com

Printed on Recycled Paper

Printed in the United States

We recently lost our beloved pet "Bear," who was not only our best and dearest friend but also the "Vice President of Sunshine" here at Atlantic Publishing. He did not receive a salary but worked tirelessly 24 hours a day to please his parents. Bear was a rescue dog that turned around and showered myself, my wife Sherri, his grandparents  Jean, Bob, and Nancy and every person and animal he met (maybe not rabbits) with friendship and love. He made a lot of people smile every day.

We wanted you to know that a portion of the profits of this book will be donated to The Humane Society of the United States.   —*Douglas & Sherri Brown*

The human-animal bond is as old as human history. We cherish our animal companions for their unconditional affection and acceptance. We feel a thrill when we glimpse wild creatures in their natural habitat or in our own backyard.

Unfortunately, the human-animal bond has at times been weakened. Humans have exploited some animal species to the point of extinction.

The Humane Society of the United States makes a difference in the lives of animals here at home and worldwide. The HSUS is dedicated to creating a world where our relationship with animals is guided by compassion. We seek a truly humane society in which animals are respected for their intrinsic value, and where the human-animal bond is strong.

Want to help animals? We have plenty of suggestions. Adopt a pet from a local shelter,

join The Humane Society and be a part of our work to help companion animals and wildlife. You will be funding our educational, legislative, investigative, and outreach projects in the U.S. and across the globe.

Or perhaps you'd like to make a memorial donation in honor of a pet, friend, or relative? You can through our Kindred Spirits program. And if you'd like to contribute in a more structured way, our Planned Giving Office has suggestions about estate planning, annuities, and even gifts of stock that avoid capital gains taxes.

Maybe you have land that you would like to preserve as a lasting habitat for wildlife. Our Wildlife Land Trust can help you. Perhaps the land you want to share is a backyard— that's enough. Our Urban Wildlife Sanctuary Program will show you how to create a habitat for your wild neighbors.

So you see, it's easy to help animals. And The HSUS is here to help.

2100 L Street NW • Washington, DC 20037 • 202-452-1100
www.hsus.org

Dedication

This book is dedicated to my mother, Jean Ellsworth Brown, who has supported and stood beside me all of my life. Thank you for being there for me, forgiving my mistakes, encouraging me to succeed, and being there for me every time I needed you.

"Captain, I do not believe you realize the gravity of your situation."
— Spock

"Logic is the beginning of wisdom; not the end."
— Spock

"The best diplomat that I know is a fully-loaded phaser bank."
— Lt. Cdr. Montgomery Scott

CONTENTS

Chapter 6: Automation of Your Website   105

Chapter 7: E-mail Marketing   111

Chapter 9: Google AdSense   187

Chapter 10: Google Base and Google Product Search   205

Chapter 11: Blogs   217

Introduction

When I first wrote this book over four years ago, I had no idea that it would become a bestseller, receive numerous awards, and propel my career as an author and marketing consultant. Since the publication of that first edition, I wrote an additional ten books about Internet marketing and search engine marketing. Times have changed, and technology has advanced, so it is time to dust off this book and update key elements and topics to ensure it is still relevant today and captures the latest information.

To retain the competitive edge and marketing advantage in today's business environment, you must incorporate Internet marketing, Web presence, e-mail advertising, and other forms of e-commerce-driven marketing and sales campaigns. I wrote these same words five years ago, and they are truer today than they were back then. Internet use has expanded to every corner of the globe. Billions of dollars exchange hands over the Web, and the number of e-commerce-powered websites is staggering. A Web presence is an absolute must. This is no longer simply the case for online or storefront businesses; rather, this is now true for any type of business. When you want to research a product, read reviews, find restaurants, browse products, compare prices, and make purchasing decisions, you do not shop at five stores in town to compare; you do it online. The search engine is more powerful than ever. Who knew that Google would be king and other new powerful engines, such as Microsoft® Bing™ would become available?

The Internet allows you to promote, advertise, and market your business in a cost-efficient manner so that you can spend your money on other areas of your business. What other marketing tool do you have at your disposal where billions of people have the ability to reach out directly to your business or organization from anywhere in the world, where you have the capability of advertising to all of these potential clients for practically no cost or minimal capital investment?

In my series of books, I covered a wide variety of topics, such as search engine optimization, the use of blogs, social marketing, and pay-per-click marketing. I captured the very best of these free and low-cost marketing tools in this new edition, arming you with a handy reference you can use to harness the power of the Web — for little or no money. I said it in each of my previous books: You do not have to be an information technology specialist, webmaster, or marketing expert — this book will show you how you can master these no- and low-cost techniques. You do not need to possess a great deal of Web design knowledge or experience online to use the Internet in an effective manner that will push your business forward, increase sales, and promote your business and products to a global customer base. This book will help you maximize and harness the power of the Internet to promote and market your business and products at little or no cost. The concepts and steps outlined in this book are easy to implement and can be managed at the small-business level. This book is ideal for the small business owner who does not have an IT staff or a large marketing and promotion budget. It is perfect for sole proprietors and is also useful for large corporations seeking a lesson in the "back to basics" approach to low-cost marketing.

The bottom line is that you do not need a professional marketing firm to promote and market your online business; you can do it yourself and put the saved funds toward other business needs. This book provides you with all the industry secrets, practical knowledge, and time-tested methodology. It also includes numerous tricks of the trade to help ensure that your site ranks at the top of the search engines and will therefore generate money for you, grow your business, expand your customer base, and help you achieve online success. By implementing these procedures, you will reduce costs while increasing your online business sales and profits dramatically.

The concepts in this book are simple and will help you reach your current customers as well as find new customers in ways that you could not achieve before the advent of the Internet. Many of the advertising and promotional concepts outlined in this book will cost you little or nothing to implement, and in many cases you will see immediate and substantial results. In addition, it will provide you with additional tools, marketing suggestions, and other venues with which you can inexpensively expand your online business and increase customer visibility and profitability.

If you are the owner, proprietor, or manager of a traditional brick-and-mortar business, you need to tap into and harness the power and potential of the Internet. You will save the thousands of dollars in costs that before you spent sending out flyers, postcards, or other forms of offline or postal advertising. These antiquated methods only reach a small customer base, are costly to produce and distribute, and typically fail to generate the return required to break even. The explosive growth of e-mail marketing, blogs, websites, and social marketing sites has changed the landscape forever. This book will show you how you can use your website to (a) advertise current specials; (b) inform customers about what products or services are new and hot; (c) let your customers know how to find you by providing contact information and directions to your business; (d) provide your customers with additional information about your business, your products and services, and how to use your products; and, most importantly, (e) reach a potentially unlimited customer base at little or no cost and use social and viral marketing to generate new revenue streams.

No matter what type of business you have, the possibilities are endless when it comes to Internet advertising and online business promotional solutions. It is critical that you understand the concepts, rationale, and procedures for each solution or suggestion provided. This book will provide you with all the information you need to advertise on the Internet — with little or no money — so that you can successfully promote your online business or your traditional brick-and-mortar business.

This book is written for anyone who is considering designing and developing a website, whether they are a small business, large business, or sole proprietor. It is intended to act as a guide for anyone who is interested in making money, increasing website traffic, driving up revenue, and improving the financial posture of his or her organization through establishing a Web presence at little or no cost. Although this book is not an intense Web development guide, it will help you understand website design, search engine optimization, and other essential components of a website, as well as overall marketing campaigns. This will ensure that your website is highly effective, visible in search engines, and ultimately achieves your goals.

This completely revised second edition updates older content in the book and adds extensive new content designed to help you achieve online success. I am excited to update this book and hope that you find it as useful as others found it previously; here are just some of the awards the first version of this book won:

- The National 2007 Indie Excellence Book Awards Business Finalist

- 2007 Independent Publisher Book Awards Computer/Internet Bronze

- ForeWord Magazine's Book of the Year Awards Finalist

- USA Best Books Awards 2007 Business: Marketing & Advertising Finalist

- Library Journal: Best Business Book 2006 Marketing/Branding

The Internet is the ultimate marketing tool, giving you immediate access to billions of people worldwide. By having an online presence, you can take advantage of this marketplace for little or no investment. With the help of this book, both the novice and the expert can discover the easiest and least expensive ways to harness the power of the Internet to maximize search engine visibility and successfully promote themselves through websites, blogs, and social media.

CHAPTER 1

Developing a Successful Marketing Plan

Marketing and advertising a traditional business can be a costly venture. Postage and mailing costs are high, return rates on mailings are typically less than 1 percent of the total mailing, and most catalog and direct sales marketing techniques are considered successful if they merely break even. However, this is not the case with advertising your business and website on the Internet. Expanding your business to the Web exposes your products or services to a dramatically larger customer base; however, without proper advertising and marketing skills and techniques, few will ever find your website. You can advertise and market your website in this enormous marketplace at little or no cost using the techniques provided in this book. Internet marketing is more important than and has a higher return on investment (ROI) than any other form of advertising, including newspaper, television, and radio.

Every facet of business has been affected by the Internet. No matter what type of business you have, chances are you are going to want to use the Internet to promote your products and services. The Internet is not just for selling products online. Most people visit a Website to solve one or more of the following three basic fundamental problems:

- They want/need information.

- They want/need to make a purchase/donation.

- They want/need to be entertained.

The Internet is different from other mediums of advertising and marketing in several ways. Not only is the Internet a channel for communication, but it is also a channel for distribution and transactions. This is because consumers are able to get all the information that they need to make their purchases and their payments online — and companies are actually able to process those transactions. There is no other advertising medium that is able to accomplish all these goals at once. The Internet is able to meet the needs of people looking for product information in a way that other advertising mediums are unable to do. With so much interactive information, and with such a vast number of resources available at their fingertips, consumers are able to make informed and educated choices as to what they want to buy and how much they are willing to pay.

The other way that the Internet is significantly different from other marketing and advertising mediums is that it is full of multimedia-rich content such as images, videos, and flash animations. Consumers can interact with websites, and as a business owner, you can communicate with your customers. The Internet can be used for all types of interesting advertising techniques that leave the consumer with high-impact marketing images, including audio and visual. Some of the Internet marketing techniques that rely on multimedia include banner ads, interstitials, advertorials, and 3-D visions.

A sales and marketing kit will go hand-in-hand with the marketing strategy you develop. Assuming you are just starting on the road to developing your strategy, you will have to ask yourself some questions:

- Who or what are your target markets?

- In what ways do you plan on advertising and promoting your business?

- Are you going to have a central focus for your business promotion?

- What goals are you trying to reach with your plan?

- Are you highlighting your best assets, and what you can offer to your future clients?

- When you are approached with a potential client, what are your plans for responding to them? Do you have a clearly defined way that you would like to follow up? Through e-mail or phone is good, but can you visit their business in person?

- How will you be generating leads on new clients on a consistent basis? Are there resources you can use to build your clientele?

- Will you be keeping a record of how your advertising is working or not working for your business? What areas can be expanded, and what should be cut out?

People often try inaccurate methods of measuring the success of marketing. Increased sales, for instance, are how you measure the success of your sales, not the success of your marketing campaign. Likewise, increased brand awareness is a measure of the success of your brand agencies and media buyers. Customer satisfaction is a difficult thing to measure, and it only tells you how well your company is performing. Marketing metrics can generally be based upon scientific analysis. Marketing is about market development, the process of reaching out into new markets, and segments of products and services provided by your business. The objective of your marketing should always be, in the broad sense, to find and tap new markets and segments.

The measurement of marketing needs to be both concrete and objective. You need to evaluate how many new markets and segments you are able to add or strengthen over a period of time, tracking your efforts in an objective manner: mathematically, calculating the cost dollar for dollar. The type of advertising that works best for your company will depend upon numerous factors. In particular, you must take into consideration your target market. Who or what businesses will you target to get the best response? Will you stick to Internet advertising, or will that not be enough? The best approach for your business depends upon the precise nature of your target market, your ability to network and make connections, and how actively you want to go beyond your own network of contacts.

This chapter delves into overall business plans, whether traditional or online, and is a building block for a successful online business venture. A good marketing plan is critical for you to map out your future goals and achieve success. Writing a marketing plan is a fairly straightforward process that requires you to set clear objectives and determine how you will achieve them. A marketing plan must be achievable, realistic, cost-effective, measurable, and flexible. One of the main objectives in developing a marketing plan is to establish your budget. Your marketing plan may consist of the following:

- Market analysis
- Business objectives
- Marketing strategies
- Steps to achieving business objectives
- A realistic budget
- A realistic timeline

Performing a Market Analysis

You need to be flexible based on your budget, marketplace competition, business objectives, and both internal and external influences. Market analysis helps you determine if there is a need for your supplies or services. Understanding the marketplace, consumer desire for your products, and your competition will help you better understand how to establish a successful business in a competitive environment. If there is no need for your products, you will likely fail unless you establish your presence in the marketplace. Likewise, if there is a high level of competition, you must develop a marketing plan that allows you to compete in product, quality, availability, or price. Knowing the marketplace needs and how they are currently serviced is essential in developing your marketing plan. You cannot realistically expect customers to find you. If there is no demand or desire for your products or services, you will fail. Marketplace analysis must be done in advance to ensure there is a viable market for your products or services in the first place.

The following questions will help you perform a basic market analysis:

- What market am I trying to enter?
- What or who is my current competition?
- How successful is my competition?
- What is the market share for my competition?
- Is the market saturated or open?
- What is the market size? Is there room to grow?
- Is there stability in the market or is it volatile?
- How are my competitors marketing their goods or services?
- What do customers seek in regards to my products?
- What is most valuable to my customers?
- What are customers willing to pay for my products or services?
- What do I offer that my competition does not?
- What effect will the current economy have on my business goals?

You should analyze current or previous marketing strategies as well as those of your competition, both successful and unsuccessful. Understanding failure is as important as understanding success factors. These questions may help you analyze your potential for success in a competitive marketplace:

- Am I offering a new or unique product line or service?

- What marketing strategies have I used successfully? What was unsuccessful? Have I used online marketing in the past? What was the success rate or return on investment?

- Have I evaluated the results of previous marketing plans? What was the impact on sales?

- Are we currently using any strategies?

- What strategies are my competitors using?

- How much money is allotted in my current budget? How much am I currently spending? How much was my marketing budget in the past?

- Why would someone choose my product over my competition's?

- What do I do to distinguish myself from my competition?

- Why would someone trust me more than my competition?

- Who are my customers?

- Where do my customers come from?

You must perform what is known as primary and secondary research. Primary research includes phone interviews, telephone surveys, Web-based surveys, and focus groups. Primary research is the most current information available. Secondary research is data that has already been collected for other purposes but may assist you with your market research. Examples of secondary research may be found in journals, magazines, blogs, or other online resources.

Establishing Marketing Strategies

You must establish a clearly defined, written strategy and marketing plan for your online business. Consider all marketing strategies, and implement those that are most relevant to your business operations and offer the most potential for increased customer base and return on investment. Implement and evaluate your marketing strategy as it relates to achieving your corporate business objectives. Some marketing plans may take significant time and investment; think long-term, and do not be too quick to change your objectives because you are not meeting the goals in your specified timelines. Be flexible, but allow time for your marketing strategies to grow and mature. Your online marketing plan does not need to be overly complex. It should not be a time-consuming process, but it is important to map out your objectives, budget, and critical success factors so you can measure and evaluate your success in achieving them. An average marketing plan may be less than a couple of pages in length. It acts as a map for your company to achieve success on the Internet.

Media exposure is a key component in developing a successful marketing profile and strategy. Your customers will form their opinions, either positive or negative, based on what they hear and see in print, on television, on the radio, or on the Web. Recognizing the importance of media exposure and dedicating resources to promote your online business can boost the sales of your products or services. That positive media exposure is also a major step toward maintaining credibility in your online marketplace and channeling more traffic to your website.

Developing a tactical approach to media exposure should be part of your overall business objectives and marketing plan. There are several things you can do to promote your offline media exposure. These may include:

- Approaching your local chamber of commerce and requesting that they write a short article about you and your business. Even if you are an online-only business, local exposure is important. You can then take that article and publish it on your website as another promotional tool or use it in an online e-magazine, also known as e-zine, campaign.

- Offering to be a speaker at a seminar or lead a workshop in your area of expertise. This is a great way to gain media exposure that is incredibly positive and community-oriented, thus earning you credibility and trust among potential clients. Circulate your URL and business information at the seminar. Put your website URL on everything you distribute: flyers, promotional items, business cards, and letterheads.

- Following up on any correspondence or phone calls from the media with a letter or phone call. Make sure to leave your website URL on their voicemail. This strategy will earn you a reputation as a conscientious, courteous entrepreneur with the media.

Share your knowledge by writing articles and professional opinions for online publications, and upload them to automated e-zine syndication sites. These syndication sites are perfect for having immediate hotlinks back to your website and other specific landing pages. Remember to include your e-mail or picture in the byline as well as brief biographical information on yourself and your business. The more exposure you generate, the more successful your business will become. Give permission to authors and editors to use your articles in their books, magazines, or other publications, and be sure to require them to include a corporate biography and contact information in exchange for the permission.

Develop tactics to make media exposure and coverage work for you. Make media friends wherever and whenever the opportunities present themselves, all in an effort to increase media awareness and promote public relations for your business. You have to earn and work for media exposure, but the time and effort you expend will be your investment in having a positive public profile both online and offline. Most columnists give their e-mail address in their byline or at the conclusion of their articles. Send them notes with your comments and views while offering your expertise as a source for future quotes. Optimize your media exposure whenever possible; the returns for your business will be substantial.

Gaining the trust of your customers is extremely critical in developing a continuing relationship that rewards your online business with repeat customer sales. The one-time sale may boost your immediate sales numbers, but returning customers are what take your business from mediocre to fantastic profits. Your goal is to build quality customer relationships and then maintain them.

Media exposure, both online and offline, opens the door to a potentially long-term relationship with customers by using implied third-party credibility. Recognition from a credible media source legitimizes you as an expert in your field. Once you attract customers, you still have to deliver your goods and/or services and ensure that the customer is completely satisfied. One of the major advantages of using Google™ marketing tools, for instance, is that the Google name is already equated with trust. Google's reputation is superior, and you can leverage that reputation and trust in your marketing campaigns.

Increasing Your Public Profile

The more positive your public profile, the more success you will have both online and offline. This is how you gain credibility with the public and with your customers. Your public profile is your trademark for success and profits, and your online profile and business rating are critically important in how customers perceive you. Local and state Better Business Bureaus are great organizations to join to obtain positive ratings. Other online business profile ratings services worth considering are ResellerRatings (**www.resellerratings.com**), Epinions (**www.epinions.com**), and Consumer Reports® (**www.consumerreports.org**). Do not underestimate the impact of a review of your business and/or products and services. You must ensure 100 percent customer satisfaction in both service and product quality to ensure you garner only positive reviews for you and your company.

Positioning yourself and becoming an expert in your market takes time, patience, and personal confidence. Just knowing the advantages of effective marketing is half the battle. The combination of media and marketing communicates the benefits and unique aspects of your business, which in turn drives customers to your website. When you establish yourself as an expert in your market, others will be drawn to you for advice, sponsorship, professional opinions, and branding — all of which will have dramatic, positive impacts on your online business.

When it comes to sharing your expertise, your goal should be to publish for free, thereby allowing many other organizations, news services, and other publications to distribute your article in return for links back to your website and direct product promotions to thousands of potential new customers. There are ways that you can publish a full-page ad promoting yourself and your business without spending a dime. Contact editors of publications and offer them your press release to add content to their next publication. Many editors are looking for useful and relevant content so they can meet deadlines. Take advantage of this opportunity and create the perfect article for publication. Always ensure that you require a corporate biography and full contact information to be published with your articles. You should target newspapers, magazines, newsletters, websites, and e-zines.

CHAPTER 2

Website Branding

Branding is something that is talked about frequently in the world of marketing and advertising, both on and off the Internet. But just what is this "branding" all about? In a nutshell, branding is when you give your business or product a unique identity by using one or more of a combination of (a) a design, (b) a name, (c) a sign or symbol, or (d) a specific term. It is this "brand" that will make you stand out among the competition and make your customers remember who you are. Branding is a promise, a pledge of quality. It is an image. It is the essence of a product, including why it is great and how it is better than all competing products. It is a combination of words and letters, symbols, and colors. Branding is a way to uniquely identify your product or your business so that you stand out among the competition. The information in this chapter can be applied to new businesses that are developing a brand for the first time, as well as already-established businesses that need a facelift.

There are many companies, both online and offline, that successfully use branding so that you can easily identify them over their competitors. Some of these companies that successfully use branding are Walmart, IBM, The Gap, Travelocity, eBay, Amazon, and Microsoft. These names are trusted among consumers throughout the world. With the huge increase in business activity conducted on the Internet, more companies now use branding to help customers find them and remember who they are. When it comes to your own business, you may wish to use branding in such a way that your service or product stands out among the many Internet websites that are all vying for attention and customers.

Branding is a mixture of creativity and the type of relationship that you strive to establish with your customers. The creative part of branding is all about the logo or other branding that you choose to use and the way that you advertise both on and off the Internet. The relationship part of branding is all about the way you make your customer feel when they come to your website. You want your customers to feel that they can trust you and your products or services so that they generate sales for your business. In summary, branding is all about:

- How your product or service looks when it is on a website or on a shelf in a traditional store

- How your customers feel when they access your website

- How you handle customer orders

- The credibility and trust that you earn with your customers using a combination of branding and successful Internet marketing

Developing your own branding for your business is an important step when it comes to the success of your company. This means that you need to spend quality time coming up with the right branding for your products and services.

Developing or Reinventing a Company Image

When you are developing or reinventing a company image, it means that you will be creating a "personality" for your company with which customers can identify and want to do business. The personality of your company will be a combination of many things, such as the facts of your business, the goals of your business, the style of advertising that you choose to use, and the history of your business. All these elements tie together to leave a lasting impression on your customers that can make the difference between the success of your business or its failure. You want to leave a positive and lasting impression on the public and your potential customers.

Many large and successful companies work hard to develop their company image. Part of this image is having a logo, or brand, with which customers identify. McDonald's has a successful logo that people all over the world identify with: Ronald McDonald and the golden arches. Some of the most effective logos are by the following companies: Coca-Cola, Sony, Google, Dell, Yahoo!, and America Online. These companies maintain corporate images that appeal to customers and help generate large sales figures each year.

Developing your company image means that you need to identify many aspects of your business, including

- Knowing just who your target market is and how to reach them

- Developing a company image that is constant and revolves around your target market.

How to determine your target market

It is important that you define your target market. You need to know who you are trying to reach as customers and why you are trying to reach them. From the first day that you launch your business, you need to know who your customers are and who you want them to be. Many businesses make the mistake of not focusing on a specific market segment. This means that they waste much time and money with advertising campaigns trying to attract customers that will probably never buy from them.

When you are developing your company image, you need to focus your time, energy, and money on the portion of the market that you know will be the most likely to buy your product or service. There are certain things that you need to identify about your customers so that you can attract the right kind of sales to your business. Some of the things that you need to know about your potential customers include:

- The buying habits of your customers

- The type of lifestyle that your customers have, including their age, sex, and marital status

- Where your customers live and what types of jobs they have

- What type of budget your customers have

- What customers like and do not like about your product or service

- What customers like and do not like about your competitor's product or service

Any information you gather about your potential customers and your target market will be a big factor in the success of your business.

The importance of your business name

You might think that a name is just a name and that it will have little impact on the success of your business. This is the mistake that many businesses make as they come up with a name for their companies. What you call your company can be very important in providing you with a business identity that is strong and will leave a lasting impact. You want to choose a business name that is going to be a reflection of what your product or service is all about. If you choose a name for your business that is too unique and creative, you may find that customers have a harder time finding you on the Internet or associating your name with your products or services. The same theory applies to your domain name selection on the Web — keep it relevant to the business, tied to the business name, and easy to remember.

Another thing that you need to keep in mind when you are choosing a name for your business is that this name will be your first contact with your customers. The first impression that you present to your customers can often be a lasting one. If you have a business that is selling scrapbook products, you will want to have a business name that lets customers know that your business is about scrapbooks. For example, "Creative Scrapbooks" lets customers find you easily on the Internet and describes the product that you are selling. A name such as "Creative Crafts" will not be as definitive when it comes to the core of what your business is all about. Some people choose to name a business after themselves, and although this may work for companies that already have an established presence, it will not work well if you are just starting your company, unless you include mention of the product that you are selling as well.

An example of a business that includes your name would be "Carter's Creative Scrapbooks." This not only uses your personal name, but it also lets your customers know what your business is selling. There are some benefits that come from using your name in your business title, such as the following:

- Customers will be able to associate your personal name, corporate name, and your product together.

- You will become better known in the business community, both online and offline.

- Your credit rating may be higher and stronger when your personal name is associated with your business. Keep in mind that if your business is not successful, your credit rating may also pay the price. This is why many people, when they are first establishing a new business, choose to keep their personal finances separate from their business finances, which is typically recommended.

You should research the name you are considering carefully before finalizing and selecting it as your business identity. You need to make sure that you are

not infringing on another company name, or you may find yourself faced with a lawsuit in the future.

How to choose your company logo

The logo that you choose for your company will be how you are visually identified in the business world. There are many companies that have logos that are instantly recognized around the world, such as McDonald's and Tommy Hilfiger. These logos help promote the corporate image and increase product recognition and profitability, both on and off the Internet.

You may want to choose a logo that not only identifies your business but that also ties your product to a symbol or image. If your product is scrapbooks, you may want to include an image of a scrapbook in your logo. This symbolic identification can be a big advantage when it comes to establishing yourself in your target market as an emerging corporate entity. You may wish to draft a mission or purpose statement to help you design your corporate logo.

When it comes to creating your company logo, there are some things that you should keep in mind:

- Your logo should be functional and multi-purposed, and it should work well in color, in black and white, printed, on letterhead, or on vehicles.

- Make sure that your business logo is tasteful and not offensive in any way.

- Try to make your logo as original and creative as possible without copying some of the other logos that fall into your target market.

- Many times, simplicity is the best rule to follow. You want to leave a clear and precise image with your customers — and potential customers — that will allow you to stand out from the rest of the competition. Studies show that customers are more able to remember companies that have simple logos that they can identify.

- Make sure that the logo you choose for your business has a marketable value. This means that you need to have a logo that you can use for the sale of your product or service, for advertising purposes, and for any future public relations.

- Use vector graphics, which can be resized easily without distortion.

- Protect your logo. You may find details at the U.S. Patent and Trademark Office (**www.uspto.gov**).

When you are ready to create your company logo, remember that simplicity and tastefulness go a long way, including the colors that you use, the shape and dimensions of the logo, and the typeface on the logo. You will want a logo that performs and looks good on the Internet. The color of your logo will often convey a certain message to the public, and you want to choose colors that send a clear message to your customers. As a general rule, dark colors are usually associated with conservative companies that are selling serious and functional products, while companies that are selling unique and fun products tend to choose logo colors that are bright. If you are selling scrapbooks, you will want to use bright and fun colors to get your message of creativity across to your customers.

Although the shape of your company logo may seem to be a small thing, just look at the many logos out there and the shapes to which they conform. Straight-edged logos are often used by more conservative companies, while circular logos are seen more often for businesses that sell unique and creative products. Typeface follows the same rules of convention. You can use typeface that is conservative, modern, or classic. You may want to come up with your own typeface that is unique to your company and logo. If you consider this route, you will want to make sure that you trademark it for your exclusive use. No matter what method you choose to use for finding the right typeface for your logo, make sure that the letter characters match the logo that you choose. Your company logo is a cornerstone of corporate branding, and the investment spent carefully designing a logo will reap dividends with branding, corporate identification, and product familiarity.

Branding is an important step to developing a successful business, both on and off the Internet. You will want to make sure that the impression that your company presents to the public is as precise as possible and one that customers will remember when they are looking for the product or service that you are selling. You want to communicate with your target market in such a way that they know who you are, that they trust you, and that they keep coming back time and time again.

Branding has one aim: to earn the trust of your customers so that they buy from you, buy repeatedly from you, and refer you to family and friends. You will want to develop a brand for your business website that lets your customers quickly recognize who you are and the products or services you sell. Brand recognition should be a direct reflection of the products and services that you are selling as well as the personal style of your business. There are different methods that you can infuse into your branding marketing strategy so you can gain that all-important recognition for your business:

- **Packaging that is creative**. You want to create packaging for your products that can be easily identified by your customers and that they will remember when they see your product.

- **Communication that is visual**. You want to create a logo for your business that can be displayed on the packaging of your products or that symbolizes the services that you are selling. This type of visual communication with your customers will help them to recognize your business in an instant. Not only should your logo be displayed on your packaging, it should also display prominently on your business cards, catalogs, letterhead, brochures, and any other type of media that you use for the marketing of your business.

- **Advertising campaigns that boost your business**. Take every opportunity to expose your business to all kinds of media exposure. You want to encourage and improve your company profile whenever you can so that customers trust and rely on you and your products. Inclusion of a recognizable logo is extremely important in a healthy and profitable e-mail marketing campaign.

The bottom line is that branding allows you to sell your products or services to customers in a way that makes you stand out from the crowd of competitors, each of whom are looking for their share of Internet business.

Other consideration when naming your business

You will need a name that sets you apart from others in the in your industry. Do not choose a name that is already out there. Make sure your name is different but still easy for people to remember. Once you find a perfect name, you will need to use that in branding your business with a distinctive image, like a logo and slogan that will be remembered. Steer away from anything overly cheesy. Your slogan should express your business image. Naming your business may be more complicated than it sounds. Much time and effort will go into finding the perfect name, and there may be some things that you have not thought of that will play a major role in choosing your website business name. It will need to be memorable and also represent your business properly. There are also legal matters that need to be considered during the naming process. In small business, your name can play a big part in your success. A perfect business name can make the difference between your business being talked about or being forgotten in the shuffle. In coming up with your business name, you will need to put in considerable effort, maybe even as much as you did in planning for your business and how you were going to put your ideas into action. Your name should reflect your business purpose, your vision, and the specialties that your business will provide customers.

Everyone has ideas about what makes a successful name. Some are more straightforward than others. Some people might say the best names for businesses are not even real words at all. These people believe that such names can be remembered much more easily than conventional names like "Sally's Website Design Business." Some experts think this idea is genius, while others think it is less than perfect. Some believe that people like to be able to relate to words and understand them and that by extension, real words are more effective.

Take time and brainstorm adjectives that you want to be associated with your business. These adjectives will be able to spark inspiration for you to come up with unique but identifiable names. An example of using this technique would be a store that offers handspun rugs and one-of-a-kind home furnishings. The generic name for such a place could be called "Rug and Home Shop." But an even better name that evokes the senses would be "Handspun Home." It conveys the message that what is inside is unique and has a specialty shop atmosphere. Try thinking about what adjectives convey what you want your business to be.

When you are ready to start brainstorming, look everywhere you see words. Try your dictionary, magazines, and newspapers. Enlist the help of friends and family who will understand your vision and be able to help you come up with some key words and phrases that will help. When naming firms start working on a business name, they start out with a list of anywhere from 500 to 1,000 names. Do not worry; you should not need to come up with that many. After all, you understand your business vision better than any strangers would. A list of 25 names would be a good start. Critique each name carefully, one at a time. You will probably lose half of the list after one sweep.

Since your business will be global from the beginning through the World Wide Web, you may want to make sure your name will not offend someone who speaks another language or lives in a different culture. Also, assuming your business name will be in the phone book, you might choose to have a name that is closer to the beginning of the alphabet. Even though it is not recommended, that is why some businesses have names such as "AAA Refrigerator Company," because it will put them first in the phone book.

When you are deciding on your business name, you should also look at your immediate competition. You do not want a name that is very similar to other businesses in your area of expertise. Trademarking is another issue that will come into play when choosing your name. Your business name should be screened in the trademark database to see whether it is already taken. You can even go to a search engine and type in your prospective business name and see how many true matches are returned. This can eliminate the ones that should be screened from the ones that are obviously already taken. If you find a few matches for your name, do not assume that the name is already trademarked. Some people never register their business names, and you can go ahead and use the name that you have your heart set on. That should be a lesson as to why you should trademark your business name once it is chosen — someone might come up with the name later and trademark it.

There are attorneys who specialize in trademarks who can help if you need legal guidance. If you are going it alone in the trademarking process, you can conduct your own trademark search online through the United States Patent and Trademark Office (USPTO) website (**www.uspto.gov**). Also, you can search the Internet for any businesses that may not be trademarked but use the business name that you want to use. Checking through domain name registers like GoDaddy® (**www.godaddy.com**) can give you a good idea as to whether your name is being used by another business. Keep in mind that if a name you want is being used by someone else's business, you could possibly still use it.

You could only end up with a few names that meet all the requirements and are available to be used. If you have a particular affinity for a name, then go with it if it meets all the standards. If you like it, chances are other people will also. If you are stuck on a few names, you can try to research within your city to see what people outside your family and friends think about your potential business names. If you have a design that fits in better with one name than the other, you may choose that one because it will incorporate well with the logo.

The last legal bit of naming bears mentioning. A DBA, also known as "doing business as," is something you may have to file. If your business is a sole proprietorship or a partnership, you will need to file a DBA. This could be required at various levels, including your county, city, or state. Each state is different when it comes to DBAs. It may be as simple as going in and paying a small fee. Other states can be more complex. Check with your local business association or government offices to get the most accurate information for your place of business.

Personality in branding

Confidence when meeting potential customers is crucial to gaining a client's trust in your abilities. If you come across as meek and unsure of yourself, they will be unsure of you also. Be positive of your skills, and do not be afraid to brag about what you are capable of. Projecting an assertive, self-assured front will make clients feel that you are more than competent to handle their needs.

Be accessible to your new customers. Answer calls or e-mails promptly. If you leave your customers waiting for days, they may choose someone else in the time that it takes for you to get back to them. This is why it is important to share different ways of communicating with you when giving out your information. Some people may prefer to speak with you over the phone instead of dealing with e-mail. If a potential client is not Internet savvy, he or she may not have the access or knowledge to reach you by your e-mail. Provide a phone number that will allow clients or customers to reach you.

Having strong references that you can supply to clients will give them assurance that you are trustworthy and can deliver a quality product. By offering a better service to clients than your competition, you will pull in more business. Whatever your competition is doing, find out how you do it better and stress that to potential customers. Do not criticize your competition, but find a way to politely state how you can offer a better service. Keeping the conversation on your services and your strengths will increase your business.

Whenever you offer quality work on a consistent basis, others will take notice. Performing to the best of your ability on every single project will help you gain a winning reputation. Let your work speak for itself. If you are not happy with work you do, then fix it so it becomes something you are proud of.

Moving with the times

Keep an eye on the industry. New gadgets and techniques are constantly emerging, and you want to be on the cutting edge of your field. This will keep you abreast of new trends that are hot at the moment and give you some creative inspiration. What is your competition doing? Do they have a new service that you can also offer your clients? Start with trade magazines or by subscribing to a news feed that is centered on your industry.

Become visible in your particular business or industry. Attend trade shows or conferences that can also offer some courses and workshops to improve your resume and skills. Just as you need to be visible, you also need to start making contacts with others in the field. Befriend the competition. Having other people you know in your field will open doors for you that otherwise would have been unknown. Having someone who is more experienced and established in the business on your side will give you a mentor to go to with questions. Advice from someone who has been in your position is a wonderful learning tool. Name recognition and reputations are important, no matter what line of business you are in. Having a brand name, trademark, or image that is recognizable by others as representing a company that stands for honesty, value, and excellent customer service is very important in a competitive marketplace.

CHAPTER 3

Generating Website Traffic — Proven Online and Offline Techniques

O ne of the primary goals of your online business venture will be to obtain the highest search engine rankings possible. To be successful in your advertising and marketing strategies, you need to be visible, and if you are visible, you will receive more visitors to your site. Website traffic is determined by the number of visitors you garner and the number of pages they visit. Website traffic is measured to see the popularity of websites and individual pages or sections within a site. Most quality Web hosting companies provide you with detailed Web statistical analysis and monitoring tools as part of a basic Web hosting package.

Your website traffic can be analyzed by viewing the statistics found in the Web server log file or using website traffic analysis programs. Any quality Web hosting company will provide free, detailed statistics for website traffic. There are many ways to increase your website traffic, all leading to greater sales and profit potentials. This chapter will discuss a variety of options you can utilize that will lead to increased website traffic.

Proven Techniques for Generating Website Traffic

The following proven techniques may be employed to increase website traffic.

- Create a "What's New" or "New Products" page. Site visitors like to see what is new, trendy, or just released. Make it easy for them.

- Establish a promotion program. You can offer free products, trial samples, or discount coupons. Everyone loves a bargain, so provide this for your customers.

- Establish a contest. Create an online contest to promote anything. Be creative; you do not have to market your products in a contest. The main goal is to draw visitors.

- Add content-relevant professional articles, news events, press releases, or other topics of interest on a daily basis to draw visitors back to your site. Fresh material ensures that visitors will keep coming back and not grow bored with your site.

- Establish a viral marketing campaign or embed viral marketing techniques into your current advertising programs or e-zines. Viral marketing incorporates such things as a "forward to a friend" link within the advertisement. In theory, if many people forward to many more friends, it will spread like a virus and eventually reach many potential customers.

- Use signature files with all e-mail accounts. Signature files are basically business cards embedded within e-mail, so send your business card to all your e-mail recipients. Signature files are included with every e-mail you send out and can contain all contact information, including business name and website URL. Signature files can be created in all e-mail applications.

- Start an affiliate program and market it. Include your affiliate information in e-mails, newsletters, e-zines, and on websites to promote your program. A successful affiliate program will generate a significant increase in website traffic. For an example of a highly effective affiliate campaign, visit Atlantic Publishing Group's website (**www. atlantic-pub.com/affiliate.htm**).

- Include your website URL on everything, such as business cards, letterhead, promotional items, and e-mails.

- Win some awards for your website. There are quite a few award sites that are nothing more than link exchange factories, but there are some reputable award sites.

- Everyone loves search engines, so put Google right on your website. Simply visit Google (**www.google.com**) to add a free search feature to your website. This is a tool that site visitors will love.

- Implement Google AdSense on your website to increase revenue and traffic.

- Implement Google AdWords to increase website traffic and generate sales revenue.

- Put your website URL on your business card.

- Register your site with online directories relevant to your content.

- Write free articles and submit them to other newsletters.

- Post often on content-related forums and message boards, and post your website URL with each entry.

- Submit content often to relevant e-mail discussion groups, and post your website URL with each entry.

- Establish links from other sites to yours. Create a "Links" page or directory on your website, and offer your visitors a reciprocal link to your site for adding a link to your site on theirs.

While you do not have to follow all of these tips, simply incorporating a handful of these strategies in your online advertising and marketing campaign will prove extremely beneficial.

Use Press Releases to Generate Website Traffic

An online press release is part of the online medium of communication, and online communication is all about timing. Your press release, whether printed and faxed or online, is one method of communicating with your customers and your industry. It is up to you to make the most of a press release so that it has as much impact as possible.

Most companies use press releases to alert the public about a new product or service they offer. These press releases, while informative, tend to be somewhat dry, and consumers typically skim over them, sometimes missing the key points. The bottom line is that if it is not newsworthy, then you will not be covered by the media. That said, a press release promoting specific events, specials, or newsworthy items can be quite effective.

As an alternative to a written press release, you could try a multimedia approach. If you are giving a live press release, you can incorporate the audio or video files onto your website, either to complement a written press release or replace it altogether. It is highly recommended that you have a media section on your website to serve reporters, columnists, producers, and editors with your latest press release information. Many people find listening to an audio clip or watching a video clip preferable to reading a written press release. There is so much written on the Internet that trying another medium to get your message across could be just the boost your company needs. You should also think of other website owners as another form of a media channel, since everyone is looking for fresh content and expert advice.

Consider using an online press release service, such as PRWeb® (**www.prweb. com**), to generate successful media exposure for your online business. This free service is another tool you can use to distribute your press release information to thousands of potential new customers or clients.

Keep in mind the value of using highly relevant keywords often within the content of your online press release in order to use the benefits of search engine optimization (SEO), which is how you improve your site's visibility. Including live links within your online press release is another way to ensure increased media coverage. Linking to relevant websites increases the credibility and functionality of your online business.

Make sure that you give your customers a reason to visit your site, spend time browsing it, interact with it, and most importantly, return to it. Offer incentives by showcasing featured products or promotions, and use creative Internet tools, such as video and audio, to create an interactive experience. You can also import video clips from promotional products, CDs/DVDs, or create your own video clips and add them to your website.

Publishing Articles to Generate Website Traffic

Writing articles is amazingly effective for generating website traffic and increasing your ranking in search engines because you can embed links to your site into articles, which may be published and re-published on several websites. The viral effect of this generates quality inbound links, promotes awareness of your website, and increases your reputation as an expert in your specialty, since you are publishing articles on the subject. Embed keywords into your article, as well as links to your website. Keep your articles fairly short, generally no more than 750 words. If you need to write longer, break the content up into a series of articles. Draw readers to your website by giving them enough information to at least instill an interest in visiting your website.

For all articles, ensure that you include a biography that includes contact information and information about your experience, education, company, and products, as well as links to your website. Establish yourself as an industry expert, and you will be recognized as one by your peers. Below are the most popular free article-listing websites. When you do submit your article, send it to each of the following:

- Article Alley (**www.articlealley.com**)

- Ezine Articles (**www.ezinearticles.com**)

- ArticleCity (**www.articlecity.com**)

- eArticlesOnline (**www.earticlesonline.com**)

- Article Cache (**www.articlecache.com**)

- GoArticles (**www.goarticles.com**)

You must first visit these sites and sign up as an author, which will provide you with an account login and simple instructions to publish your articles. It could not be easier or more effective. Note that most of these sites have an approval process to ensure that your article meets their content standards.

Publish Testimonials on Your Website

Using customer testimonials is a good way to promote the quality and reliability of your website and, more importantly, promote your products or services. This is an amazingly effective tactic. The media coverage you get is a subtle, third-party referral to you. However, the strongest, most effective sales assistance comes from direct customer testimonials. It is highly recommended that you use audio and video testimonials as well as printed quotes on your website. You should include your customer's name, e-mail address, and Web address with each unsolicited testimonial to increase believability. No matter how flashy or impressive your website may look, it is customer service, satisfaction, and reliability that keep customers coming back.

Link Exchanges and Website Traffic

A link exchange is when two or more websites exchange links and point to each other. Be careful here — do not sign up with link farms, which do nothing more than exchange links with thousands of websites. Link exchanges can be effective when they are selective, relative, and used in moderation. It is not uncommon for sites to establish a "Link With Us" page, such as the one at the Atlantic Publishing Group website (**www.atlantic-pub.com/links.htm**).

Link exchanges can be done manually or automatically, but only the manual method is recommended to ensure strict quality control over who you link with. Be selective, and ensure that you get a quality reciprocal link. For example, if you sell books about how to become a home inspector, linking to the state regulations on home inspection or websites with hurricane standards in the state of Florida is fine. Also, you may want to link with companies who provide related services and supplies, such as hurricane shutters and roofing. If you link to companies that sell flowers, Web hosting, or shoes, you may be penalized by search engines because these topics are not relevant to your content.

A quick search on the Internet reveals many companies you can use for paid link exchange programs, but it is recommended that you stay away from them all. Yes, manual links take some labor to create, and you may only add a link or two a week. This may also require you to initiate the link request with relevant companies you want to exchange links with, but the benefits are well worth the time investment.

When you initiate a link request, ask for the exchange in a natural e-mail; do not use a canned template, which sounds like a robot is asking for the exchange. You will find few responses to this.

Using Web Directories to Generate Website Traffic

A Web directory is simply an organized cataloging of websites by subject. The best examples of this are the Open Directory Project (**www.dmoz.org**) and the Yahoo!® Directory (**http://dir.yahoo.com**), which is also the largest human-maintained Web directory. You should submit your website to Web directories. Most provide you with a simple "Add URL" link (such as **www.dmoz.org/ add.html** and **https://ecom.yahoo.com/dir/submit/intro**).

While Web directories are often free, some, such as Yahoo!'s, will charge you for the listing. When adding your website to directories, embed key words or key phrases into your title and description so your website shows up in various searches. There are programs that can automate this process for you, such as SubmitEaze (**www.submiteaze.com**).

CHAPTER 4

Search Engine Optimization

Search engine optimization (SEO) is one of the proven methods that you can use to push up the ranking of your website within your target market on the Internet by using keywords that are relevant and appropriate to the product or services you offer. To achieve success with major search engines, you must achieve high rankings in search results. One of the most critical steps in designing and implementing a successful online marketing campaign is to invest in an SEO plan for your website to ensure that it is designed to work effectively with all major search engines. SEO should be an ongoing process that you consistently reevaluate on a periodic basis. There are over two billion Web pages on the Internet, meaning that there are many websites that are directly competing with yours for potential customers. You need to take realistic, time-proven measures to ensure that your online business is noticed and obtains search engine rankings that will deliver the results you desire.

When developing keywords for your website, focus on the content on each Web page, and strive to include at least 200 content-related words on the pages of your site. Integrate your keywords into the content you place on each page, but be cautious of "keyword stuffing," which is where you overload the pages with keywords. Doing so may result in your site being blacklisted from major search engines.

Google uses PageRank™, which measures the quality of a Web page based on the incoming and outgoing links from that page. This has led to a huge increase in the emphasis on links to and from websites in efforts to increase PageRank scores. Google has since changed its algorithm to eliminate links it deems low in quality, lacking Web content, or being topically irrelevant. PageRank is not just based upon the total number of inbound links. PageRank considers some links more important than others; therefore, all links are not equal. The ranking algorithm for Google is complicated, but in general, a higher PageRank score equates to better search engine placement in the Google search engine — therefore, quality inbound links are critical.

You can check the ranking for any website, page, or domain name at the Page-Rank Checker website (**www.prchecker.info/check_page_rank.php**).

How Search Engines Work

Before diving into SEO, it is important that you first know the way search engines operate and how they will rank your site. There are several different types of search engines: crawler-based, human-powered, and mixed. This section will explain how each one works so you can optimize your website in preparation for your paid placement program. Your paid placement advertising campaign will ensure your website shows up with the top search engine rankings based on your keyword bidding.

Crawler-based search engines

Crawler-based search engines, such as the Google search engine, create their listings automatically. They "crawl" or "spider" the Web and index the data, which is then searchable through Google. Crawler-based search engines will eventually revisit your website; therefore, as your content is changed, your search engine ranking may change. A website is added to the search engine database when the search engine spider or crawler visits a Web page, reads it, and then follows links to other pages within the site. The spider returns to the site on a regular basis, typically once every month, to search for changes. Often, it may take several months for a page that has been spidered to be indexed. Until a website is indexed, the results of the spider are not available through the search engines. The search engine then sorts through the millions of indexed pages to find matches to a particular search and ranks them in order based on the formula it uses to find the most relevant results.

Human-powered search directories

Human-powered directories, such as the Open Directory (**www.dmoz.org**), depend on humans for their listings. You must submit a short description to the directory for your entire site. The search directory then looks at your site for matches from your page content to the descriptions you submitted.

Hybrid or mixed search engines

A few years ago, search engines were either crawler-based or human-powered. Today, a mix of both types is common in search engine results.

Successful Search Engine Optimization

The concepts and actions necessary for successful SEO can sometimes be confusing and hard to grasp when you are first starting out using SEO techniques. There are several steps that need to be followed so that you get the most out of your SEO:

- Making sure that your website is designed correctly and set up for optimal SEO

- Choosing the right keywords that are going to bring the most hits to your website

- Using the right title tags to identify you within search engines

- Ensuring appropriate content writing on your website

- Using properly formatted meta tags on your website

- Choosing the right search engines to submit your website to and understanding the free and paid listing service options available

- Having quality inbound links to your website

- Ensuring that every image on your site has an **<alt>** tag

Once you know which areas to focus on, your ranking in search engines will increase dramatically. The main problem with SEO — and the No. 1 reason most site builders fail to properly ensure a site is optimized — is that it requires significant time investment and patience to obtain high rankings in search engines. SEO will not net you immediate visibility in search engines. You need to be realistic in your expectations; expect it to take months to see tangible results.

Meta Tag Definition and Implementation

A meta tag is a tag that is placed within an HTML document to provide additional information about that Web page, usually for search engines or databases. Meta tags are key components of any overall SEO program. There remains controversy surrounding the use of meta tags and whether their inclusion on websites truly impacts search engine rankings; however, they are still widely held as an integral part of a sound SEO plan, and some search engines do use these tags in their indexing processes. You need to be aware that you are competing against potentially thousands of other websites that are often promoting similar products, using similar keywords, and employing other SEO techniques to achieve a top search engine ranking. Meta tags have never guaranteed top rankings on crawler-based search engines, but they may offer a degree of control and the ability for you to impact how your Web pages are indexed within the search engines.

When you implement keywords and key phrases in your meta tags, use only those keywords and phrases that you included within the Web content on each of your Web pages. It is also important that you use the plural forms of keywords so that both the singular and the plural will end up in any searches that people do in search engines using specific keywords and key phrases. Also include any misspellings of your keywords and phrases, since many people commonly misspell certain words — this ensures that search engines can still find you.

Do not repeat your most important keywords and key phrases more than four to five times in a meta-keyword tag. If your product or service is specific to a certain location geographically, you should mention this location in your meta-keyword tag.

Meta tags comprise formatted information that is inserted into the "head" section of each page on your website. To view the head of a Web page, you must view it in HTML mode, rather than in the browser view. In Internet Explorer, you can click on the toolbar on the "View" menu and then click on "Source" to view the source of any individual Web page. If you are using a design tool such as Adobe® Dreamweaver® CS3, Microsoft® SharePoint® Designer 2007, or Microsoft® Expression® Web, you will need to use the HTML view to edit the source code of your Web pages. You can also use Notepad to edit your HTML source code.

This is a simple basic layout of a standard HTML Web page:

```
<!DOCTYPE HTML PUBLIC "-//W3C//DTD HTML 4.01//EN"
<HTML>
 <HEAD>
```

```
<TITLE>This is the Title of My Web Page</TITLE>
</HEAD>
<BODY>
<P>This is my Web page!
</BODY>
</HTML>
```

Every Web page conforms to this basic page layout, and all contain the opening **<head>** and closing **</head>** tags. Meta tags will be inserted between the opening and closing head tags. Other than the page title tag, which is shown above, no other information in the head section of your Web pages is viewed by website visitors as they browse your Web pages. The title tag is displayed across the top of the browser window and is used to provide a description of the contents of the Web page displayed. We will discuss each meta tag that may be contained within the head tags in depth.

The Title Tag

The title tag is the first tag a search engine spider will read, so it is critical that the content you put in the title tag accurately represents the content of the corresponding Web page. Whatever text you place in the title tag — between the **<title>** and **</title>** tags — will appear in the reverse bar of an individual's browser when they view your Web page. In the example above, the title of the Web page to the page visitor would read as "This Is the Title of My Web Page." Titles should accurately describe the focus of that particular page and might also include your site or business name.

The title tag is also used as the words to describe your page when someone adds it to their "Favorites" list or "Bookmarks" list in popular browsers, such as Internet Explorer or Firefox. The title tag is the single most important tag in regard to search engine rankings. The title tag should be limited to 40 to 60 characters of text between the opening and closing HTML tags. All major Web crawlers will use the text of your title tag for the title of your page in their result listings. Since the title and description tags typically appear in the search results page after completing a keyword search in the Web browser, it is critical that they be clearly and concisely written to attract the attention of site visitors. Not all search engines are alike; some will display the title and description tags in search results but use page content alone for ranking.

The Description Tag

The description tag enables you to control the description of your individual Web pages when the search engine crawlers index and spider the website. The description tag should be no more than 250 characters. This is an important meta tag, since all major search engines use it in some capacity for site indexing. A page's description meta tag gives Google and other search engines a summary of what the page is about. Google Webmaster Tools, which are described later in this chapter, provide you with a content analysis section, which will notify you if your meta tags are too short, too long, or duplicated too many times.

It is important to understand that search engines are not all the same, and that they index, spider, and display different search results for the same website. For example, Google ignores the description tag and generates its own description based on the content of the Web page. Although some major engines may disregard your description tags, it is highly recommended that you include the tag on each Web page, since some search engines do rely on the tag to index your site.

The Keywords Tag

The keywords tag is not used much anymore, as it has been heavily abused in the past. Today, page content is critical, while keywords tags are limited or not used at all by spiders indexing your site. However, it is recommended that you at least use the keywords tag in moderation. Using the best keywords to describe your Website helps Internet users to find your site in search engines. The keywords tag allows you to provide relevant text words or word combinations for crawler-based search engines to index.

The keywords tag is only supported by a few Web crawlers. Since most Web crawlers are content-based, meaning they index your site based on the actual page content instead of your meta tags, you need to incorporate as many keywords as possible into the actual content of your Web pages. For the engines that support the description tag, it is beneficial to repeat keywords within the description tag that appear on your actual Web pages — this increases the value of each keyword in relevance to your website page content.

The keywords you want to use in the tag **<meta name="keywords" content="** should go between the quotation marks after the **"content="** portion of

the tag. It is suggested that you include up to 25 words or phrases, with each word or phrase separated by a comma.

To determine which keywords are the best to use on your site, visit the Wordtracker website (**www.wordtracker.com**). Wordtracker's suggestions are based on over 300 million keywords and phrases that people have used over the previous 130 days. However, this is a paid service. A free alternative for determining which keywords are best is Google Rankings (**www.googler-ankings.com**).

The Robots Tag

The robots tag lets you specify whether a particular page within your site should or should not be indexed by a search engine, or whether links should or should not be followed by search engine spiders. To keep search engine spiders from indexing a page, add the following text between your tags:

```
<meta name="robots" content="noindex">
```

To keep search engine spiders from following links on your page, add the following text between your tags:

```
<meta name="robots" content="nofollow">
```

You do not need to use variations of the robots tag to get your pages indexed since your pages will be spidered and indexed by default; however, some Web designers include the following robots tag on all Web pages:

```
<meta name="robots" content="all">
```

ALT Tags

The **<alt>** tag is an HTML tag that provides alternative text when non-textual elements, typically images, cannot be displayed. The **<alt>** tag is not part of the head of a Web page, but proper use of this tag is critically important in SEO. The **<alt>** tags are often left off Web pages, but they can be extremely useful for a variety of reasons:

- They provide detail or text description for an image or the destination of a hyperlinked image.

- They enable and improve access for people with disabilities.

- They provide information for individuals who have graphics turned off when they surf the Internet.

- They improve navigation when a graphics-laden site is viewed over a slow connection, enabling visitors to make navigation choices before graphics are fully rendered in the browser.

Text-based Web content is not the only thing that increases your ranking in the search engines; images are just as important because these images can also include keywords and key phrases that relate to your business. If any visitors to your website have the image option off, they will still be able to see the text associated with your images. The **<alt>** tags should be placed anywhere where there is an image on your website. It is key to avoid being too wordy when describing your images, but include accurate keywords within the tags. The keywords and key phrases that you use in **<alt>** tags should be the same keywords and phrases that you use in meta description tags, meta keyword tags, title tags, and in the Web content on your Web pages. A brief description of the image, along with one or two accurate keywords and key phrases, is all you need to optimize the images on your Web pages for search engines.

Most major Web design applications include tools to simplify the process of creating **<alt>** tags. For example, in Microsoft Expression Web, right-click on the image and choose "Properties" and the "General" tab; you can then enter **<alt>** tag text information. Most website development applications actually prompt you for **<alt>** tags as you add images. To enter **<alt>** tag information directly into a Web page, go to the HTML view and enter them after the **<img>** tags in the following format:

```
<img border="0" src="images/cftec.jpg" width="300"
height="103" alt="ChefTec Software helps you save
money"></b></font></p>
```

Optimization of Web Page Content

Web page content is by far the single most important factor that will affect and determine your eventual website ranking in search engines. It is extremely important that you have relevant content on your Web pages that is going to increase the status of your website in search engine rankings. The content on your Web page is what visitors are going to read when they find your site and start to browse your Web pages, whether they browse to a page directly or via a search engine. You need to optimize your website with all the right keywords within the content of each Web page so that you can maximize your rankings within search engines. You can use software tools to find out what keywords people are using when they search for certain products and services on the Internet.

Not only are the visitors to your website reading the content on these pages, but search engine spiders and Web crawlers are reading this same content and using it to index your website among your competitors. This is why it is important that you have the right content, so that search engines are able to find you and rank you near the top of the listings for similar products. Search engines look for keywords and key phrases to categorize and rank your site; therefore, it is important that you focus on just as many key phrases as you do keywords.

The placement of text content within a Web page can make a significant difference in your eventual search engine rankings. Some search engines will only analyze a limited number of text characters on each page and will not read the rest of the page, regardless of length; therefore, the keywords and phrases you may load into your page may not be read at all by the search engines. Some search engines do index the entire content of Web pages, but they typically give more value, or "weight," to the content that appears closer to the top of the Web page.

Optimizing Your Website

To get the best results from search engines, here are some tips for optimizing your website:

- Make sure you have at least 200 words of content on each page. Although you may have some Web pages where it may be difficult to put even close to 200 words, you should try to come as close as you can, since search engines will give better results to pages with more content.

- Make sure that the text content you have on your Web pages contains those important keywords and key phrases that you researched, that you know will get you competitive rankings, and that are the most common phrases potential customers might use to search for your products or services.

- After incorporating keywords and phrases, make sure that your content is still understandable and readable in plain language. A common mistake is to stuff a website full of so many keywords and phrases that the page is no longer understandable or readable to the website visitor — a sure way to lose potential customers quickly.

- The keywords and phrases that you use in the content of your website should also be included in the tags of your website, such as meta tags, **<alt>** tags, head tags, and title tags.

- Add extra pages to your website, even if they may not at first seem directly relevant. The more Web pages that you have, the more pages search engines will have to be able to find you and link to. Extra pages can include tips, tutorials, product information, resource information, and any other information or data that is pertinent to the product or service that you offer.

Optimizing your Web content and Web pages is one of the most important things you can do to ensure the success of your website. If you are unable to optimize your website yourself, you should hire an expert so that you get the most out of your Web content.

Website Optimization Tips, Hints, and Secrets

It is critical that you explore and implement the wide range of suggestions provided in this chapter to give your website the most competitive edge and obtain the highest possible rankings with search engines. The following pages contain various best practices, tips, and secrets:

- It is important to use keywords heavily on your Web pages. Use key phrases numerous times, placing them close to the top of the page. Place key phrases between head tags in the first two paragraphs of your page and in bold type at least once on each page. Repeat keywords and phrases often to increase density on your pages.

- Design pages so they are easily navigated by search engine spiders and Web crawlers. Search engines prefer text over graphics and HTML over other page formats.

- Never use frames. Search engines have difficulty following them, and so will your site visitors.

- Limit the use of Adobe Flash® and other high-end design applications, as most search engines have trouble reading and following them, which will hurt in search engine listings.

- Consider creating a sitemap of all pages within your website. While not necessarily the most useful tool to site visitors, it does greatly improve the search engine's capacity to properly index all your website pages.

- Many websites use a left-hand navigational bar. This is standard on many sites, but the algorithm that many spiders and Web crawlers use will have this read before the main content of your website. Make sure you use keywords within the navigation, and if using images for your navigational buttons, use **<alt>** tags loaded with the appropriate keywords.

- Ensure that all Web pages have links back to the homepage.

- Use "Copyright" and "About Us" pages.

- Do not try to trick the search engines with hidden or invisible text or other techniques. If you do, the search engine may penalize you.

- Do not list keywords in order within the content of your Web page. It is fine to incorporate keywords into the content of your Web pages, but do not simply cut and paste keywords from your meta tags into the content of your Web pages. This will be viewed as spam by the search engine, and you will be penalized.

- Do not use text on your Web page as the page's background color. This is another way of keyword "stuffing," and all search engines will detect it and penalize you.

- Do not replicate meta tags. In other words, you should only have one meta tag for each type of tag. Using multiple tags, such as more than one title tag, will cause search engines to penalize you.

- Do not submit identical pages with identical content with a different Web page file name.

- Ensure that every Web page is reachable from at least one static text link.

- Ensure that your title and **<alt>** tags are descriptive and accurate.

- Check for broken links and correct HTML.

- Try using a text browser, such as Lynx, to examine your site. Features such as JavaScript™, cookies, session IDs, frames, DHTML, or

Flash keep search engine spiders from properly crawling your entire website.

- Implement the use of the **robots.txt** file on your Web server. This file tells crawlers which directories can or cannot be crawled. You can find out more information on this file by visiting The Web Robots Pages (**www.robotstxt.org/wc/faq.html**).

- Have other relevant sites link to yours. This is an often overlooked but extremely important way of increasing your search engine rankings, especially with the Google search engine. This is also known as backlinking, and it is critically important in gaining search engine visibility.

- Design Web pages for site visitors, not for search engines.

- Avoid tricks intended to improve search engine rankings. A good rule of thumb is to decide whether you would feel comfortable explaining what you have done to a website that competes with you. Another useful test is to ask, "Does this help my users? Would I do this if search engines did not exist?"

- Do not participate in link schemes designed to increase your site's ranking. Do not link to Web spammers, as your own ranking will be negatively affected by those links.

- Do not create multiple pages, sub-domains, or domains with substantially similar content.

- Do not use "doorway" pages created for search engines.

- Consider implementing cascading spreadsheets (CSS) to control site layout and design. Search engines prefer CSS-based sites and typically score them higher in the search rankings.

If you follow the above advice, your site should do well in search engines, which will in turn bring more potential customers to you.

Web Design and Optimization Suggestions

There are a few more steps you can take to ensure optimal search engine rankings. Implement a few or all of the below suggestions to make your site as search engine-friendly as possible.

Establish a reciprocal link program

You should try to find quality sites that are compatible and relevant to your website's topic, and approach the webmasters of those sites for link exchanges. This will give you highly targeted traffic and will improve your score with search engines. Your goal is to identify relevant pages that will link to your site, effectively yielding you quality inbound links. However, be wary of developing or creating a "link farm" or "spam link website" that offers massive quantities of link exchanges, but with little or no relevant content for your site visitors or the search engines.

NOTE: Do not link to your competitors.

Begin your link exchange program by developing a title or theme to use as part of your link request invitations. This should be directly relevant to your site's content. Since most sites use your provided title or theme in the link to your website, be sure you include relevant keywords that will improve your website optimization and search engine rankings. Keep track of your inbound and outbound link requests.

Begin your search for link exchange partners by searching a popular engine, such as Google, and entering key phrases, such as "link with us," "add site," "suggest a site," or "add your link." If these sites are relevant, they are ideal for your reciprocal link program, since they too are actively seeking link partners. Make sure that the webmasters of other sites actually link back to your site, as it is common that reciprocal links are not completed. If they do not link back to you in a reasonable amount of time, remove your link to them, as you are only helping them with their search engine rankings.

You may want to use LinkPopularity (**www.linkpopularity.com**) as a free Web source for evaluating the total number of websites that link to your site.

Establish a website privacy policy

Internet users are becoming increasingly concerned with their privacy. You should establish a "Privacy" Web page and let your visitors know exactly how you will be using the information you collect from them.

You may also wish to develop a P3P privacy policy. This may be necessary to solve the common problem of blocked cookies on websites, as well as with shopping carts and affiliate programs. Details may be found at the World Wide Web Consortium website (**www.w3.org/P3P/usep3p.html**).

The privacy web page should include the following information for your potential customers:

- For what purpose do you plan on using their information?

- Will their information be sold or shared with a third party?

- Why do you collect their e-mail addresses?

- Do you track their IP addresses?

- Notify site visitors that you are not responsible for the privacy issues of any websites you may be linked to.

- Notify site visitors that you have security measures in place to protect the misuse of their private or personal information.

- Provide site visitors with contact information in the event that they have any questions about your privacy statement.

Establish an "About Us" page

An "About Us" page is an essential part of a professional website for a variety of reasons. Your potential customers may want to know exactly who you are, and it is a great opportunity to create a text-laden page for search engine visibility. An "About Us" page should include:

- A personal or professional biography

- A photograph of yourself or your business

- A description of you or your company

- Company objectives or a mission statement

- Contact information, including your e-mail address

Establish a "Testimonials" page

Another way to develop credibility and confidence among your potential customers is to include previous customers' testimonials. You need to make sure your testimonials are supportable, so include your customers' names and e-mail addresses for validation purposes.

Establish a money-back guarantee

Depending on the type of website you are operating, you may wish to consider implementing a money-back guarantee to completely eliminate any potential risk to customers who purchase your products. By providing them with a solid, no-risk guarantee, you build confidence in your company and products with potential clients.

Establish a "Feedback" page

There are many reasons to incorporate a feedback page into your website. There are times when potential customers will have questions about your products and services or may encounter problems with your website, and the feedback page is an easy way for them to contact you. Additionally, it allows you to collect data from the site visitor, such as name, e-mail address, or phone number. A timely response to feedback is critical in assuring customers that there is a real person on the other end of the website, and this personal service helps increase the likelihood they will continue to do business with you.

Establish a "Copyright" page

You should always display your copyright information at the bottom of each page. You should include both the word "Copyright" and the © symbol. Your copyright should look similar to this:

Copyright © 2009 Bruce C. Brown, LLC.

Using a Search Engine Optimization Company

If you are not up to the challenge of tackling your website's SEO needs, it may be to your benefit to hire an SEO company so that the optimization techniques you use are properly implemented and monitored. There are many SEO companies on the Internet that can ensure your rankings in search engines will increase when you hire them. However, be wary of claims of anyone who can "guarantee" you top-ten rankings in all major search engines; these claims are baseless. If you have the budget to hire an SEO company, it may be extremely beneficial since you will know that the experts at SEO are taking care of you, and you can focus your energies on other important marketing aspects of your business. To find a good SEO company, follow these basic rules:

- Look at the business reputations of the SEO companies you are considering. Ask the companies for customer references you can check out on your own. You can also contact the Better Business Bureau (**www.bbb.org**) in each company's city or state to confirm its reputation.

• Do a search engine check on each company to see where it falls into the rankings of major search engines, such as AOL®, MSN®, and Google. If the company that you are considering does not rank highly itself in these search engines, you cannot expect it to launch your business to the top of the ranks.

• Choose an SEO company that has *people* working for it, not just computers. While computers are good for generating the algorithms that are needed to use search engine programs, they cannot replace people when it comes to doing the market research that is needed to ensure that the company uses the right keywords and phrases for your business.

• Make sure that the SEO company uses ethical ranking procedures. There are some ranking procedures that are considered to be unethical, and some search engines will ban or penalize your business website from their engines if they find out that you, or the SEO company that you hired, are using these methods. Some of these unethical ranking procedures include doorway pages, cloaking, or hidden text.

• The SEO company you decide to hire should be available to you at all times by phone or e-mail. You want to be able to contact someone when you have a question or a problem.

• Once you decide to hire an SEO company, it is important that you work with the company instead of just handing over all the responsibility to them. How much control over your website you should allow your SEO company is debatable, but since you will be controlling your PPC advertising campaign, you must have control over your SEO efforts. Use these tips to work effectively with your SEO provider:

• Listen carefully to the advice of the SEO account manager. He or she should have the expertise to provide factual, supportable recommendations. SEO companies are expected to know what to do to increase your ranking in the search engines; if your chosen company fails to deliver, you need to find another company.

- If you are going to be making any changes to your website design, let your SEO account manager know. This is because many times, any changes you make can have an effect on the already optimized Web pages. Your rankings in search engines may start to plummet unless you work with your SEO account manager to optimize any changes to your website design that you feel are necessary to make.

- Keep in mind that SEO companies can only work with the data and information that you have on your Web pages. This means that if your website has little information, it will be difficult for any SEO company to pull your business up in the search engine rankings. SEO relies on keywords and key phrases that are contained on Web pages filled with as much Web content as possible. This may mean adding two or three pages of Web content that contain tips, resources, or other useful information that is relevant to your product or service.

- Never change any of your meta tags once they are optimized without the knowledge or advice of your SEO account manager. The SEO company is the professional when it comes to making sure that your meta tags are optimized with the right keywords and phrases needed to increase your search engine ranking. You will not want to change meta tags that have already proven successful.

- Be patient when it comes to seeing the results of SEO. It can take anywhere from 30 to 60 days before you start to see your site pushed into the upper ranks of search engines.

- Keep a close eye on your ranking in search engines, even after you reach the top ranks. Information on the Internet changes at a moment's notice, and this includes your position in your target market in search engines.

Search Engine Optimization Checklist

There are many aspects to SEO that you need to consider to make sure that it works. Though each of these topics has already been covered in this chapter, the following checklist can serve as a helpful reminder to ensure that you have not forgotten any important details along the way.

- **Title tag**: Make sure that your title tag includes keywords and key phrases that are relevant to your product or service.

- **Meta tags**: Make sure that your tags are optimized to ensure a high ranking in search engine lists. This includes meta description tags and meta keyword tags. Your meta description tag should have an accurate description so that people browsing the Internet are interested enough to visit your website. Do not forget to use the misspelled and plural forms of words in your meta tags.

- **ALT tag**: Add <alt> tags to all the images that you use on your Web pages.

- **Web content**: Use accurate, rich keywords and key phrases throughout the content of all your Web pages.

- **Density of keywords**: Use a high ratio of keywords and key phrases throughout your Web pages.

- **Links and affiliates**: Make sure that you use links, and affiliates if you are using them, effectively for your website.

- **Web design**: Make sure that your website is fast to load and easy to navigate for visitors. You want to encourage people to stay and read your website by making sure that it is clean and looks good.

- **Avoid spamming**: Double-check to make sure that you are not using any spamming offenses on your website. This includes cloaking, hidden text, doorway pages, obvious repeated keywords and key phrases, link farms, or mirror pages.

- **ALT tags**: Make sure all images have <alt> tags on your website.

Always be prepared to update and change the look, feel, and design of your Web pages to make sure that you are using SEO techniques wherever and whenever possible.

Search Engine Registration

It is possible to submit your website for free to major search engines, including Google. You can also pay for this, and when you use paid search engine submission programs, you will find that the process of listing will be faster, but results are often unacceptable, as many search engines reject automated Web submissions. Other than PPC and similar advertising programs, such as Google AdWords, it is not necessary to pay for search engine rankings if you follow the optimization and design tips contained in this book and have patience while the search engine Web-crawling and indexing process takes place. Provided at the end of this chapter is a wealth of tools and methods to submit your website to search engines for fee. If you do decide to hire a third-party company to register you with search engines, there are some basic guidelines to ensure you get the most value for your investment.

Submitting to human-powered search directories

If you have a limited advertising budget, you will want to make sure that you have at least enough money to cover the price of submitting to the directory at Yahoo! This is called a "directory" search engine because it uses a compiled directory; it is assembled by human hands, not a computer. With this directory, you will be able to ensure that crawler search engines will be able to find your website in the Yahoo! directory. You will also want to submit your site to the Open Directory, which is free. Crawlers consistently use directory search engines to add to their search listings. If you have a large budget put aside for search engine submissions, you might want to list with both directory search engines and crawler search engines. When you first launch your website, you may want it to show up immediately in search engines, rather than waiting the allotted time for your listing to appear. If this is the case, you might want to consider using what is called a "paid placement" program. Your PPC advertising campaigns will show up with the top search engine rankings based on your keyword bidding.

Submitting to crawler search engines

Submitting to crawler search engines means that you will likely have several Web pages listed within the search engine. One of the top Internet crawler search engines is, of course, Google. Google is extremely popular because it is not just a search engine; it is also the main source of power and information behind many other search engines, such as AOL. The best thing that you can do when getting your website listed at Google is to make sure that you have links within your website. When you have accurate links on your website, you ensure that crawler search engines are able to find you, drill down through your site, and index your pages accordingly.

You can submit your URL to Google yourself (**www.google.com/addurl. html**) or sign up for Google AdWords, which triggers an indexing of your site. Because a higher PageRank in search results equates to better placement in the Google search engine, quality inbound links are critical.

Using search engine submission software

There are dozens of software applications that can submit your website automatically to search engines, the preferred program being Dynamic Submission™. You can find a trial edition at their website (**www.dynamicsubmission.com**). Software programs like Dynamic Submission were developed to offer website owners the ability to promote their websites to the ever-increasing number of search engines on the Internet without any hassle or complication. This type of software helps you submit your website to hundreds of major search engines with just a few clicks and drive traffic to your website.

Since nearly 85 percent of Internet traffic is generated by search engines, submitting your website to all the major search engines and getting them to be seen on the search engine list is extremely important, especially in concert with your PPC advertising campaign. It is essential to regularly submit your website details to these Web directories and engines. Some search engines de-list you over time, while others automatically re-spider your site.

However, you should be aware that the success of these submission applications has decreased over time as search engines began to reject these "auto-bot" submissions in favor of human submissions or paid submissions. Google and most other search engines do not recommend the use of products such as WebPosition® Gold or Dynamic Submission, which send automatic or programmatic queries to Google. It is in violation of their terms of use and quality guidelines.

Free Website Search Engine Submission Sites

- The Open Directory (**www.dmoz.org**)

- Submit Corner (**www.submitcorner.com/Tools/Submit**)

- Quickregister (**www.quickregister.net**)

- ScrubTheWeb.com™ (**www.scrubtheweb.com**)

- Web.com® Search Agency (**www.submitawebsite.com/seo-tools/search-engine-submission.html**)

- Web Launch (**www.nexcomp.com/weblaunch/urlsubmission.html**)

- SubmitShop (**www.submitshop.com/freesubmit/freesubmit.html**)

- BuildTraffic (**www.buildtraffic.com/submit_url.shtml**)

- AddPro (**www.addpro.com/submit30.htm**)

There are many other free services available on the Internet, and there is no guarantee as to the quality of any of these free services. It is recommended that you create and use a new e-mail account just for search engine submissions, such as **search@yourwebsite.com**, to avoid spam, which is prevalent when doing bulk submissions.

Free Website Optimization Tools

These free tools evaluate different aspects of your website to ensure it is user friendly and shows in searches.

- **Website Optimization (www.websiteoptimization.com/services/ analyze)**: Contains a free website speed test to improve your website's performance. This site will calculate page size, composition, and download time. The script calculates the size of individual elements and sums up each type of Web page component. On the basis of these page characteristics, the site then offers advice on how to improve page load time. Slow load time is the No. 1 reason potential customers do not access websites.

- **SiteSoluntions.Com (www.sitesolutions.com/analysis. asp?F=Form)**: A free website that analyzes your page content to determine whether you are effectively using meta tags.

- **Mike's Marketing Tools (www.mikes-marketing-tools.com/ranking-reports)**: Offers instant online reports of website rankings in seven top search engines and the top three Web directories for free.

- **Keyword Density Analyzer (www.keyworddensity.com)**: Free, fast, and accurate keyword density analyzer.

- **Wordtracker (www.wordtracker.com)**: The leading keyword research tool. It is not free, but there is a limited free trial.

- **Google AdWords Keyword Tool (https://adwords.google.co.uk/ select/KeywordToolExternal)**: Gives ideas for new keywords associated with your target phrase, but does not indicate relevance or include details on number or frequency of searches.

- **HTML Basix (www.htmlbasix.com/meta.shtml)**: Free site that automatically creates properly formatted HTML meta tags for insertion into your Web pages.

Google's Webmaster Tools

Google's own Webmaster Tools include powerful applications that help you achieve better, higher rankings in the Google search engine. These tools provide you with a free, easy way to make your site more Google friendly. The tools show your site from the perspective of Google and let you identify problems, increase visibility, and optimize your site.

To increase your website's visibility on Google, you need to learn how their robots crawl and index your site. Webmaster Tools (**www.google.com/Webmasters/tools**) shows you exactly how to do this. You can see when your site was last crawled and indexed, view the URLs that Google had problems crawling, and then take corrective action to ensure all of your pages are indexed. You can also see what keywords Google validates and which sites link to yours. In addition, you can see which queries have been performed that are driving traffic to your site and where your site lands in the search engine result for those queries. Finally, you can review how your site is indexed and whether you have any violations that Google is penalizing you for.

To take a closer look at each of these amazing Google tools, first you must sign up with Google and log into your account.

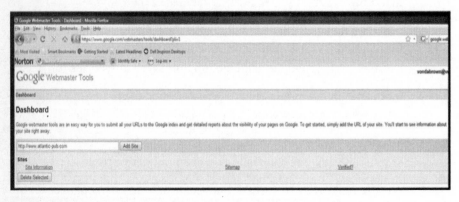

Google screenshots © Google Inc. Used with permission.

Add your URL into the "Add Site" box and click the button.

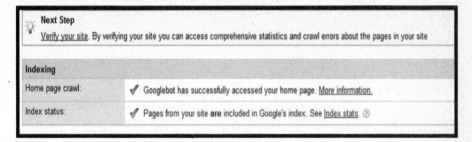

Google screenshots © Google Inc. Used with permission.

Google requires proof that you are the site owner, to prevent you from using the same tools on your competition's site. You can do this by adding a meta tag to your website, which Google provides, or by uploading an HTML file. In the example, the meta tag is added to the HTML code in the **index.asp** Web page. Once you add the code, simply click on the "Verify" button to continue.

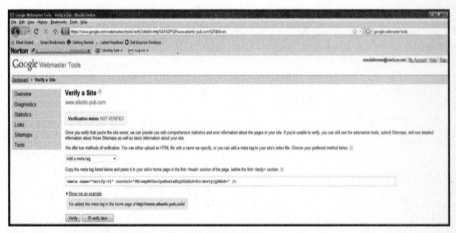

Google screenshots © Google Inc. Used with permission.

Once the site is verified, you can review the status of indexing and Web crawls. As you can see in the following screen shot, the site has been verified, and has been included in Google's index. You can look at the index statistics, and you can also submit a sitemap. By examining the Web crawl errors, you can see that the site has 14 URLs not followed.

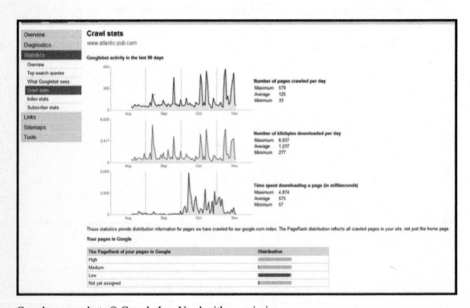

Google screenshots © Google Inc. Used with permission.

Detailed statistics about the Web crawls are available to you, as is PageRank information. This site is ranked "low" in Google PageRank, so there is some work to do.

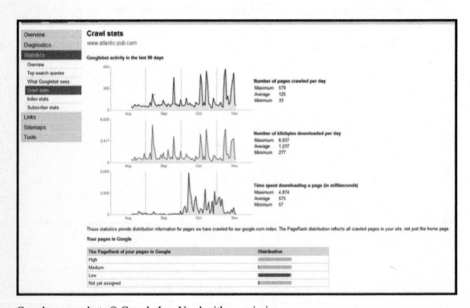

Google screenshots © Google Inc. Used with permission.

You can review your top search queries and the relative position in which your results were ranked on the Google search engine.

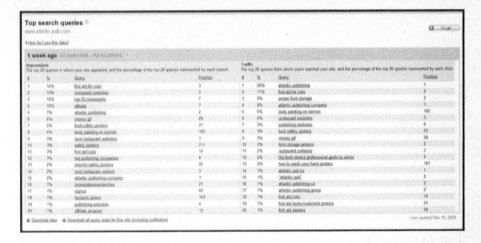

Google screenshots © Google Inc. Used with permission.

Spend some quality time with Google Webmaster Tools. They are all simple enough to use and understand as you analyze your site. You can even set up Google Webmaster Tools to monitor your site from your desktop, providing you with constant information about the performance of your site in relation to the Google search engine. The following is a screen shot of just some of the many tools available to analyze your website:

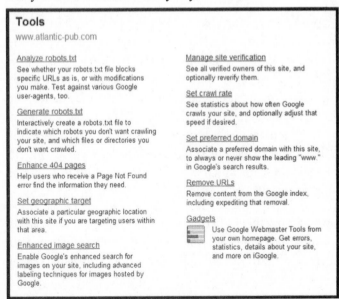

Tools

www.atlantic-pub.com

Analyze robots.txt
See whether your robots.txt file blocks specific URLs as is, or with modifications you make. Test against various Google user-agents, too.

Generate robots.txt
Interactively create a robots.txt file to indicate which robots you don't want crawling your site, and which files or directories you don't want crawled.

Enhance 404 pages
Help users who receive a Page Not Found error find the information they need.

Set geographic target
Associate a particular geographic location with this site if you are targeting users within that area.

Enhanced image search
Enable Google's enhanced search for images on your site, including advanced labeling techniques for images hosted by Google.

Manage site verification
See all verified owners of this site, and optionally reverify them.

Set crawl rate
See statistics about how often Google crawls your site, and optionally adjust that speed if desired.

Set preferred domain
Associate a preferred domain with this site, to always or never show the leading "www." in Google's search results.

Remove URLs
Remove content from the Google index, including expediting that removal.

Gadgets
Use Google Webmaster Tools from your own homepage. Get errors, statistics, details about your site, and more on iGoogle.

Google screenshots © Google Inc. Used with permission.

Remember those 14 URLs that Google reported could not be followed? Often, this error is caused by a problem with the HTML coding of a page or by a link to a page that does not exist, which is the case with the example. Clearing up this problem is a simple matter of fixing the URLs:

Google screenshots © Google Inc. Used with permission.

Sitemaps & Google

Submitting a sitemap to Google is a critical step toward achieving top rankings in the Google search engine. If you do nothing else with Google Webmaster Tools, submit a sitemap. To do so, first you must log back into Google Webmaster Tools, select the URL you want to work with that you have already verified, and click on the link "Sitemaps." A sitemap is an HTML page listing of all the pages in your site — it tends to be designed to help users navigate your site, and it is especially beneficial if your site is large. In the case of Google, you should create an XML sitemap, which provides Google with information about your site and improves your rankings with Google.

Essentially, a sitemap is an organized list of every page on your website. It helps Google know which pages are on your site and ensures that all your pages are discovered and indexed. According to Google, sitemaps are particularly helpful if:

- Your site has dynamic content.

- Your site has pages that are not easily discovered by Googlebot, Google's crawler, during the crawl process.

- Your site is new and has few links to it.

- Your site has a large archive of content pages that are not well-linked to each other, or are not linked at all.

Your sitemap can include additional information about your site, such as how often it is updated, when each page was last modified, and the relative importance of each page. You must create your sitemap and either submit to Google the sitemap itself or a URL to the sitemap. You can create a sitemap in the following three ways:

1. Manually creating it based on the sitemap protocol.

2. Using the Google Webmaster Tools' Sitemap Generator. If you have access to your Web server, and it has Python® installed, you can use a Google-provided script to create a sitemap that uses the sitemap protocol.

3. Using a third-party tool.

The easiest way to create an XML sitemap is to use the free tool at the XML Sitemaps Generator Website (**www.xml-sitemaps.com**). This is an incredibly easy site to use; simply type in the URL, and it does the rest for you. You upload the XML file to your website, and in the Google sitemap tool, add the URL for the new file you placed on your Web server. Simply add your sitemap URL into the form, as shown in Google Webmaster Tools in the next screenshot, and click the "Add General Web Sitemap" button.

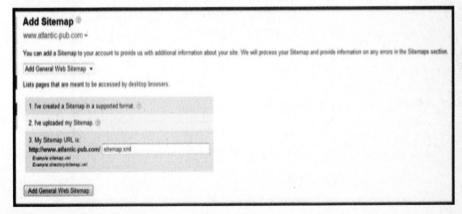

Google screenshots © Google Inc. Used with permission.

Google confirms that your sitemap has been added and will update in several hours. It is important that you check back to ensure that your sitemap completed processing with no errors. The tool at this site creates an HTML sitemap that you can place on your website. It also creates the feed format to submit to Yahoo! as well as a generic XML format for other major search engines.

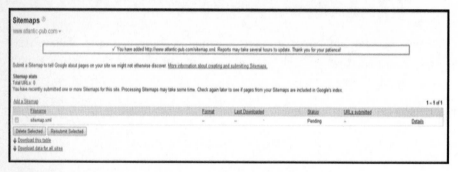

Google screenshots © Google Inc. Used with permission.

Creating a sitemap with Google is a must for every website, and it is one of the most important things you can do to improve your site rankings with Google. You will not find a more useful set of applications than you will with Google Webmaster Tools to ensure your site is optimized, error-free, and properly indexed by the Google search engine.

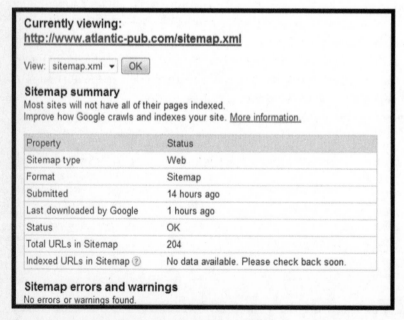

Google screenshots © Google Inc. Used with permission.

You can view your sitemap results at any time. In the preceding image, you can see that the 204 URLs in the sitemap were indexed properly, and there are no errors or warnings. With Google Webmaster Tools, you can view a wide variety of analytics and statistics.

Snippets

A snippet is simply the text excerpt that appears below a page's title in the Google search engine results and describes the content of the page. Words contained in the snippet are bolded when they appear in the query results. The premise is that these snippets will give the user an idea of whether the content of the page matches what they may be looking for. The description snippet is taken directly from the description meta tag. If no description meta tag is provided, Google may extract a description from the page content. One source Google uses for snippets is the Open Directory Project (ODP). It is possible to tell Google to not use the ODP for generating snippets by using a piece of meta tag code. To do this, use the following code on any Web page you want this rule to apply to:

```
<meta name="googlebot" content="noodp">
```

The Problem with Navigation Bars and Spiders

You already know you need to have excellent navigation menus on your site to ensure that your customers can easily find your products and services. One problem you may face regarding SEO is that your website navigation menu, which is commonly on the top or on the left-hand side of each page, is indexed by the search engine and can hurt you in search engine rankings when it indexes words from your menu rather than from your page content. You need to get the search engines to index your content, not your navigation menus. You may want to put the navigation menu to the right of each page, which can be effective, although it is non-standard navigation and may turn site visitors off. There are a few options you can use to overcome this challenge if you want to keep your traditional navigation menus. One option is to use CSS to place your navigation menu later in the code, or you can use Web accessibility settings to have the search engine skip over the navigation menu and go right to your Web content.

Breadcrumbs

Breadcrumb navigation is good for user-friendly site navigation and SEO. Essentially, breadcrumbs are a form of text-based navigation that shows where the current Web page you are viewing is located in the site hierarchy. It contains shortcuts to the next level of a website and lets you jump multiple layers at one time. An example of breadcrumb navigation may be: "Home > Real Estate > Home Inspections > Books." Microsoft Expression Blend™ features a breadcrumb trail tool, which allows designers to quickly and easily create breadcrumb trails.

Inbound and Outbound Links

Since Google values quality Web links, Google Webmaster Tools includes the ability to search for relevant sites. To get links, you often must give out links. Reciprocal links are fine, as long as you link to quality, relevant sites. Create outbound links as text-based links and use keywords in the text.

Google TrustRank

Google uses a concept known as TrustRank to give higher search engine rankings to trusted sites and lower rankings to sites that are not trusted. Exactly how this works remains a bit of a mystery, so use the advice provided here as you strive to optimize your site for Google.

Here are some factors that may affect your TrustRank ratings:

- **Performing routine updates to your site**: Adding content shows your site is maintained and current.

- **Inbound links**: Ensure your site is stacked with quality links from websites that have content relevant to your site.

- **Domain name age**: Having an established domain name for several years shows credibility and should give you a benefit over newly established domain names.

- **Use sitemaps**: Use XML sitemaps to ensure that search engine spiders can easily index your website.

- **Avoid spam**: This means spam e-mail as well as other techniques designed to trick search engines into giving you higher rankings, such as doorways, landing pages, hidden text, and stuffed keywords.

404 Pages & Search Engine Optimization

Even the best Web designers inevitably leave a link to a page that no longer exists. This is known as a 404 Error. Make sure you have a custom 404 page to redirect users back to a page from which they can navigate your site. Often, 404 pages will redirect you to the homepage. You may also wish to have links to your most popular pages. An auto-redirect will give site visitors a few seconds to click on a link, and if they take no action, it will bring them to the website homepage.

Sample 404 Error Page. Reprinted with Permission of Atlantic Publishing Company.

Google simplifies the processing of creating 404 pages by providing a Google 404 Widget in Google Webmaster Tools. You can also use the widget to identify which page has the links to the nonexistent page so you can take corrective action.

Section 508 and Website Accessibility

In 1998, Congress amended the Rehabilitation Act to require federal agencies to make their electronic and information technology accessible to people with disabilities. Inaccessible technology interferes with an individual's ability to obtain and use information quickly and easily. Section 508 was enacted to eliminate barriers in information technology, to make available new opportunities for people with disabilities, and to encourage development of technologies that will help achieve these goals. The law applies to all federal agencies when they develop, procure, maintain, or use electronic and information technology. Under Section 508 (29 U.S.C. 794d), agencies must give disabled employees and members of the public access to information that is comparable to the access available to others. You should design Web pages with accessibility in mind, as there are benefits for everyone. While the Section 508 rules are quite involved and apply to much more than Web pages, here are the essential requirements for website design:

§ 1194.22 Web-based intranet and Internet information and applications.

- A text equivalent for every non-text element shall be provided.

- Equivalent alternatives for any multimedia presentation shall be synchronized with the presentation.

- Web pages shall be designed so that all information conveyed with color is also available without color; for example, from context or markup.

- Documents shall be organized so they are readable without requiring an associated style sheet.

- Redundant text links shall be provided for each active region of a server-side image map.

- Client-side image maps shall be provided instead of server-side image maps except where the regions cannot be defined with an available geometric shape.

- Row and column headers shall be identified for data tables.

- Markup shall be used to associate data cells and header cells for data tables that have two or more logical levels of row or column headers.

- Frames shall be titled with text that facilitates frame identification and navigation.

- Pages shall be designed to avoid causing the screen to flicker with a frequency greater than 2 Hz and lower than 55 Hz.

- A text-only page, with equivalent information or functionality, shall be provided to make a website comply with the provisions of this part, when compliance cannot be accomplished in any other way; the content of the text-only page shall be updated whenever the primary page changes.

- When pages use scripting languages to display content, or to create interface elements, the information provided by the script shall be identified with functional text that can be read by assistive technology.

- When a Web page requires that an applet, plug-in, or other application be present on the client system to interpret page content, the page must provide a link to a plug-in or applet that complies with §1194.21(a) through (l).

- When electronic forms are designed to be completed online, the form shall allow people using assistive technology to access the information, field elements, and functionality required for completion and submission of the form, including all directions and cues.

- A method shall be provided that permits users to skip repetitive navigation links.

- When a timed response is required, the user shall be alerted and given sufficient time to indicate more time is required.

To check your site for Section 508 compliance, visit the HiSoftware® Cynthia Says™ Portal (**www.contentquality.com**).

Google's Quality Guidelines

Google's quality guidelines address most of the common techniques employed to overcome and trick search engines in order to achieve higher rankings. This list is not all-inclusive. Use your time and energy to implement proven website design techniques and SEO standards to improve your site in Google's rankings. If you believe another website is abusing Google's quality guidelines, you may report it at **www.google.com/webmasters/tools/spamreport**.

Here are Google's quality guidelines:

- Make pages primarily for users, not for search engines.
- Avoid tricks intended to improve search engine rankings.

- Do not participate in link schemes designed to increase your site's ranking or PageRank.

- Do not use unauthorized computer programs to submit pages, check rankings, or perform other functions.

- Avoid hidden text or hidden links.

- Do not use cloaking.

- Do not load pages with irrelevant keywords.

- Do not create multiple pages, sub-domains, or domains with duplicate content.

- Do not create pages with malicious behavior, such as phishing or installing viruses or trojans.

- Avoid "doorway" pages created just for search engines.

- If your site participates in an affiliate program, make sure that your site adds value and has content a person would visit based on the content, regardless of whether it has an affiliate program.

CHAPTER 5

Website Fundamentals

In many cases, websites are built by business owners to save the cost of professional Web design. This is a viable option in many cases, and you can certainly be your own Web designer, Web master, and business owner. Web design applications such as Microsoft Office FrontPage®, NetObjects® Fusion™, and early versions of Adobe Dreamweaver were amazing technological advances for Web designers. If you are a beginner working with basic HTML code or using the latest products such as Microsoft Expression Web, you are a Web designer, though your skill level may be less than others. Many times it may be too difficult for you to create your own website, or you may just want that professional, polished look that only a real designer can deliver. You can sink an enormous amount of money into Web design, and in some cases, you may need to if you have a truly complex site. However, it is possible to design a highly effective site with little or no money.

There are four main components of a website:

1. **Domain name**: This name is registered and corresponds with where your website is physically located on a Web server and is also used for your e-mail accounts.

2. **Web hosting**: This is the physical "storage" of your Web pages on a server that is connected to the Internet. This machine "serves" your Web pages as they are requested by a Web browser.

3. **Web pages**: These are the Web pages you created and published to your Web server. Your individual Web pages collectively create your website. Your website can be as small as one page, or it can be thousands of pages. All websites have a homepage. The homepage is the page that site visitors are taken to when they type in your website domain name into a browser. From your home site, visitors can navigate your site and visit other Web pages on your site.

4. **Optional items**: These might include shopping carts, forms, or databases. While none of these are required for websites, you will find your needs may change over time, so keep that in mind during the planning process.

All websites consistently change as new content and other Web pages are added; so while you may complete your initial design and publish your Web page, typically your site will require further maintenance, updating, and revisions. The most challenging part of creating a website is developing a blueprint for how you want your site organized, what pages it will contain, how content will be organized, and how your pages will be laid out in relation to others as you design your navigation and page relationships. Design your pages individually, formulate what each page should include, and then you can flesh out the actual content and site design later. One of the first things to recognize when building a website is that you will either need some type of software program or you will have to learn HTML coding and build your site from the ground up.

Web Design Hardware Requirements

You do not need to invest significant funds to be able to create your own website. You only need to have a reliable computer. Websites can be designed and tested on your personal or business computer, and you do not need to have your own Web server — in fact, you should avoid this cost. Many Web designers work exclusively from their laptop computers, which is a great way of having mobility so you can keep working on your Web pages no matter where you are.

You also need to have a fast, reliable Internet connection. It really does not matter what you choose, as long as it is high speed broadband that is reliable and cost-effective. Do not cut corners on your Internet speed, and do not use dial-up because it is far too slow and you will become frustrated with its limitations very quickly. You may want to use an external 1TB hard drive for regular backups, while programs like Carbonite™ are extremely useful for full backups of Websites. You can get a free trial at the Carbonite website (**www. carbonite.com**).

For graphics editing, popular options include Corel® Paint Shop Pro® X2 and Adobe Photoshop® CS5. Some well-known examples of Web design software include Microsoft Office FrontPage, Microsoft Expression Web, and Adobe Dreamweaver CS5. Other design applications such as Serif WebPlus X2 offer great tools for the novice designer. That said, you do not need to invest significant funds into advanced Web design applications. There are also many freeware, or free software, offerings for both your Web design and graphics editing needs, which will be discussed later on. Also, it is important to recognize that most Web hosting companies also provide easy to use website templates as part of your hosting package, enabling you to create a great looking site quickly and very easily.

In the Web design and development communities, you will see two distinct groups: the Microsoft group and the Adobe group. The Adobe group uses Adobe Dreamweaver CS5. Most Web developers consider Dreamweaver to be the professional Web designer's product of choice. In comparison, many used to consider Microsoft Office FrontPage to be the beginner's tool. Microsoft changed that with the release of Microsoft Expression Web, which matches up favorably with Dreamweaver. FrontPage is no longer officially supported by Microsoft, but it is still readily available for purchase. It is a good beginner tool that provides you with the what-you-see-is-what-you-get (WYSIWYG) environment where you create in design mode and the software writes the HTML code for you. WebPlus X2 is also a great design application for those without any HTML experience.

Website Hosting

Web hosting is a bit more complex than simply buying storage space, though that is essentially what you are doing. You are paying a provider to "host" your website on their Web server. As pages are requested from your website, it "serves" them to the website visitor. A Web server can host hundreds of websites simultaneously, which is how you can buy Web hosting services relatively inexpensively.

In most cases, you will buy hosting from a commercial service provider, though you can host your own website on your own servers. But hosting is cheap and reliable, and buying hosting services puts the burden of supporting the equipment, leased high-speed Internet connections, and back-up services and applying patches and upgrades on the service provider. Let your hosting provider deal with all the costs and challenges associated with keeping your website available; it is not worth investing in your own Web server equipment.

A Web host is the foundation you will need to build your website; you cannot begin to implement your design plans without it. The Web host provides you with disk space, e-mail accounts, and secured shopping carts. It is not recommended that you use a free Web hosting service because going the free route might end up costing you more money and headaches in the long run. One of the key factors in using a free Web host might include limiting your ability to create interactive pages or having enough space to build the site you have designed in your planning stage, and in most cases, none will support e-commerce or other advanced Web development needs.

You can use Google or any other search engine to find reputable hosting service providers, both free and cost providers. As you will find, feature-rich Web hosting packages can be readily obtained for under $100 a year. With Go-Daddy.com® (**www.godaddy.com**), for instance, hosting plans are relatively cheap, and you can upgrade to a virtual dedicated server with full administrative access or sign up for a dedicated server with administrative access. A virtual dedicated server has several businesses using it, but all are separated from each other by allotments of space and security, whereas a dedicated server is all yours — no one else uses any portion of it. A virtual dedicated server is suitable 99 percent of the time. All plans offer full customer support and include routers, servers, firewalls, and Google Webmaster Tools. As with most hosting sites, the costs can rise exponentially if you pile on the extras.

No matter what site you use, research and read the fine print to understand exactly what you will get with the different packages. One thing to look for is whether any site-building tools and templates are included in the package you choose. Also be sure to find out what types of customer service they offer, whether you can update your site when you want to, and what types of e-mail accounts and support the host provides.

Domain Names

You must own your own domain name if you want to have a serious Web presence. Your domain name is your brand name on the Web. It is the address every site visitor will type in to visit your website, and it is critical that you choose a good domain name and host it with a reputable provider. There are dozens of companies you can purchase your domain names from. Most offer convenient control panels that let you update settings.

Your domain name should uniquely identify your business. The general rule of thumb is that the shorter the domain name, the better, and it should be relevant to your company name, service, or products. If you already have an established corporate name or identity, you should try to base your domain name on that corporate identity. This will allow customers to identify your company name with your domain name. For example, Atlantic Publishing Company's domain name is **www.atlantic-pub.com**. We also highly recommend that you secure any similar domain names, the main reason being to protect your identity from others who may use a similar or identical domain name, with a different extension. Using the example above, you would also want to tab **www.atlanticpub. com**, **www.atlanticpub.net**, and **www.atlanticpublishing.com**. Your primary domain name should be the domain name that is "hosted," while others may be parked at no additional cost and pointed to the main domain name URL. This way, you only pay for one hosted domain name but utilize many domain names on the Internet, all directing site visitors to your main hosted site.

It is important that you name your website after your domain name. The primary reason for this is so that people know your website and business by name. CNN® stands for Cable News Network, but no one calls it that. CNN is simply known as CNN, and the domain name is **www.cnn.com**. While this may be a simplistic explanation, your domain name should easily relate to your company name so your "brand" or company name can be easily recognized or memorized.

Domain names should not be extremely long; this is going to be your URL address for your website, and the last thing you need is a long address no one can remember. Although some people may bookmark your page in their Internet browser, just as many, if not more, will not. You could lose valuable traffic if your website address is too long. If you are determined to have a long URL address, hyphenating the words will make it easier to read.

There was a time when domain names were readily available, but today you will find that many domain names are already registered by someone else. Typically, there are variations of your desired domain name available, or perhaps other domain name extensions such as .org, .net, or .us. You can check the availability of a domain name by going to the GoDaddy.com "WhoIs" database (**http://who.GoDaddy.com/WhoIsCheck.aspx**).

Advantages of Owning Your Own Domain Name

- You have full creative control over your domain name.

- It is easy to get it listed with the major search engines, which in turn makes your site easier to find.

- You can have multiple branded e-mail addresses, i.e. **you@yourdo-main.com**.

- There is plenty of Web page space for site expansion when hosted.

- There are no worries of your site being removed unexpectedly when hosted on a free hosting provider with a virtual domain name.

- It looks more professional than virtual domain names.

- You have more flexibility for design and functionality.

Website Design Fundamentals

On one level, a website design is an art form. It is a presentation of a concept or an idea through the use of HTML coding, just as a painting is the presentation of an idea rendered using paints of various colors and other such mediums. To determine what type of pages you need for a Web design project, begin by determining what you expect your site to look like. Below are some considerations to take into account.

- Consider the amount of information you have and how to organize it. Under no circumstances should the site visitor be overwhelmed by the content. If there is too much information, you will probably have to think about creating a database to manage it all. Ordinarily, however, you should just think about developing a reasonable amount of information per page.

- Consider how visitors are likely to use the information. Most websites allow the user to simply sit back and read information. Most people spend their time online reading e-mails, catching up on the latest news, or occasionally tracking the financial markets. Online banking is big, too. Most of these activities fall somewhere between being entirely passive and being moderately passive, but that does not mean that people do not enjoy interactive websites and online activities. Also consider whether there is going to be any need for visitors to download content, such as video or audio files.

- Consider users' expectations. It is important in your design process, as you develop a concept for a site, to have a fairly clear idea of what people are going to want from the site when they visit. Since most users have a pretty clear idea of what they expect when they go looking for a particular website, it pays to look closely at what features are common among sites that are relevant to your project.

For the layout and multimedia content of the site you design, think about the best way to organize the information you need and the best way to meet the expectations of site visitors. Most sites have a unique homepage layout and two or three subordinate page designs. Uniformity is important as an aesthetic element, too; people do not want to be overwhelmed by too many different page layouts any more than they want to be overwhelmed by too much information or too many multimedia features. Select the best elements — the top three or four page layouts, the best three or four colors, a single font style — and stick with them, applying a single resolution to all the pages.

Websites are always a work in progress. There will constantly be products or information to add and updates to liven up your page and garner more page views. Aim for a site that is content-rich with images that catch the eye but is still easy to load and navigate. Many buttons, icons, and frames are good if they serve a purpose and make the site better, but if they serve as a distraction or a nuisance, people will look for a site that is less complex. However, just as there are some sites with too much, there are sites that are full of "under construction" pages and black holes. A messy, incomplete site will also steer the average browser to a better place, even if you do offer a better product or service. You never want to put a site up that is not ready for potential clients to see. A small, comprehensive website is a good foundation for better, more complex features as you learn more and grow. You can add things after you establish your basic website with all the necessities.

Plotting out how your website will be seen is another vital part to creating a winning website. No amount of advertising or quality content can make up for an unattractive or sloppy design and layout. Many websites have amazing content but rarely get seen because they are not appealing to a user at first glance. Take some time and plot out what you want to do on paper. List all of the links you want to have on your homepage. Color is crucial and should be given plenty of thought. A dark or heavily patterned background with a light text is hard to read and can divert people's attention from your products. Backgrounds should be white or a light color that dark text can stand out on. A dull website with no personality is not going to win you regular visitors either, so go with a combination that is universally liked by most people. Brightly colored text should only be used for highlighting words. If you choose to use a color other than black for your main text, make sure it is dark. If black is too plain, opt for a chocolate brown or navy on a light background. It is crucial to find something most people will like, combinations that appeal to the eye and are easy to read. Black text with a white background is not the only option. Some combinations that work well, for instance, are a light blue with a dark chocolate-colored text or a light green background with a navy blue text.

The layout of a page and its components will make or break your website. You have limitless options in the layout of your website, but there are some general rules to follow that will make your page standard enough for even the extreme novice to use and understand easily. Avoid making things so busy no one can focus on a single piece of your website. Including plenty of space where there are no graphics, text, or links is key to making a website clear and easy to maneuver. If you make it easy for your visitors to completely explore your site without any problems, they will come back for more.

The top of a page should be reserved as a marker for the name of the website or business. Think of it as a small billboard or a calling card. You can include a logo or another identifying image of your brand. Keep it simple and concise. The best positioning is in the middle third of a page. It will be front and center and impossible not to notice when a homepage loads.

Links to other pages on a website, called navigation buttons, are typically positioned in one of three ways. You can place them across the top, down the left side, or down the right side of each page. If you choose, you can place two sets of links at the top and bottom, allowing the visitor to click on links even if they scroll all the way down or up the page.

Give your visitors options to increase the likelihood that they will move on to other pages on your site. If you have many different links on your homepage, you may choose to place them vertically on the left or right side just because of how many there are. A list down either side of the page is much neater than having several that stretch across the screen and out of the main view. If you have several links and the top of the page looks like a large block of links clustered together, go with a listing on the side.

Labels for links should also be short. They should convey the message of what it connects them to without being too wordy. For instance, instead of "All about us and our history as a company" go with "Company Bio" or just "About Us." Keep it short and sweet. Look at other websites and see what phrases pop up. It is a good idea to go with the grain. If you want to be unique, you can come up with your own link words, but make sure that people can make the connection you intend.

Every computer will view a page differently as well. Your site should be designed to look good no matter what the resolution or page view settings of any computer are. Using a percentage setting on your website can make it look good on a wide range of screens, not just yours. With 80 to 90 percent, your page will fill 80 to 90 percent of the screen width of every computer. Keep in mind that most monitors sold today are high-resolution, wide-screen LCDs. You should still check your page in all possible resolutions whenever you are going live for the first time or after you add new pages.

One of the great benefits from using programs such as Dreamweaver or Expression Web is that they come with an arsenal of powerful tools for creating very impressive websites fairly easily. With these programs, it is also easy to create advanced effects such as rollover buttons, forms, navigation menus, and database integration. With the click of your mouse in Expression Web, you can create HTML pages, ASPX, PHP, CSS, master pages, Web templates, JavaScript, XML, and .ASP Web pages.

Expression Web and similar applications can create styles for you, and you can customize your style sheets as you work through them. By using CSS to lay out your website, you eliminate the need to use HTML tables. Expression Web even lets you create dynamic rollover buttons quickly and easily. You can also create amazing rollover navigation menus in a matter of minutes.

Make sure you are consistent throughout your website. Text which is "clickable" should be a different color than standard text. Fonts should be standardized throughout your site, and generally, your Web pages should be based on the same template so they appear seamless as they are served by the Web server. CSS sheets give you enormous control over the look and organization of your Web pages, but you can still achieve this without the use of CSS. Make sure you test out your pages in a variety of browsers on a variety of monitor sizes and resolutions. Design for a 1024 by 768 resolution, which is the "standard" today.

There are dozens of software applications on the market to help you create Websites quickly and easily. Some of these help automate the creation of HTML if you want to work in an HTML environment, while others let you create Web pages in a design environment where the HTML is written for you. This chapter will provide you with an extensive review of several of the most popular Web design applications on the market, such as Dreamweaver CS5 or Expression Web 3. Often it simply comes down to personal preference or what you are most comfortable with. Another available avenue is to use a content management system (CMS), such as Joomla! These programs offer tools to create, modify, and organize information on your website. However, they do require some technical savvy to install and set up, so unless you truly need a CMS, this option is not highly recommended for beginners.

Other suggestions for simple website development may be through your Web hosting provider. Many offer custom templates and simple applications to expedite Web development and let you get a site created and hosted within hours. Hosting providers like PowWeb (**www.powweb.com**) and Applied Innovations (**www.appliedi.net**) offer free page-building tools, a large amount of space for your website, and all of the interactive capabilities you may want to incorporate either now or later. The only drawback of free applications such as these is you are limited in creativity since you have a limited set of options to manage and design your website, and often it can be very difficult to move your site to another hosting platform if required at a future date.

This chapter will also give you an overview of some free HTML editors, such as Nvu, and whether you need these editors once you build your site. Other topics will include learning what open-source software programs such as WordPress and Joomla! offer, how they work, and how you can use them to create a platform for your website. It will also touch on the hosting systems some of these open-source software programs need to be fully functional.

Joomla!

Joomla! is a CMS that helps users build websites. Not only is this software free to use, but the Joomla! site (**www.joomla.org**) also provides a forum where users can find additional support and answers to their questions. Joomla! allows users to download an easy-to-install package that provides website builders with the ability to add, edit, and update images. It utilizes a simple browser interface that allows users to upload new items, job postings, images, and staff pages. It also allows users to create a subscriptions feature, which is helpful in learning who visits your website.

This software offers multiple applications to allow website builders to create add-ons and extensions. Some of the examples listed on the website include form builders, business or organizational directories, document management, image and multimedia galleries, e-commerce and shopping cart engines, calendars, forums and chat software, blogging software, directory services, e-mail newsletters, data collection and reporting tools, and banner advertising systems. Joomla! is a great free, open-source application you may wish to consider if you want a robust, flexible CMS.

WordPress

WordPress (**www.wordpress.com**) is another free open-source option for building a blog. Blogs can be — and often are — used as websites. This is an attractive option to some people because blogs are free and easy to use. Many businesses have abandoned the idea of maintaining both a blog and a website in favor of just a blog. This is also a good option for creating personal websites. *Blogs will be discussed in greater depth in chapter 11.*

Homestead®

Homestead (**www.homestead.com**) offers many options for making your site extremely simple, interactive, and user-friendly. Homestead is designed to work with small businesses and help them reach out to find new customers while also getting their sites noticed by some of the major search engines like Yahoo! and Google. This site provides more than 2,000 website templates, which you can either use individually or use to create your own customized template. You can also start from scratch and build your own template if you so choose.

A unique aspect of Homestead is that it offers you the capability to edit text right on the Web page or completely replace it with your own content by pasting it on the page. You can upload images from your computer's hard drive or use some of the more than 250,000 images available to you for free. Homestead will also provide support in transferring your current domain name and even help you to create a link to redirect your traffic to your new site. You can add forms to collect information from your visitors so that you can send them e-mail promotions and newsletters, or you can get a guest book and allow your visitors to post comments. The site includes a PayPal shopping cart you can set up to make it easy for your customers to purchase items or services without having to use a credit card, and it has an e-commerce option if you want to set up a larger business site. Homestead is a great option if you do not want to learn a Web design application and want to create an attractive site quickly.

Nvu

Nvu, pronounced "en-view," is an open source software program designed exclusively for the Linux computer operating system. If you are a Linux user and need an easy-to-use Web authoring system, Nvu may be your solution. Nvu is free and originated from the Mozilla® Composer code base. According to the Nvu website (**www.nvudev.com**), it takes the basic functionality offered by Composer and adds new levels that allow "integrated website management, better form and table support, and better browser compatibility." One of the advantages of using Nvu is that it allows an easy-to-use system for Web file management and WYSIWYG Web page editing, which makes this software a good choice for someone with little or no HTML code experience.

Although Nvu was primarily designed for the beginning Web builder, the site explains that it is also a great tool for advanced Webmasters because it reduces the amount of time required to build a professional-looking site. Nvu is not an exact clone of FrontPage and Dreamweaver, which use the Windows operating system, but it is similar because it incorporates many of the same easy-to-use features of these products.

Microsoft Office Live

Another website hosting service that offers free site building software is Microsoft Office Live Small Business. This host offers free hosting, domain registration, e-mail, and tips for getting traffic to come to your site. When you sign into the site (**http://smallbusiness.officelive.com**) and click on the "Design a Website" tab, a design window pops up that allows you to use a predesigned table format to build your site. You just type in the information you want included on your site. It comes with a navigation bar set up on the left with pre-labeled tabs for "Home," "About Us," "Contact Us," and "Site Map." At the top of the design page, there are options such as fonts, colors, font sizes, site themes, styles, navigation options, inserting your logo, headers, and footers. There are also image, document, and template galleries that you can browse and select from to build your page.

This option for hosting and building your website is self-explanatory, and everything you need to build a personal and small business site is available. You will need to log in using your Windows Live™ ID or register for a free Windows Live ID to access the site and begin building your own Web pages. There are definite limits to this option: You cannot use your own domain name because Live assigns one to you, and you have limited control over the content of your site.

The SeaMonkey® Project

As an open-source project by Mozilla, the company who manages and distributes the popular browser FireFox, the Seamonkey Project (**www.seamonkey-project.org**) includes: a Web browser, an e-mail and newsgroup client, an HTML editor, Internet relay chat (IRC), and Web development tools. The SeaMonkey Internet Suite is completely free and is a great way to learn HTML. The SeaMonkey Internet Suite is available for Windows, Mac, and Linux-based systems. It also supports CSS and other advanced languages. The HTML editor produces HTML 4.01 compliant code, but it does not produce XHTML or XML. The HTML editor does not support all elements, but does allow for elements from other HTML documents to be pasted in.

The SeaMonkey Composer, its WYSIWYG Web design program and HTML editor, features four different views in its user interface: Normal (WYSIWYG), HTML tags, HTML code, and browser preview. Because the program is open source, there is a large community of support and plenty of documentation to help people who are working with SeaMonkey.

There are many other free Web design applications and solutions you can use. You can do a search on your favorite search engine with the keywords "open source HTML editors" or "open source Web building software." This will pull up thousands of sites to choose from. However, use caution and read all the fine print to ensure you are not downloading and building your site on a software program that is just a free trial version with a 30-day usage. Many of the trial or demo software programs do not provide the full software capabilities, and they will shut down your entire usage capabilities at the end of the free trial, leaving you with a completely built site that you no longer have access to unless you pay for the full version of the software.

Now that you have an overview of the free options, this next section will give you an in-depth review of some of the most popular commercially available Web design applications on the market and compare features among these applications. You must choose which path you are willing to take to build your own website. If you want a quick, easy site and do not want to spend money, there are plenty of options for basic websites or blogs. If you want to create highly customized or advanced websites and avoid using templates, you need to use a more advanced Web design application such as Dreamweaver, Microsoft Expression Web, or WebPlus X2.

Microsoft Expression Web, part of the Expression Studio suite, works with the SharePoint® Designer to replace the Microsoft Office FrontPage product previously included in the Microsoft Office suite. The Microsoft Expression Web program is a WYSIWYG and Web authoring program meant to help people design websites and Web applications that use ASP.NET or PHP.

Microsoft Expression Web is currently in its third version. The Microsoft Expression Studio suite includes: Expression Web, Expression Blend, Expression Design, Expression Encoder, and SketchFlow. All of these programs work together similar to the programs in the Adobe CS5 Design Suite. When compared to its major competitor, Adobe Dreamweaver, many believe Expression Web is the better program for designers and Dreamweaver is the better program for coders.

Microsoft Office FrontPage

Microsoft Office FrontPage is a WYSIWYG Web design and website administration program produced by Microsoft. The most recent version of this program is FrontPage 2003. This program is meant for those who are not familiar with HTML and Web design technology. FrontPage is integrated with a Microsoft Office interface so as to make the program work seamlessly with the other programs many people are already familiar with from the Microsoft Office suite. Microsoft FrontPage has several benefits, including a shared office interface, a WYSIWYG editor, help for novice designers to learn HTML code, and a low-cost availability.

It was designed for Windows-based systems, though a Mac version was released in 1998. The Mac version of the program came with fewer features than the Windows version, and because of this, the program never received any updates. Though it is no longer supported by Microsoft, there is no shortage of support for the program from other users, so those who are looking to save some money and still want a Microsoft-based product may be satisfied with FrontPage. You can upgrade to Expression Web in the future, if you so desire. The automatically generated HTML is non-complaint with HTML standards set forth by the W3C. The code is hard to edit for compliance and is proprietary to Microsoft.

Adobe Dreamweaver CS5

Adobe Dreamweaver is a combination WYSIWYG Web design program and text editor to allow for both visual design and line-by-line hand coding. Originally owned by Macromedia®, the program debuted in December 1997. Macromedia was acquired by Adobe in 2005, and since the acquisition, Dreamweaver has been updated to version 10.0, more commonly known as CS5. Dreamweaver is considered an industry standard for Web design because it is widely used in many institutions. Adobe chose to discontinue its GoLive® competitor product when it acquired Dreamweaver from Macromedia.

People without any HTML or coding knowledge at all can use this product with ease, and there is plenty of support to be found. Dreamweaver is also suitable for Web designers who use other programs in the Adobe suite, including Flash, Fireworks®, Photoshop, and Illustrator®. There are several integration tools, meaning you can use a file from one program in another. Dreamweaver formats and color-codes the actual scripting of the pages to make learning the code and editing the code easier for the designer.

One of the drawbacks of Dreamweaver is that it comes with a steep learning curve and is also pricier than its competitors. While this is a drop in the bucket for Web design firms and larger corporations, this cost is not very feasible for many small businesses, let alone individuals who want to learn how to code and design their own websites.

Web Page Content

Content drives search engine visibility and is vitally important to achieving success on the Web. Content is critical not only in drawing visitors into your site, but also in enticing them to return. Writing solid, comprehensible content means two things: You have to know your topic, and you have to have a good grasp of how to build your content into something of value.

Search engines look for well-written, interesting, and unique content and information that is updated and relevant. Content should be written so that it can be easily scanned because site visitors may not have time to read lengthy text. Include bold-faced headlines with text to make it easier for visitors to find what they are looking for without having to read everything. Four basic tips for writing good Web content are: include keywords, use clear titles, keep it short and sweet, and forego the sales pitch so your visitors can get to the real meat of the site.

Your first sentence and paragraph is going to determine whether your visitors will read the entire Web page. One of the first things you learn in journalism is how to write a lead, which is that first sentence you see in most newspaper stories. It must be something that grabs the reader's attention and is best served with a solid verb to describe what the article is about. Make sure your content is not only timely but also relevant to your readers. Remember to spell check everything. Do it as you write and again when you are finished. Also make sure to check your grammar closely. Using fancy fonts will not help you to retain visitors because they are just too difficult to read and often not Web-friendly.

It is imperative to write about something you know and have researched extensively. Just throwing words on a page is not the way to write your content. You must have a clear focus on what you are trying to sell or offer to your clients. If you do not understand the topic you are attempting to write about, neither will your audience. Do not be too wordy; use clear, concise descriptions. That does not mean you cannot write longer copy when necessary — it just means you do not want to write more than is required to explain your product or service. When using the Web, potential clients want the information to be quickly and easily digested.

Only hyperlinks to other pages or websites should be underlined. There are many other ways to emphasis a specific area of your content, such as bolding or italicizing sub-headlines to divide your content into predetermined areas. You can also implement bullets or numerical lists. Within the text and in sub-headers, you may create links to different areas of your website, single pages on your site, different sections of a document on the same page, or to other websites. In doing so, however, remember to use the keywords you have chosen to promote your site with search engines. Another factor to remember is to leave enough space between your content and graphics or images. Do not allow your content to flow under or over these items. If you have content that is buried or unreadable, you will irritate your readers and may lose current and future customers because the site looks unprofessional.

People seldom read Web pages word for word; instead, they sweep the page, selecting various words and sentences. In researching the way in which people read websites, it was discovered that only 16 percent read word-for-word. Consequently, Web pages must use analyzable text and employ accentuated key words. Additionally, Web pages must contain significant sub-headings, bulletized lists, and ideas organized by paragraph.

Rules of Web Writing

Your website is your professional calling-card. A well-written Web page explains what your website is all about, who you are, and what products or services you offer. It must be captivating and easy to read. People often make instantaneous decisions based on what they see, and websites are no exception. The following are some general guidelines for creating Web page content.

- **Create content for the site visitor:** Perhaps the hardest part about creating a website is determining what is important for your readers, which may be in opposition to what is important for the business. Ensuring that you create content for the website visitor is critical.

- **Convey the advantages:** Content must clearly convey the advantages and benefits of visiting your site or using your products or services. Give visitors the information up front.

- **Write to reach your visitors:** Write your content in a conversational tone. This ensures a much clearer model of writing.

- **Format pages for ease of scanning:** Web pages are often filled with long, uninterrupted paragraphs that are often nearly impossible to read. Site visitors typically only sweep these pages. Capture the main ideas, concepts, and key points in your copy so the reader can skim the content without losing the main purpose.

- **Use images with Web page content:** The use of images is necessary to seize the attention of site visitors. You must gain their attention immediately, and the creative use of images is one of the best ways to do that. Once you do so, your content should provide them with the information they are seeking. Images should be used strictly to enhance your content.

Website Graphics

The saying "a picture speaks a thousand words" still holds true in this digital age. When used properly, pictures and images are able to convey ideas and concepts in ways that words cannot. But they can just as easily become a distraction and an eyesore. The use of images in the right places on a website can enhance the user experience, but you must ensure that your images do not detract from your keyword-rich Web page content.

Images can define the character of a website at first look. Excessive use of images can characterize a page as an amateur page, while a reserved use of images is usually correlated with information and news-related sites. Images can be used for representations of data in forms such as graphs and charts without having to script the necessary code to parse and display such information dynamically. They can be used to set the tone of an article through pictures and photographs. The importance of graphics and images on the Web is undeniable.

Images and graphics are key components to website design. You must balance text with graphics and white space. You do not want to drown out your written content with too many pictures or graphics. Most webmasters believe the rule of thumb is to use no more than three pictures or graphics on any given page and resize them to no more than 72 dots per inch (DPI) to ensure that they load quickly. Balance and space images so that the written content is clearly visible on the page, which allows your visitors the opportunity to begin reading your content as the pictures load. These can add a touch of class to your Web page, but they do usually require a subscription fee.

Images provide an added value to your site, but if there are too many, they can also detract from your site and make it look less professional. Clipart should be used with extreme caution because it tends to make your site look amateurish in nature. Most of the clipart and graphics available for free download are of low quality. One of the best website investments you can make is to obtain royalty-free stock photos. These can add a touch of class to your Web pages and are absolutely free.

Use CSS when possible to control font size, color, and layout. External style sheets are typically used for this purpose because they control the entire site. The style sheet is actually a file on your Web server that stores all your CSS preferences. You embed HTML code into each Web page, and your style sheet is applied when the page is loaded in the browser. You can also use internal style sheets, which control only the page they are on; this is useful if you need one page to function or appear differently than the others.

Image File Formats

The three main formats of images seen on the Web are JPEG, PNG, and GIF. TIFF and BMP are other familiar formats. Although they might all look the same at first glance, each has its own advantages and disadvantages.

JPEG stands for Joint Photographic Experts Group, the committee that created the standard. Its most common file extensions are .JPG or .JPEG. This is one of the most popular graphic formats on the Web because it is usually the default output format for most cameras and other imaging devices. However, default and most popular does not always mean the best. Certain versions of JPEG use an interlaced, progressive loading style. The rough outline of the image is displayed first before the details slowly start filling in. The difference is almost unnoticeable for smaller images, but on larger JPEG images viewed through slow connections, you can see the image slowly being formed as it loads. The advantage of this is that the user can view a low-quality, but full, version of the image before the high-quality version of the image loads. This is contrary to the linear loading style used by PNGs and other formats, where the image is loaded line by line, pixel by pixel, in its full quality.

One disadvantage of JPGs is that they do not support an alpha component, so this format can only be used for full-sized images without any transparency. This is one of the main reasons why JPEGs are not often used in features like menus and navigation bars that use irregular shapes like round edges or circles with transparent backgrounds. JPEGs can be compressed to your bandwidth needs, though this is at the cost of quality. Quality also varies based upon the system, since some browsers take shortcuts to decompress the file faster. The lossy compression, or losing of data, is one of the main problems with JPEG. It is infamous for leaving behind artifacts. You can notice the JPEG artifacts by comparing the original and the compressed version of the file and looking for blocks of color and loss of minor details.

Portable Network Graphics, or PNGs, are a newer file type with support for many features. They stand apart from JPEGs because they have an alpha channel, which allows transparency. They also support indexing options that allow you to reduce the file size of an image by narrowing down the number of colors used in the image pallet. PNGs also differ from JPEGs in that they have support for lossless compression, which preserves the original quality of the image. The advanced preprocessing techniques this format utilizes for compressing files come at the minor cost of speed. It also comes with a gamma channel to adjust the brightness of the image. The main highlight of this format is its extremely efficient compression. If you are looking for a small file size that is light on bandwidth without any loss of quality, then PNG is your format.

The Tagged Image File Format, or TIFF, is a universally accepted file format for images compatible with most Window, Mac, and UNIX™ operating systems. TIFF images incorporate a lossless compression, giving you small file sizes without loss of quality. This is an important factor to consider when storing any quality-sensitive images. Compression always comes at the cost of speed in opening and saving files. Although the difference is minute with modern processors, the speed might be a factor to consider for images and files that need to be repeatedly opened or saved. TIFF files are used mainly for the purpose of printing and archiving.

Bitmap, or BMP, is another common file format. Bitmaps are usually uncompressed, leaving their file sizes much larger than equivalent PNG or JPEG files. There are multiple versions of BMP available, including a 32-bit version supporting an alpha channel for transparency. BMP files can be manually compressed into a fraction of their original size using free compression programs such as 7-Zip.

GIF images are one of the original image formats of the Web. They are usually used for animations. Their use is limited because GIF images limit your pallet to 256 colors. Because of this, gradients and other shades are often hard to achieve within the limits of GIF, unless it is used for small images such as logos. Programs such as GIMP, the GNU Image Manipulation Program, allow you to draw your graphics in full color and then reduce the pallet down to the essential 256 colors. This often results in grainy pictures. The main advantage of GIFs is that they offer a simple alternative to bandwidth-intensive video. GIF files also support JPEG-like interlacing options that allow a rough image to be downloaded before the full detail image. This is especially useful for users with a slow Internet connection. The format also uses a lossless compression technique to compress the images into a smaller file size.

SVGs are Scalable Vector Graphics files. Unlike JPEG or PNG files, SVG files store information as vectors. This allows you scale the image indefinitely without losing any of the quality of the image. This makes it an optimal file type for logos and other images that are repeatedly resized, since resizing often causes blocky pixelization with most other file types. The features of SVGs are limited when it comes to more advanced enhancements, so consider saving a basic outline of your image as an SVG and then doing the final touch-up on it and saving it as a high-resolution JPG or PNG.

Images and HTML

The way an image is incorporated into a page is very important when it comes to SEO, usability, and accessibility. The following is an example of how to embed an image into an HTML document. Open Notepad or another HTML editor and create the following Web page:

```
<head>
<body>
<img src = "Images\SampleImage.png"></img>
</body>
</head>
```

Save it to your desktop or local folder. In the same location, create an "Images" folder and place a sample image in the folder from your system. You can edit the **src** attribute of the image to point to your particular image. It is also possible to add in an image without the end tag **</img>** by using this format:

```
<head>
<body>
<img src="Images\SampleImage.png"/>
</body>
</head>
```

Run the sample Web page file in a Web browser to see the output. The code displays the image **SampleImage.png** from the Images folder in the local directory. The default position of the image is at the top left corner. You can move the image around the screen by doing this:

```
<head>
<body>
<div style = "position:absolute;left:40px;top:20px;">
<img src = "Images\3.png"></img></div>
</body>
</head>
```

The line **<div style = "position:absolute;left:40px;top:20px;">...</div>** moves the image 40 pixels right and 20 pixels down. You can also align text as top, bottom, middle, left, or right by doing this:

```
<div style = "align:center;position:absolute;left:20p
x;top:350px;">
```

It is possible to add borders to images by using the border attribute with the number of pixels as the parameter:

```
<img src = "Images\3.png" border = 10>
```

If you want to set an image as the background of a page, just add the background attribute linking to the background image to the **<body>** tag:

```
<html>
<body background="Images\background.jpg">
</body>
</html>
```

Although it is recommended that you format images beforehand, it is sometimes necessary to do basic adjustments to the image while it is being displayed. You can adjust various properties of an image such as its source, width, height, and border though these lines:

```
<img src = "Images/sampleImage.png" width=1024
height=768 hspace=0 vspace=0></div>
```

The **"width = 1024"** and **"height = 768"** attributes resize the image to 1024 by 768 pixels. Keep in mind that it can sometimes reduce the quality of the image if the original ratio is different from the new one. The **hspace** and **vspace** options adjust the vertical and horizontal spaces around the image. Setting these to 0 will align the image to top corner of the page. Adjusting this value is also a way to move the image around the page without relying on the **<div>…</div>** tag.

Search Engine Optimization & Images

Naming your image properly will help optimize it for search engines, allowing users to easily find the image. The mouseover text description, or tooltip, of an image is another factor to consider for SEO. Properly tagging images drives search engine traffic to your website. Proper tagging will also aid users with images disabled to navigate the site without trouble. Try the following code without having **"SampleImage.png"** in the local directory:

```
<img src="SampleImage.png" alt="Sample Image" />
```

The Web page will display a blank square with the image not found symbol and the text from the **alt** tag. The **alt** tag still shows up whether or not the image is there. This adds an extra layer of protection to your Web page since it is still usable even without the images. The **alt** tag will also make your website more accessible to users with disabilities since it is compatible with most assistive software such as Microsoft Narrator. You can further improve accessibility while optimizing for search engines like Google and Yahoo! by using "D" links and **longdesc**.

```
<img src="SampleImage.png" alt="A sample image show-
ing the use of HTML attributes" longdesc="sampleImage
Description.htm"><a href="sampleImageDescription.htm"

title="Sample Image">D</a>
```

The page that the **longdesc** points to can contain a further description of the image, allowing you to describe the image in higher detail while squeezing in a few more keywords related to the image. A sample description could look something like this:

"The image shows a sample image used commonly to demonstrate sample features. The sample image is ambiguous in nature. The blank background blends in nicely with the blank foreground. It also uses the PNG format, referring to another part of the article. The image shows how simple tags can be decorated to make it more accessible while also optimizing it for search engines."

The **alt** tag can contain a basic description of the image with a few keywords, while the **longdesc** should either be a longer sentence or should link to a better description of the image. One of the main differences between **alt** and **longdesc** is that the description in the **alt** tag is visible when you mouse over the image, while the description in **longdesc** is not. Do not, however, stuff either of the descriptions with keywords. Modern search engines use spam filters that look for the excessive use of catch phrases without any real content. The **alt** and the **longdesc** should be a textual replacement for the image without being simply a list of tags. Also note that decorative eye candy is usually not tagged. This is to help keep the HTML page simple and clean without any unnecessary information. Ask yourself if the speed and bandwidth costs are worth the extra tag.

Another factor that search engines consider is the file type. JPEGs are often associated with photographs, while GIFs are assumed to be site graphics. Make sure to choose the right file type so that your images are categorized correctly.

Using just one copy of an image and then referencing it consistently throughout your website could help its page rank in search engines like Google. This is one reason you should always license your images correctly so as to protect them from being leeched to other sites. External sites can, however, link to them. This improves your page rank while protecting your Web property.

Copyrights and Licenses

When using content from other sites, always give proper citation. A simple link with credit to the photographer and a short note about the license is usually enough, but check with the original author to see if he or she has any special preferences. Properly cite content using an accepted format, such as the Modern Language Association (MLA). Properly citing is another one of the factors that search engines consider when ranking. This is one reason why Wikipedia® pages often get a high page rank.

You should always host all important image files on your own server. Files hosted on free image hosting servers are convenient for larger, more bandwidth-intensive elements of the site, but should not be used for main components such as navigation and logos, since many of these sites are prone to downtime and file loss. Image leeching is considered bad manners on the Web. Never use an image from another website without the expressed written permission of the website owner to make sure you are not violating any copyright laws. Hosting images on your own server will protect crucial content. You can find many free images online that are released under free and open licenses. Look for images marked "copyleft" or those released under the Creative Commons License. Be sure to read the license carefully to make sure you comply with the requirements listed before using the image for your website. If you cannot find what you are looking for, consider using one of the following programs to create new and original graphics for your website.

Free Graphics Editing Software

GNU Image Manipulation Program (GIMP) is a widely used graphics editing program. It is a free, open-source graphics program released under the GNU General Public License (GPL). Its functionality is similar to Photoshop in the sense that its main focus is to edit and enhance photos and other pictures. It supports all of the basic features such as cropping, color filtering, brightness and contrast, hue and saturation, and color modes. It also comes with many filters and plug-ins for the more advanced editing requirements. These include blur, sharpen, oilify, edge detect, lens flare, fractal rendering, solid noise, plasma, ripples, and waves. Additional plug-ins can be created or downloaded from the official GIMP website. GIMP allows you to open and save your files in a variety of file formats. Note that you can work with Photoshop files in GIMP since it supports .PSD, the Photoshop file format. One disadvantage is that, like Photoshop, GIMP can sometimes be very resource heavy. If you plan to add more plug-ins and external features to do more advanced editing, make sure you have a system that can support the RAM and processing needs of GIMP. The support for brushes, patterns, and add-ons combined with a myriad of built-in features make GIMP a serious alternative for Adobe Photoshop. You can download the latest version of GIMP for free from the GIMP website (www.gimp.org). It is also possible to download past versions of GIMP if the current version is not working for you.

Microsoft Paint, also known as MS® Paint, is the built-in graphics program for Windows. Although it comes with the bare minimum in features, it is an easy-to-use option for simple tasks. The main focus of Paint is pixel-based drawing. It will take much more work to get the same effects from Photoshop or GIMP in Paint since almost all of the work done by filters in GIMP must be done manually in Paint. Paint does allow you to switch between three modes of painting: pencil, brush, and airbrush. You can zoom in and work on individual regions of the picture in detail and then zoom out for a higher-quality finished product. There are tools to create ovals, rectangles, polygons, straight lines, and curvy lines. If you are running a Windows system, MS Paint should already be on your system. Go to **Start > Run >** and type in "MS Paint." It should launch the Paint program.

Inkscape® is a vector graphics editor. It is used to create SVG files. It is the perfect tool for creating buttons, logos, and other simple graphics in a snap. You can also create a custom character set to use as a font for your site in Inkscape. The Calligraphy Tool is perfect for such tasks. If your mouse handling is not so great, draw rough outlines in Inkscape, then use the Node Tool to edit it to your liking. Since SVG files are actually XML files, it is actually possible to edit SVG files with any text editor. That, however, can be very tedious. Inkscape is an easy-to-use program that allows you to create amazing artwork using simple shapes and tools. Inkscape can be downloaded for free at the Inkscape website (**www.inkscape.org**).

Paint.NET is another graphics program that offers features similar to GIMP and Inkscape. It comes with the simplicity of MS Paint, the usability of Inkscape, and some of the advanced features of GIMP. Its main use, like GIMP, is photo manipulation, and it supports all of the popular file formats. The two programs are almost exactly same in many aspects, but the interface of Paint. NET is different than GIMP in the sense that it only displays the basic tools and features. It offers features similar to, but better than, regular MS Paint, but without the high-tech features of GIMP. You can download Paint.NET at the website (**www.getpaint.net**).

The decision between these four free programs is the simple matter of personal taste. Each offers unique features and capabilities that, when combined, can allow you to create eye-catching graphics without the cost of expensive and bloated software like Photoshop. All of these programs are being actively developed at their corresponding sites, so expect bigger and better features to be added to the bundles in the future.

Commercial Graphics Editing Software

Adobe Photoshop is the most popular graphics editing software on the market. It is geared toward professionals and is incredibly complex and expensive. However, it stands out among the competition for its incredible depth of features, functionality, and power. It is the best graphics editing software on the market.

Corel Paint Shop Pro Photo X3 is a much cheaper, yet still feature-rich, alternative to Adobe Photoshop. The bottom line is that it is an excellent program that will meet the needs of most graphics challenges and is not overly complicated to learn. Corel Paint Shop Pro Photo X3 balances user-friendly design with powerful features at a reasonable cost.

Logos and Banners

Logos and banners are another aspect of Web design that is intertwined with graphics and animation. Creating a logo requires a great amount of patience and care. There are plenty of options for creating an outstanding logo. You can create it yourself or contract it out to a graphics design professional. There are also many software packages designed to help you create them yourself. AAA Logo (**www.aaa-logo.com**) is one of many companies that allows you to download the latest trial version of the software. Although this is not free software, AAA Logo is reasonably priced and provides the user with more than 8,000 unique logo objects and logo templates that can help you build your own logos, business cards, banners, headers, and icons for your site. This software allows you to create nearly any graphic you might need for your business or personal use. AAA Logo offers industry-specific logos in its pre-built templates, including technology, finance, health care, general business and retail, education and training, travel and tourism, organizations, sports and fitness, and food and beverage.

Website banners and advertisements are often the first impression a website has on a potential visitor. The two most common sizes for banners are 728 by 90 pixels and 468 by 60 pixels. Banners and advertisements must be interesting enough to capture the audience's attention. It is often a good strategy to ask a question or offer a sneak preview of the full content available at the website through headlines or catchy topic titles. This is enough to intrigue the audience, but not enough to satisfy its curiosity. Flashy, distracting advertisements are associated with scams and spyware more often than not, so their effectiveness has decreased dramatically. It is better to attract new users through content than through manipulation because it ensures that they will keep coming back.

Colors and Themes

When picking a color scheme, keep the feeling you want to create for the website in mind. Warm colors such as red, orange, and yellow can represent passion and energy, while cool colors like blue, green, and violet are used to create a sense of peace and serenity. Neutral colors like gray and brown are, of course, neutral. Colors have meaning and emotions tied to them just like words and images. Look for colors that complement each other to give your website a nice flow.

The choice of colors is usually a personal one, as everyone has his or her own individual preferences regarding color. However, there are some basic rules that seem to be universal. Primary colors like red, yellow, and blue tend to emphasize simplicity as well as speed. Secondary colors are created by mixing two primary colors together. These include green, orange, and purple. Tertiary colors can be created by mixing secondary and primary colors together. When choosing the colors, first decide what parts of your website you want to stand out and what parts should flow. Use colors that are adjacent to each other to create a sense of consistency to your website. Use colors that are opposite of each other in the color wheel to highlight content by making it stand out. Over-contrasting everything could become an eyesore, so be picky in choosing what to emphasize.

Shades of gray are created when the red, green, and blue values are all the same (Ex: 127, 127, 127). Bright neon colors are created when one value is a lot higher than the two others (Ex: Neon Green: 0, 255, 0). Softer colors are created when the colors are closer together (Ex: 255, 200, 150). These should be used mainly for backgrounds and other large, solid-colored spaces. The colors on the foreground of the page should be at the opposite end of the color wheel so they are easily visible against the background. Look around at other websites to find complementary images and colors.

Website Typography

Typography is another factor to consider when designing a Web page. There are many free fonts available online. You can also design a character set for personal use in Inkscape or GIMP. Choosing the right fonts and using them in the right places can really add to the style of a page. The choice of font can help set the mood and tone for the content. Be creative with titles, but be sure to choose a simple and easily readable font for the main text of the page.

The choice of font size is another important aspect of typography. Size 24 is commonly accepted as a good size for headlines, and size 12 is common for regular text. Keep your audience in mind when choosing the font size. Font sizes should be relative. If your main text is going to be in a bigger text, then the headline must be much larger also. The standard ratio between the body text and the title text is two to three times larger. Always follow the basic rules of grammar and sentence and page structure.

Website Templates

There are thousands of website templates available for you to use when developing your website. Many of these are of high quality and are designed specifically for Dreamweaver, FrontPage, or Expression Web. These applications also come with built-in templates, as does WebPlus X2. Even when you create your own website, you will create a template for your site, which you reuse as you add new Web pages, whether this template is created from the ground up, is purchased from a design company, or comes with your website hosting package or your design application software. Template is not a bad word, and you should consider commercial templates as a starting point for your Web design efforts. You can use these or customize them to meet your design needs.

There are dozens of websites that also sell customized templates, such as PixelMill™ (**www.pixelmill.com**). Most templates take advantage of include pages, which allow you to have portions of a Web page "call" data from other pages and display it on that page. To the site visitor, it is seamless, but for you, it simplifies maintenance and changes. If your entire site navigation is an include, and you have 300 Web pages, you edit the one navigation page, and it is updated instantly on 300 pages. The alternative is that you update 300 pages individually.

CHAPTER 6

Automation of Your Website

One of the important aspects of advertising online is the ability to automate as much of the work that you have to do as possible. The more parts of your business that you can automate, the more time you can spend taking care of other parts of your company business. There are many work tasks that you can automate, including:

- Automation of the way that you take payment for orders
- Automation of the way that you process those orders
- Automation of your e-mail lists and database
- Automation of the way you deliver your product or services
- Automation of your invoicing
- Automation of the "Help" section of your website
- Automation of e-mail marketing campaigns
- Automation of Web forms

There are many areas of your website that you can automate to make your job as easy as possible and avoid the possibility that some important tasks might fall between the cracks.

Using Auto-Responders

An e-mail auto-responder is a software program that sends a pre-written reply to anyone sending a message to the auto-responder's e-mail address, typically an e-mail address that is accessible from your website. If someone sends an e-mail to an auto-responder's e-mail address, it automatically and immediately e-mails this person the reply — for example, "Thank you for contacting the Atlantic Publishing Group." The auto-responder is one of the most popular ways to automate your website. You will have the ability to set up the response messages to your customers in a way that will most benefit your company.

You will also be able to send out reminders to those customers that have not visited your website in a certain amount of time, perhaps offering an incentive to return to your website and purchase items.

Methods of Payment and Payment Gateways

When you have an automated system that lets you accept credit card payments, you will not only be simplifying your business, but you will also be making sure that you have all bases covered when it comes to your payment plan. There are typically fees for using online credit card authorization services; however, you reap the benefit of instant credit card approval or denial. One no-cost option for businesses with a limited number of products is to utilize the free PayPal system to accept credit card transactions. But even if you do not use PayPal as your payment processing system, you should ensure that your shopping cart is capable of accepting PayPal payments as the use of PayPal has increased dramatically in recent years. Shoppers do not necessarily have to have a PayPal account to pay with a credit card.

Managing Your E-mail Names

We discussed the importance of growing an e-mail customer database and mailing list. When your business is first starting out, you will have time to manage your mailing list, which will most likely be very small as you begin your online venture. However, as your business grows, so will your mailing list, and you will find that management of the database and e-mail list is time-consuming. You should incorporate an automated method to collect your e-mail addresses. The use of Web forms soliciting customers to "join our mailing list" on the website is the best place to start. Instead of having customers e-mail you with their contact information, you can connect the form to a Microsoft Access® database on the Web server and allow the database to automatically capture that data for you or automatically populate your opt-in mailing list. *Chapter 7 discusses e-mail marketing campaigns at length.*

How to Automate Your Website

If you are operating an e-commerce website to complement your existing brick-and-mortar business, then you most likely recognize the importance of Internet marketing and the integration of shopping cart solutions as part of the overall approach to website management. If you are going to sell online, you need a combination of powerful marketing systems and credit card processing systems to be efficient and profitable.

One of your goals should be to have as close to a hands-free sales and marketing system as possible. Automation of your website processes enables you to focus on other areas to grow your business, travel, do charitable work, spend more time with your family, or enjoy a favorite recreational pastime or hobby, all while your business continues to market and sell your products and services. You simply check in to ensure that your website is operating properly, credit card orders are processed, and other automated processes are working as designed.

The benefits of automation are so numerous that you cannot afford to ignore them. If you automate your online processes correctly, then you will reap the rewards from this type of "hands-free" marketing that lets you sell to customers 24 hours a day, seven days a week. The importance of implementing a reliable automated order processing, marketing, and advertising system is of crucial importance to sustained website expansion.

- **Cost reduction:** Automation reduces your costs across the board, including everything from long distance phone bills, to direct mail postage in your sales and marketing department, to reducing the need for additional staff to handle customer service and support.

- **Easy to run:** The number one complaint of most business owners is their inability to get away from the business. With automation, your online business becomes much easier to run, requiring little attention and maintenance. With a properly implemented automated e-commerce solution, you can check your sales and customer orders from anywhere with a Web browser.

- **More time:** You can free up more time than you ever expected to focus on priorities for the strategic growth of your company, addressing all those small problems that pile up and eat away your day.

- **Satisfied customers:** Automation lets you serve your customers faster and more efficiently. Staff can focus on other high-value functions that require human intervention, or you can reduce the high cost of customer service representatives.

- **Targeted marketing:** When your e-mail lists are compiled, your prospects can be segmented according to the offers and promotions to which they respond based on demographics. When they join your e-mail list, or as they e-mail you for a specific offer or question, they can be put on a demographics list that identifies them, the products they want, and their personal preferences. This will allow you to market to your prospects more effectively, efficiently, and personally.

Automation could be just what your business needs to give you the edge over your competition. The following steps will help you build a successfully automated business website.

Taking orders online

When you are taking online orders for your business, there are a few things that you can do to push sales to even higher levels:

- Set up a merchant account and gateway, which will approve your credit card orders automatically through the bank.

- Create custom, branded order forms unique to your business to provide a highly professional image.

- Consider limited use of audio/video to sell your products/services. Do not use background music on your website, or you will quickly lose customers.

- Incorporate cross-selling to promote additional products to customers at checkout.

- Offer incentives to close the transaction, such as free promotional items.

The final stage of checkout is where most customers are going to change their mind about buying your product and thus abandon your website. Shopping cart abandonment can be as high as 60 to 80 percent. You need to make sure your online ordering process is as efficient and streamlined as possible so that the remaining 25 percent of customers make repeat purchases.

Affiliate programs

An affiliate program is a Web-based pay-for-performance program designed to compensate "affiliate" partner websites for driving qualified leads or sales to your website. Typically, you will pay a percentage of any sales resulting from any click-through, via banner or text link, to your website from an affiliate partner's website. However, you should understand that once established, the majority of the processes are automated and require minimal manual intervention. The incorporation of an affiliate program into a website's marketing and sales portfolio allows you to market and sell your products through thousands of content-related websites throughout the world.

Ad tracking

Ad tracking is a great way for you to know how many times a person clicks on a certain link on the Internet. This is extremely valuable data because not only does it allow you to determine how many times a banner was clicked, but it also lets you know how much revenue was generated. This simply means that you can tell how many times a visitor was directed to your website from a link and made a purchase. Most affiliate programs provide tracking and click-through data, as do some search engines. *Pay-per-click advertising is explained in further detail in Chapter 8.*

Using Software for Automation

There are many different types of software that will help you to automate your website efficiently and effectively. Some of the tedious tasks that need to be completed each day include keeping track of your passwords, making submissions for your websites to search engines, monitoring traffic to your website, and testing new features of your website. When you use automation software, you will be able to have these tasks automated by a running script or functionally specific software applications.

Different types of automation software will provide you with different functions, depending on the software bundle that you purchase, and many are included in the major website design packages, such as Microsoft Expression Web 3. There are many different companies on the Internet from which you can choose. Make sure to research before you make your final choice so that you are completely happy with the features you purchase. You can expect to pay anywhere from $100 to $1,000 for the right software bundle; however, most automations can be found for free or for a minimal charge at the following websites:

- Scripts.com™ (**www.scripts.com**)

- The JavaScript Source (**http://javascript.internet.com**)

- Dynamic Drive (**www.dynamicdrive.com**)

Developing Positive Relationships with Customers

Developing positive relationships with your customers is crucial to your long-term success and profitability. Once you have a customer's e-mail address, it is important to communicate with him or her frequently. You want to follow your leads and convert more of the visitors to your site into customers. When you use auto-responders, you can personalize the messages that you send to customers. This can be accomplished in both the subject line and in the content of the e-mail you send.

E-mail newsletters are a great way to communicate with your customers since there is an endless amount of information you can include in a newsletter. Remember to provide information that is relevant and factual. Studies show that when companies send out newsletters that contain nothing more than sales pitches for their products or services, customers tune out these sales pitches and discard the newsletter. When this scenario occurs, you have no chance of developing a positive relationship with your customer.

If you have a budget that allows it, consider sending out postcards to reach your customers and communicate with them on a personal level. Do not target all the suspects, prospects, customers, and advocates in your database since that type of a marketing program would take too much money, time, and effort and would likely yield little results. Instead, choose one customer segment on which to focus, such as parents of small children. Postcards are a cost-effective way to send useful information to a select group of customers.

It is important that you do what you say you are going to do. This means honoring all special offers and bonuses that you promise. When you or your products fail to deliver on their promises, you lose credibility, which is crucial in establishing a trusting relationship with your customers.

When a customer makes an effort to contact you, make sure that you return the communication as soon as you can. Follow the three basic rules when drafting e-mails to customers: professionalism, efficiency, and protection from liability. Draft a corporate e-mail policy that addresses e-mail etiquette to ensure that all employees are on the same page.

CHAPTER 7

E-mail Marketing

E-mail marketing, when designed and implemented correctly, can be one of your most effective advertising, marketing, and sales tools. It can also be one of your most cost-efficient means of disseminating promotional materials, advertisements, special offers, coupons, new product announcements, and relevant news to a large audience for absurdly low costs when compared to traditional print media advertising and marketing campaigns. Practically everyone now has e-mail, and most access e-mail daily both at work and at home. E-mail marketing allows you to distribute information instantly and globally while providing detailed tracking and reporting not possible with other forms of advertising and marketing.

E-mail marketing has garnered a somewhat negative reputation. E-mail marketing is not spam, when it is done properly and legally. A properly designed e-mail marketing campaign is targeted, relevant, and useful to the recipient. If you want a successful and spam-free campaign, it does take some planning, design, and organization to ensure that your e-mail marketing campaign is optimized for success. If you have a personal computer and check e-mail, then you are already familiar with e-mail marketing, since you most likely receive such messages multiple times per day, often unsolicited and unwanted.

E-mail marketing is simply defined as the promotion of products or services via e-mail. E-mail is a very versatile and widely used form of communication. Thanks to advancements in technology with e-mail clients such as Microsoft Outlook® and Mozilla Thunderbird® and the offer of free e-mail accounts from industry giants such as Google and Yahoo!, e-mail is affordable, readily available, and used by nearly everyone both at and away from their work environment. E-mail formats can be very simple text-based or more complex HTML with embedded graphics and advanced website design techniques. The content of an e-mail can be customized based on size or target audience, and you can have scheduled deliveries, nearly automating the entire process. Of course, one of the biggest benefits is that overall costs for implementing an e-mail marketing campaign are very low, especially when compared to other traditional advertising means.

E-mail marketing is ideal for:

- Businesses with products to sell

- Businesses wishing to distribute news

- Businesses that wish to maintain contact with customers

- Businesses wishing to promote new business lines, products, and services

- Businesses seeking to increase revenue

- Businesses that want to announce special events

- Businesses that seek to offer coupons or discounts to customers

- Businesses that strive to save money on advertising costs or have limited advertising budgets

- Small, independent businesses competing with industry leaders

- Businesses seeking to expand customer bases or reach into new market areas

Plan Your E-mail Marketing Campaign

The biggest challenge you will face is the actual design of your e-mail marketing campaign. You must determine what your desired results are and how best to attain them with a single e-mail. It is important that you first identify what your goals and objective are with your e-mail campaign. For example, your goal may be to distribute industry-relevant news, articles, or information, or it may be to promote specific new products that you can provide.

The best advice when designing an e-mail marketing campaign is to start small and think clearly. In other words, do not try to reach all of your business objectives in a single e-mail. Compile a list of the many objectives you would like to achieve; start with the simplest, and go from there. Sending an e-mail with an introduction, news articles, product information, discounts, subscription offers, and a variety of other potentially useful information will saturate your customers with information overload. Introduce them to your company, give them an incentive to go to your website, and let your business win them over.

As you build successive e-mail campaigns, you can target products, provide industry-relevant information, and build your e-mail client list.

The following steps will help you develop a successful e-mail marketing campaign.

1. **Target your audience and content:** One of the advantages of an e-mail marketing campaign is the ability to target your audience. It is important to realize that you may be able to — depending on your e-mail list — target a wide variety of demographic information such as age, gender, interests, or geographical information such as country, state, region, or city.

2. **Write and design your e-mail:** Writing an effective e-mail can be a challenge. You will need to decide if you want to use text-based e-mail, HTML, or both. In addition, you will need to ensure your e-mail is balanced, error-free, and properly formatted to be displayed in the recipients' e-mail client. How you deliver your message is critical to the success of your campaign. If your recipient will not open your e-mail, it is a failure; therefore, you must at least capture the interest of the recipient to open your e-mail and hopefully click-through to your website. Obviously, if your goal is to sell products through your e-mail marketing campaign, its success hinges on the ability to actually close the deal and ultimately sell products on your site as a result of your e-mail marketing campaign.

3. **Set up your online mail distribution method:** There are many companies that offer all-in-one solutions for managing your e-mail lists, creating and sending your e-mail campaigns, and tracking statistics. Many even offer exceptional templates to simplify the process of designing your e-mail campaigns. It is highly recommended that you use either an all-in-one solution provider or one of the industry experts to manage your e-mail campaigns. Do not attempt to send out e-mail marketing campaigns through your local e-mail client or you likely will find yourself suspended for "spamming" through your ISP; nor should you use one of the many "bulk" e-mail providers who offer to send your e-mail to hundreds of thousands of recipients for one low fee. Know your service provider and have confidence in the quality of your list. Do not use overseas providers to send your e-mail to recipients who did not ask to receive it.

4. **Review your e-mail list:** A quality e-mail list of opt-in recipients is a valuable asset to your company. Protect your e-mail list — it is valuable. Most all-in-one service providers provide you with HTML code for subscriptions, simplifying the process of allowing website visitors to join your mailing list.

5. **Test your e-mail:** One of the most important — and often overlooked — steps in the development of an e-mail marketing campaign is to test e-mails before you actually send them. You should open your e-mails in a variety of e-mail clients so that the format is exactly as intended. In addition, you should test each part of the document to ensure that it works properly. If you send an e-mail with mistakes, errors, or broken links, you will quickly lose potential customers. Pay special attention to the embedded graphics in your e-mails by viewing them on a computer other than the one you used to create your e-mail campaign. When you are satisfied with the quality, quantity, and functionality of your e-mail, it is time to schedule it.

6. **Schedule your e-mail blast:** You know your customers, and this chapter will help you determine the most effective time and day to schedule your e-mail blasts.

7. **Send your e-mail blast:** The act of sending your e-mail is actually the simplest. With an all-in-one solution provider or e-mail campaign manager, this will be scheduled far in advance. You will not have to do anything except wait for results once your e-mail campaign is developed, tested, scheduled, and actually launched.

8. **Analyze the results:** Similar to testing your e-mail before actually sending it, analyzing the results is often overlooked. You must do this if you want to understand the effectiveness of your e-mail campaign. All-in-one solution providers will supply you with plentiful data, including volume rates, bounce rates, open rates, and click-through rates. Understanding what is working and what is not is critical as you develop and refine your e-mail marketing campaign.

E-mail marketing is, of course, limited by the size of your advertising budget, but it is one of the most cost-effective methods of advertising you will find.

Spam, Spoofing, and Phishing

E-mail spam is the sending of unsolicited commercial messages to many recipients without the explicit permission of the recipients. Another major concern with spamming is the "spoofing" of e-mail addresses. Spoofing is a method of concealing the identity of the sender and making you believe the e-mail is in fact from a reputable business. With spoofing, the spammer modifies the e-mail message so it appears to come from another e-mail account. Spoofing can occur with any e-mail account or domain name. For example, you may get an e-mail from Bruce Brown with the e-mail address of **bruce@email. com**, which may be a legitimate e-mail account, thus avoiding spam filters and giving you, the recipient, peace of mind. Spoofing can cause you a multitude of headaches. As the recipient of the e-mails, you can become bombarded by "spoofed" e-mails, many of which appear to be legitimate. Dealing with spoofed e-mails is frustrating and time-consuming. As the website or domain name owner, it is much worse; typically, bounced e-mails are sent back to the spoofed domain e-mail account — yours. You may find you are receiving replies, bounced e-mails, and nasty grams for an e-mail you never sent. The main goal behind spoofed e-mails is to release privacy information or passwords to third parties who will use them against your business. If you suspect spoofing of your e-mail accounts or want more detailed information about spoofing, contact the CERT® Coordination Center (**www.cert.org**).

Most spammers are after privacy and/or financial data; some offer illicit activities such as pornography, get-rich-quick schemes, pirated software, or overseas business scams. The best combatants against spam are anti-spam filters, junk mail filters, and specialized software at the e-mail server and the mail client to protect your e-mail accounts.

Another major threat is phishing. Phishing is actually a variation on the word fishing, which means that "phishers" will throw out baited websites hoping someone will "bite." It is a process of sending a legitimate-looking e-mail to procure valuable, sensitive information, such as credit card or bank account numbers and passwords or a social security number. The e-mail will include a link to a phony website that closely resembles the legitimate site it is based upon. If the phishing scam is successful, the unsuspecting victim clicks on the link and enters their personal information; this information is then used to steal the victim's identity or use his or her credit card.

The key difference between operating legal permission-based e-mail campaigns and spam is the use of permission-based or "opt-in" e-mail lists. Spam or junk e-mail is e-mail that is sent to one or more recipient who did not request it.

The CAN-SPAM Act

The CAN-SPAM Act of 2003 (Controlling the Assault of Non-Solicited Pornography and Marketing Act) establishes requirements for those who send commercial e-mail, spells out penalties for spammers and companies whose products are advertised in spam if they violate the law, and gives consumers the right to ask e-mailers to stop spamming them. The law, which became effective January 1, 2004, covers e-mail with the purpose of advertising or promoting a commercial product or service, including content on a website. A "transactional or relationship message" — e-mail that facilitates an agreed-upon transaction or updates a customer in an existing business relationship — may not contain false or misleading routing information, but otherwise is exempt from most provisions of the CAN-SPAM Act, according to the Federal Trade Commission (FTC), the nation's consumer protection agency.

The FTC is authorized to enforce the CAN-SPAM Act, which also gives the Department of Justice (DOJ) the authority to enforce its criminal sanctions. Other federal and state agencies can enforce the law against organizations under their jurisdiction, and companies that provide Internet access may sue violators as well.

The requirements of the CAN-SPAM Act are as follows:

- **It bans false or misleading header information.** Your e-mail's "From," "To," and routing information — including the originating domain name and e-mail address — must be accurate and clearly identify the person who initiated the e-mail.

- **It prohibits deceptive subject lines.** The subject line cannot mislead the recipient about the contents or subject matter of the message.

- **It requires that your e-mail give recipients an opt-out method.** You must provide a return e-mail address or another Internet-based response mechanism that allows a recipient to ask you not to send future e-mail messages to that e-mail address, and you must honor the requests immediately. You may create a menu of choices to allow a recipient to opt out of certain types of messages, but you must include the option to end any commercial messages from the sender. Any opt-out mechanism you offer must be able to process opt-out requests for at least 30 days after you send your commercial e-mail. When you receive an opt-out request, the law gives you ten business days to stop sending e-mail to the requestor's e-mail address. You cannot help another entity send e-mail to that address or have another entity send e-mail on your behalf to that address. Finally, it is illegal for you to sell or transfer the e-mail addresses of people who choose not to receive your e-mail, even in the form of a mailing list, unless you transfer the addresses so another entity can comply with the law.

- **It requires that commercial e-mail be identified as an advertisement and include the sender's valid physical postal address.** Your message must contain clear and conspicuous notice that the message is an advertisement or solicitation and that the recipient can opt out of receiving more commercial e-mails from you. It also must include your valid physical postal address.

Each e-mail in violation of the CAN-SPAM Act is subject to a fine of up to $16,000. Deceptive commercial e-mail also is subject to laws banning false or misleading advertising. See the FTC website (**www.ftc.gov/spam**) for updates on implementation of the CAN-SPAM Act.

Most recipients of bulk e-mail, spam, or unsolicited advertisements view them as unwelcome, unpleasant, or offensive. However there are many mailing lists which deliver solicited (opt-in), useful information to recipients based on a variety of subjects they have expressed an interest in and have given their permission to allow companies to add their e-mail address to bulk mailing lists. The key to utilizing e-mail as a tool for marketing or advertising is to build your customer lists using opt-in methods to ensure that your e-mail lists comply with the requirements of the CAN-SPAM Act.

Spam Tools

Luckily there are numerous, reputable resources available to assist you with identifying and combating spam, spoofing, and phishing. The best of them are listed below:

- **Spam.abuse.net (http://spam.abuse.net)** — Contains an ongoing listing of spam related news, articles, and information.

- **Federal Trade Commission (www.ftc.gov/spam)** — The official spam site for the FTC, this site outlines the laws for consumers, businesses, and current penalties for violating anti-spam laws. This is the site where you can file spam complaints; just click on the "File a Complaint" link on the homepage.

- **Spam Laws (www.spamlaws.com)** — This site includes information on all the most recent legislation and laws from the United States, Europe, and other countries, as well as state laws and selected case histories.

- **CAUCE (www.cauce.org)** — The Coalition Against Unsolicited Commercial E-mail is a group whose primary purpose is to advocate for a legislative solution to the problem of unsolicited commercial e-mail.

- **SpamCop (www.spamcop.net)** — SpamCop determines the origin of unwanted e-mail and reports it to the relevant Internet service providers. Reporting unsolicited e-mail also helps feed spam filtering systems, including, but not limited to, SpamCop's own service.

As an e-mail marketer, it is critical that you understand what is and what is not spam. You do not want to be associated with spamming. This book is designed to make sure that you implement a successful, cost-effective marketing campaign. With spam being in the spotlight, there are ongoing debates about the true effectiveness of e-mail campaigns and the effect of spam regulations on the success of your e-mail campaigns. If done properly and carefully, your e-mail marketing campaign can be effective and profitable for your business.

Opt-in and Opt-out Lists

To maintain spam compliance and ensure your e-mail list is both legal and contains those subscribers who actually want to receive your e-mails, you need to understand opt-in and opt-out lists. The underlying principle behind opting in is very simple: If a customer has expressly given you permission to add his or her e-mail address to your e-mail list, then he or she has "opted in" to your list.

The following are some definitions that may help you to better understand these concepts:

- **Single opt-in:** E-mail addresses are added to your e-mail list through a subscription — such as completing a "join our mailing list" form, sending an e-mail to a subscription e-mail address, checking a box on an order to add your e-mail address, or providing your e-mail address to customer lists through business reply cards. This is a simple process and is not validated or confirmed. In other words, your e-mail address is added to one or more e-mail lists, and you do not have to perform any specific actions to confirm that it has been added. Often, the subscriber is sent a welcoming e-mail and instructions on how to unsubscribe if he or she did not intend to join the e-mail list — however, this is not always the case. While an opt-in list is effective and simple to manage, there are some potential drawbacks to maintaining such a list:

  ◊ **Subscription errors** — It is not uncommon for subscribers to mistype their e-mail addresses, making them unusable. An invalid e-mail address will bounce back when sent, or worse, may actually be delivered to someone who did not join your list. Mistyping a single character in an e-mail address can cause e-mail to be undeliverable or sent to someone else.

  ◊ **Invalid submissions** — Because of the prominence of spam in today's environment, many individuals may fill out Web forms and other subscription vehicles and enter a false or invalid e-mail address to avoid being added to potential spam lists. As with the subscription errors, an invalid e-mail address will bounce back when sent, or worse, may actually be delivered to someone who did not join your list.

  ◊ **False subscriptions** — Sometimes, a user will submit someone else's e-mail address to one or more lists. This really accomplishes nothing other than causing the recipient the frustration of receiving e-mails they did not subscribe to and also forces them to remove themselves.

  ◊ **List poisoning** — This is when invalid e-mail addresses are intentionally added to your e-mail list. In most cases, these will simply bounce back and should be removed from your list, but it does cause you extra administrative work. If your list is excessively poisoned, it may be rendered useless for its intended purpose. Another way lists are poisoned is by intentionally adding anti-spam e-mail addresses to your list, so that when your e-mail is sent to your list, these "anti-spam" e-mail addresses trigger "spam-traps" which can automatically put your IP address on a "blocklist" that keeps the sender's messages from getting through any mail servers.

- **Notification opt-in:** E-mail addresses are added to your e-mail list through a subscription. A welcoming e-mail is immediately sent to the subscriber with instructions on how to unsubscribe if they did not intend to join the e-mail list. This is very similar to single opt-in with the exception that the welcoming and opt-out e-mail is always sent. The main advantage of this over single opt-in is that you are notified of the list subscription and are given the opportunity to remove yourself from any e-mail lists to which you have been subscribed.

- **Double opt-in (closed-loop opt-in):** E-mail addresses are added to your e-mail list through a subscription. A welcoming confirmation e-mail is immediately sent to the subscriber with instructions on how to unsubscribe if he did not intend to join the e-mail list. The recipient must then confirm their subscription to be activated and added to the e-mail list. This is typically done through a hyperlink embedded within the confirmation e-mail. When the subscriber enters his or her e-mail into the "join our e-mail list" form, for example, he or she is immediately sent an e-mail confirmation. The subscriber must click on the embedded hyperlink to confirm the subscription; otherwise, he or she is not added to the list. This means the person who wishes to join your list must complete two steps to activate a subscription. While a double opt-in list is the most spam-compliant, it is not without its problems. Most of the problems are for you, not the recipient:

  ◊ **Complexity** — Double opt-in is more complex and requires a more advanced system to manage the process; thus, most small businesses or those with limited budgets often find this system is not affordable or readily available. You will discover in later chapters that many all-in-one service providers include double opt-in.

  ◊ **Negative impact** — As you now know, a person who wishes to join your list must complete two steps to activate a subscription. While this seems pretty simple, the fact is that the percentage of individuals who actually complete the double opt-in is very low.

In fact, you can expect to lose as much as 50 percent of your potential e-mail customers through this process when compared to single opt-in. Often, the confirmation e-mail is captured by spam or junk filters and is never even delivered to the recipient so he or she can confirm the subscription.

- **Opt-out:** Opt-out is simply the process where the e-mail recipient requests that a list owner take his or her name off of the list and ensures that he or she is not sent any future e-mails. You must provide a return e-mail address or another Internet-based response mechanism that allows a recipient to ask you not to send future e-mail messages to that e-mail address, and you must honor the requests. Most all-in-one providers do this for you by automatically adding opt-out features to each e-mail blast that you send.

How to Create and Grow Your E-mail Lists

The biggest challenge you will face is creating and growing an effective mailing list. There is no point in having a list with hundreds of thousands of e-mail addresses that are not relevant to your e-mail message or are invalid and will constantly bounce back as undeliverable. The most effective lists are those that contain only individuals who expressly wish to receive your e-mail marketing message and may potentially act based on the message you send. Realistically, depending on the type of message you send, you can expect between a 1 percent to 10 percent return; however, the 2 to 4 percent range is fairly typical.

There have been pushes for changes in regulations of e-mail marketing and the handling of spam, such as the creation of a "do not e-mail" list, similar to the nationwide "do not call" list used for telemarketers. Obviously, this is a hotly contested issue and would require significant changes in the management of e-mail lists. As of today, there is no such list.

One of the questions you must answer is what demographic information you wish to collect for your e-mail list. While capturing an e-mail address is the most basic, it may not be the most effective if you wish to target your e-mail blasts by region or other demographic parameters. You can collect a wide variety of demographic information, but if you try to collect too much data, you will turn off potential subscribers who do not wish to fill out a lengthy subscription form or provide too much personal information. At a minimum, if you are going to collect more than just an e-mail address, you should collect the first name, last name, gender, and state of the subscriber so you can use this information for e-mail targeting in your campaigns.

Proven methods to grow your e-mail list

There are many ways you can grow your e-mail list. This list is not inclusive of all methods, however; a little creativity can go a long way in creating an effective e-mail list.

- **Collect e-mail addresses on your website.** This is the best method of growing your e-mail list. If you have visitors on your site who have an interest in your products or services, it is an ideal time to capture their e-mail address. You can simply place a subscription form on your home page that is clearly visible and readily accessible. Since this form is directly on your website, you know that subscribers have an express interest in your products and/or services; therefore, this is a highly effective means of acquiring quality e-mail addresses.

- **Collect e-mail addresses from customer orders.** If you sell products through your website, you are most likely already collecting e-mail addresses. However, you still need to ask permission to add this e-mail address to your list. A simple method of doing this is placing a question directly on the website order form asking the customer, "Do you want to join our e-mail list?" You can customize this to provide a brief description of what the list contains as an incentive to get people to sign up. Once individuals check the "yes" box, you should still run the e-mail address through your double opt-in process to ensure that your list is completely anti-spam compliant.

- **Collect e-mail addresses through offline methods.** If you produce traditional media products or marketing campaigns such as print advertising, flyers, brochures, catalogs, business cards, and/or paper order forms, then you have an opportunity to ask them to join your e-mail list. Since such advertisements are often sent to hundreds of thousands of recipients, you have an ideal target audience from which to collect e-mail addresses. If a customer is returning something to your company, it is as simple as asking him or her to check a box and fill in his or her e-mail address, or you can put your website address on print media with instructions to visit the URL to join your e-mail list. Either way, there is no additional cost for asking for this information, and even if you only get a 10 percent return on a mailing of 100,000 individuals, you have just added 10,000 quality e-mail addresses to your list.

- **Collect e-mail addresses through surveys.** Online surveys are a great way to attract interest and draw in potential customers. Since you captured their interest in a survey, this is a great time to also ask them to join your e-mail list and capture their e-mail address. You can also do the same thing for print surveys.

- **Collect e-mail addresses through e-newsletters.** This simply means that you use your e-mail list to distribute your e-mail marketing campaigns, such as e-newsletters. One of the great things about e-newsletters is that you can include subscription forms right inside the newsletters and also incorporate a "forward to a friend" link, which can exponentially increase your distribution and potential subscriber list. Also, you should take your e-zines or e-newsletters and publish them on your website — this does two things for you:

  ◊ It gives customers the opportunity to read back issues, which may have relevant information. By including subscription information on them, you may draw in e-mail subscribers who never actually received your e-newsletter via e-mail.

  ◊ It allows you to place keyword-rich content on your website that will be scanned and indexed by search engines and spiders, so your e-newsletter can work for you by increasing your overall visibility in search engines. It is important to include proper HTML formatting, including meta-tags in each HTML newsletter, to maximize the effectiveness within search engines.

- **Collect e-mail addresses through promotions and giveaways.** Promotions, free offers, and giveaways are great ways to attract attention, draw in new customers, and acquire new e-mail leads. Some caution needs to be taken when you offer free products, however. First, the use of the word "free" in e-mail subjects is a standard target for spam filters. Your message may be flagged as spam before it ever gets to its intended target. Secondly, when you offer something for "free," you can expect much interest from people who have no real interest in your product lines and, therefore, you may not be collecting quality e-mail addresses.

- **Collect e-mail addresses through discount offers.** This is one of the most effective ways to attract potential customers and convert them into return customers. If your goal is to both collect permission-based e-mails for your e-mail list and build customers, you need to specify the terms of the offer very clearly, such as offering a 25 percent discount on any product on your website. One of the terms of your offer may be that the customers must join your e-mail list, thus converting not only a sale, but also a quality addition to your website. You can then use the e-mail list to solicit repeat business by sending your "preferred" customers another discount certificate, drawing them back to your site. If they are satisfied with the products and service provided to them, you may have just made a repeat customer for life.

- **Collect e-mail addresses through associate and affiliate programs.** For example, Atlantic Publishing Company (**www.atlantic-pub.com**) offers an affiliate program. You can become an affiliate for free and earn a flat 20 percent commission for every sale through your website. Since you now earn money for essentially doing nothing other than listing products on your website, the affiliate sponsor is hoping you will send out your affiliate links to all your friends, business associates, and others hoping they will buy the products. Obviously, the affiliate sponsor is looking for customers — and subscriptions. If you host an affiliate program, you can even ask your affiliates to include a subscription form to your e-mail list on their websites as part of the affiliate terms.

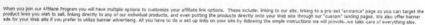

Earn an Amazing 20% Commission on ALL ELIGIBLE SALES!! The Highest Commission Rate in the Industry!!

Atlantic Publishing Company is now accepting affiliates into their brand new Affiliate Program. This program pays a minimum of 20% commission to all affiliates, with the potential to earn even more.

If you have a web site you can earn money by selling books and other Professional Food Service Industry products by linking with Atlantic Publishing Companies Affiliate Network or selling our products on your website. We have greatly expanded our product lines to include:

- Food Service & Hospitality
- Real Estate
- Entrepreneurial
- Personal Finance
- Human Resources
- Hospitality
- Internet / Web
- Spanish Products
- Professional Books
- Training
- HACCP
- Food Service Encyclopedias
- And Much More!

When you join our Affiliate Program you will have multiple options to customize your affiliate link options. These include: linking to our site, linking to a pre-set "entrance" page so you can target the product lines you wish to sell, linking directly to any of our individual products, and even putting the products directly onto your Web site through our "custom" landing pages. We also offer banner ads for your Web site if you prefer to utilize banner advertising. All you have to do is set up links on your site by following the simple instructions we will provide...we take care of everything else.

You can earn fantastic revenues by simply participating in the Affiliate Program, earning 20% of the total eligible purchase!! Our web-based Affiliate Management Program allows you to track sales and commissions online through our advanced reporting interface. The program is simple to join and easy to implement on your Web site. Technical support is available to help you maximize your affiliate setup and marketing campaign.

We feature an online Affiliate Program Application which allows you to adjust your preferences; choose different banners, entrance pages, and landing pages; as well as monitor your affiliate statistics (click-through, sales, etc.)—All for FREE!! Plus, you will receive e-mail notification after an Affiliate Sale is processed through your account, notifying you of the total purchase and your commission amount.

Please note: "Affiliate Eligible" products are those produced or published by Atlantic Publishing Company. A complete list of products is available by clicking HERE. Although all products sold on our site are not eligible for affiliate-based commissions, our system will recognize which items are eligible (even if someone orders a mix of eligible and non-eligible products on the same order) and provide you with an accurate accountability of your actual earnings through your notification emails, and online reporting tools. If you have additional questions, please review our Affiliate Frequently Asked Questions Web Page.

CLICK on the JOIN US Button to read our Agreement Terms and JOIN the
Atlantic Publishing Company AFFILIATE Program!

Make sure that if you host an affiliate program, you have a solid anti-spam policy to protect you in case one of your affiliates decides to promote your affiliate link through less than reputable e-mail distribution lists, such as the one below:

Spam: Atlantic Publishing Company has a zero tolerance policy for spam. Any affiliate accused of spamming will be immediately removed from our affiliate program. The only recourse you will have to maintain your affiliate relationship is proof of opt-in that will undermine the validity of the spam complaint. Valid spam complaints will result in the immediate termination of your account and forfeiture of any commissions owed to you.

How to keep people from unsubscribing from your e-mail list

There is no secret formula you can use to keep people from unsubscribing to your list; however, a little common sense can go a long way in solving this problem. The main reason people unsubscribe from a mailing list is that they are not receiving the material they expect or desire. You have to give your subscribers what they signed up for. You can always add additional information that may be of interest, but you must provide them with what you told them they would be getting when they first signed up for your e-mail list. Keep your list active, at least quarterly or more frequently, and keep your information fresh, relevant, and interesting.

How to Design an Effective E-mail Campaign

Writing an e-mail masterpiece is not as difficult as you may believe. While there are certain challenges you may have to overcome, the actual creation of the e-mail blast is probably easier and less time-consuming than developing and growing your actual e-mail list.

Here are some of the basics you need to review as you design your e-mail marketing campaign:

- Identify your audience so you know who you are targeting and why. You will often find your target audience varies depending on the type of e-mail you may send and often you will have multiple e-mail lists based on segmented target audiences.

- Establish the purpose and nature of your e-mails — will they be in the form of a newsletter, advertising, coupons, product announcements, press releases, articles, or a combination of any of these?

- Choose your format — will it be HTML, text, or both? This is a subject of great debate. Ten years ago, text was king. Five years ago, you should have used both text and HTML. Today it is recommended that you use HTML, with text as an alternate.

- Who is responsible for your e-mail development efforts? Are you going to manage all aspects of your campaign, or will you use an all-in-one service provider? Will you create, edit, format, and test your actual e-mails, or will you contract this out to an e-mail marketing specialist? Who will manage the administration of your program?

- What are your short- and long-term plans? Do you intend to do e-mail blasts on a regular schedule or randomly?

- Ensure that whatever method you use to manage your lists is 100 percent opt-in to maintain compliance with anti-spam laws, and always include a method for anyone to opt-out of your lists at anytime.

- What methods will you use to gather e-mail addresses and grow your current e-mail list? At a minimum, you should include a sign-up form on your website, prominently featured on your home page. You may consider additional forms on your shopping cart checkout pages and in your customer e-mails or order notifications. You may even want to include this information on print media such as brochures or business cards. Do not forget to ask customers to join your list during phone conversations, at trade shows, and at other industry events.

- Discuss the technical requirements of your marketing plan. This covers a wide variety of items, such as managing your e-mail lists, sending the actual e-mail blasts, bandwidth constraints, ISP policies, e-mail software, HTML development, automation of opt-in and opt-out techniques, and required hardware. Do not discount the expertise of the individuals who will be required to manage and administer your program, including the development of your actual e-mail blasts.

HTML vs. text format

The first issue you need to address is whether to utilize HTML-based e-mail or text-based e-mails. Several years ago, this was a fairly pertinent question as many e-mail programs were text-based and could not handle HTML-based content. Today, that is not the case, as the majority of e-mail applications effectively handle and interpret HTML code and present it in the proper format to the reader. While the trend several years ago was to cater to text-based e-mail applications, now mostly HTML-based e-mails are used; however, the issue is not entirely clear-cut. Just because these e-mail programs read HTML does not mean that they are configured to allow it; plus Microsoft Outlook 2003, by default, does not allow the download of images in e-mails. The Department of Defense, Department of Homeland Security, and several private corporations enacted security restrictions on receiving HTML formatted e-mail messages. They strip the HTML coding and convert the e-mail to a text-based format. If you are only blasting with HTML-formatted e-mail messages, your message will be received at such facilities as scrambled HTML code, which is practically unreadable. This means there is some advantage to sending both HTML- and text-based e-mails to recipients or sending HTML with an alternative link to text versions of the e-mail.

HTML-formatted messages are simply Web pages that are sent through an e-mail server, re-assembled, and presented to the recipient in his or her browser. The advantage to HTML is that you can use highly customized formatting, embedded graphics, and other dynamic features that require HTML coding. HTML allows you to use fonts, colors, graphics, and interactive, rich media technology. This format typically looks much more professional than text-based e-mails, which are simple text with little formatting, no graphics, no colors, and no special font formatting, only hyperlink capabilities.

So which is better? It is recommended to use both if possible. Most all-in-one providers allow you to craft both text and HTML formatted messages, and you generally want to give your subscribers the option to choose their personal preference. However, HTML is the more prevalent, preferred format today, and more likely than not, your subscribers will be able to view HTML e-mails.

```html
<html>

<head>
<meta http-equiv="Content-Type" content="text/html; charset=windows-1252">
<title>ATLANTIC PUBLISHING COMPANY FOOD SERVICE MAILING PROGRAM INFORMATION</title>
</head>

<body>

<!-- Begin Table -->
<table border="0" cellpadding="0" cellspacing="0" width="800">

<tr>
<td rowspan="1" colspan="1" width="266" height="200">
    <a href="http://www.atlantic-pub.com/coop_application.htm">
    <img name="apc0" src="http://www.atlantic-pub.com/ezine/apc_1x1.gif" width="266" height="200" border="0" alt="" /></a></td>
<td rowspan="1" colspan="1" width="267" height="200">
    <a href="http://www.atlantic-pub.com/coop_application.htm">
    <img name="apc1" src="http://www.atlantic-pub.com/ezine/apc_1x2.gif" width="267" height="200" border="0" alt="" /></a></td>
<td rowspan="1" colspan="1" width="267" height="200">
    <a href="http://www.atlantic-pub.com/coop_application.htm">
    <img name="apc2" src="http://www.atlantic-pub.com/ezine/apc_1x3.gif" width="267" height="200" border="0" alt="" /></a></td>
</tr>

<tr>
<td rowspan="1" colspan="1" width="266" height="200">
    <a href="http://www.atlantic-pub.com/coop_application.htm">
    <img name="apc3" src="http://www.atlantic-pub.com/ezine/apc_2x1.gif" width="266" height="200" border="0" alt="" /></a></td>
<td rowspan="1" colspan="1" width="267" height="200">
    <a href="http://www.atlantic-pub.com/coop_application.htm">
    <img name="apc4" src="http://www.atlantic-pub.com/ezine/apc_2x2.gif" width="267" height="200" border="0" alt="" /></a></td>
<td rowspan="1" colspan="1" width="267" height="200">
    <a href="http://www.atlantic-pub.com/coop_application.htm">
    <img name="apc5" src="http://www.atlantic-pub.com/ezine/apc_2x3.gif" width="267" height="200" border="0" alt="" /></a></td>
</tr>

<tr>
<td rowspan="1" colspan="1" width="266" height="200">
    <a href="http://www.atlantic-pub.com/coop_application.htm">
    <img name="apc6" src="http://www.atlantic-pub.com/ezine/apc_3x1.gif" width="266" height="200" border="0" alt="" /></a></td>
<td rowspan="1" colspan="1" width="267" height="200">
    <a href="http://www.atlantic-pub.com/coop_application.htm">
    <img name="apc7" src="http://www.atlantic-pub.com/ezine/apc_3x2.gif" width="267" height="200" border="0" alt="" /></a></td>
<td rowspan="1" colspan="1" width="267" height="200">
    <a href="http://www.atlantic-pub.com/coop_application.htm">
    <img name="apc8" src="http://www.atlantic-pub.com/ezine/apc_3x3.gif" width="267" height="200" border="0" alt="" /></a></td>
</tr>

</table>
<!-- End Table -->

</body>

</html>
```

Basic HTML e-mail (HTML view)

The HTML view below is what will be received by the user when the e-mail blast is sent:

Would you like to advertise your products to

150,000

food service professionals for only

8¢ each?

ATLANTIC PUBLISHING GROUP, INC.

FOOD SERVICE MAILING PROGRAM provides an opportunity for your company to reach food service professionals—from owners of bistros to managers of large institutions. Partner with non-competing firms to share in the cost of mailing and get results! You can choose to mail 150,000 locations across the country or target specific areas—all with proven results.

CLICK HERE FOR MORE DETAILS

Sample HTML-based e-mail

When designing an HTML e-mail, you should follow the same principles of website design. You should also follow the rules for SEO and incorporate meta-tag data and keywords into the design. Many companies place their e-mail newsletters, articles, and other e-mail blasts on their websites, which is recommended. It is also recommended that you design your HTML e-mails in a Web design application such as Microsoft Expression Web or Adobe Dreamweaver.

The process of actually creating your e-mail blast is exactly the same as designing a Web page. If you want to ensure you have a professional campaign, there are numerous e-mail marketers and Web design companies who are cost-effective and highly reputable. Your goal when creating an e-mail is to catch the attention of the recipients, captivate them with interesting and relevant content, and provide them with the ability to complete an action — fill out a Web form, follow a hyperlink, provide information, or place an order.

Options for E-mail Marketing Service Providers

Consider using an all-in-one service provider to transmit your e-mails, provide tracking, manage your lists, and perform maintenance such as managing bounces and importing new e-mails. This does not relieve you from creating your actual e-mail campaign; you will still need to do this, although the service you select will provide you with templates to simplify the process. These tasks can be daunting on your own, and it is not realistic — nor typically allowed by your ISP — to host your own e-mail lists on your local PC or domain.

An all-in-one service provider will provide you with self-managed tutorials so you can perform all management tasks. You are provided with templates and help guides, and many of the tasks are automated, such as sending the e-mails, tracking the results, generating detailed statistics, and managing e-mail lists. This method can be less costly, but it will require you to manage your accounts, create your e-mail blasts, manage your lists, and schedule your own e-mail blasts. The service provider sends out your scheduled e-mail blasts using their service with your lists.

You can also hire an e-mail marketing specialist who will perform all tasks for you, including the management of lists, creation of all e-mail blasts, sending e-mail blasts, tracking, reporting, and performing all the maintenance tasks associated with your account. This is essentially a full-service provider solution — you do nothing more than tell the specialist what you need and when to send it, and they do all the work. While much simpler for you, it is more costly. Another possibility is to purchase a commercial off-the-shelf program that can automate your e-mail campaign management on your own e-mail server or POP3 mail server.

The most difficult option is to do it all yourself. You can do this with Microsoft Outlook and a built-in contact manager/address book; however, most ISPs do not allow you to perform e-mail marketing or bulk e-mails as part of their terms of service. This is certainly the most cost-effective, but it may not be efficient or even realistic. If you have a very small business with a limited customer base and have 500 names or less on your e-mail list, you may be able to manage your entire campaign, but again, you need to check your local ISP policies and terms of service regarding e-mail use. This is also an option for new websites or businesses seeking to grow their lists to consider. Once you grow to a certain level, you may opt to use an all-in-one service provider to automate most of the processes involved or upgrade to a product that can provide you with total control of your campaign.

All-in-one e-mail marketing service providers

There are many all-in-one service providers to choose from. All of the ones listed here are reputable, cost-effective, and easily manageable without hiring specialists.

Topica (www.topica.com) — Topica's Online Marketing and Sales Solution provides data integration and analysis features, conversion optimization tools, and e-mail marketing capabilities. Topica provides customized solutions for internet retailers, online publishers, direct marketers, and interactive agencies. It is easy to manage and use. Since Topica is a fully featured provider, there are recurring monthly fees for using their service, as with other service providers. Topica offers an abundance of services at a relatively low cost, as well as a significant discount if you sign up for a yearly contract. Pricing with Topica is based on the number of e-mails you send out each month, not the number of e-mail addresses on your list. Additionally, Topica offers annual plans with 25 percent discounts. You can send out HTML, text, or multi-part e-mails, and when subscribers join your list, they can select which type they prefer to receive. There is a wide variety of user-friendly templates, which means you do not have to be an HTML expert to create HTML e-mail blasts with a professional feel. The reporting and delivery tracking tools provide you with real-time statistics, deliveries, bounces, and open rates. You can also personalize e-mails and segment or target them based on demographic data.

Lyris® HQ™ (www.lyris.com) — Formerly EmailLabs, Lyris's e-mail marketing solution is integrated with search, social, and mobile channels and enhanced with analytics to show you which of your campaigns are resulting in the most ROI. Lyris offers three editions of its HQ suite. The Essential Edition will suit most needs; this cost-effective solution grows along with your e-mail marketing needs. In addition to video training tutorials and Webinars, this edition also comes with live access to Lyris' support and e-mail deliverability team and 21 days with a personal account manager who will help get your marketing campaign on track and prepare you for future success. Lyris also offers the Power Edition for professional online/e-mail marketers who run complex, high-volume campaigns, as well as the Agency Edition for professional agencies who run such campaigns on their clients' behalf.

JangoMail (www.jangomail.com) — JangoMail is another industry leader in e-mail marketing. They provide all the standard features of most e-mail service companies, like open tracking, click tracking, HTML/plain text messaging, personalization, unsubscribe/bounce management, data import/export capabilities, e-mail list hygiene capabilities, and a double opt-in option. They also provide extra special unique features such as 24-hour support, advanced personalization, foreign language capabilities, and an advanced HTML editor. It also gives you 100 percent branding control; you will never see a "Powered by JangoMail" footer or tagline appended to the bottom of your e-mails, and you can specify all properties of your e-mail message, down to the header level details.

Constant Contact (www.constantcontact.com) — Constant Contact is highly respected and provides a robust, yet simplified interface that gives you total control over your e-mail marketing program. Similar to the other programs listed, Constant Contact is fully featured and has been very successful in meeting the needs of both small and large business for e-mail marketing. Constant Contact enables you to create and send top-notch e-mail newsletters and promotions with no technical expertise. They excel at making the process easy for you — including list management, reporting, and free live support. You will have a wealth of features, including an e-mail campaign, pre-designed e-mail templates, advanced HTML editing functionality, customizable visitor sign-up forms for websites, bounce and unsubscribe management, list segmentation functionality, e-mail tracking and reporting, and e-mail delivery management.

This list is certainly not inclusive of all-in-one service providers and is merely an introduction to some of the industry leaders. In the case studies, you will be introduced to many more highly reputable, well-respected industry leaders in e-mail campaign management.

Mass e-mail marketing software

There are numerous mass e-mail marketing applications on the market. One of the industry leaders is Arial Software's Email Marketing Director (**www. arialsoftware.com**). This professional desktop e-mail campaign software is used by marketing companies, newsletter publishers, volunteer coordinators, tourism bureaus, veterans groups, neighborhood associations, event planners, churches, service clubs, and schools. It comes with advanced HTML editing, a built-in database to support multiple lists, an e-mail template library, and the Web-based MySubscribe tool that allows subscribers to sign up from the Web and automatically adds them to your list.

Another quality product is eLoop from Gold Lasso (**www.goldlasso.com**). It was designed specifically for marketing professionals to effectively integrate e-mail as part of their promotional mix using a closed-loop concept. eLoop is a Web-based e-mail marketing system comprised of three distinct tools: Out-Bound Messaging, Data Management, and Data Collection. These tools provide all the functionality needed for a professional marketer to develop a successful e-mail marketing program with very little technical knowledge. All of eLoop's tools are integrated, providing seamless functionality and easy data flow.

Target and Segment Your Audience

Targeting your audience is a fairly simple concept. You want to send your e-mails to the recipients who will most likely respond. The more targeted your e-mail message is, the more likely it will be successful. Because most e-mail programs and all-in-one solution providers give you the capability of creating targeted e-mails, you can create highly customized and personalized messages targeting only those who are most likely to act on the e-mail message, thus increasing ROI and decreasing costs. Statistics support that personalized and targeted e-mail campaigns realize improved results when compared to generic e-mails. In general, using personalized e-mail softens the message and promotes a "friendly" exchange of information.

You need to decide how much personal data you wish to collect and how to use it. There are risks in asking for too much information. It is recommended that you only require the e-mail address and to try to collect first name, last name, and state at a minimum, where possible. You can certainly collect more data if you want, but make the fields optional so the list subscriber can choose what they want to reveal to you. Also, when using the personalization in an e-mail, be careful of overuse. Using "Dear Bruce" is fine in the introduction, but do not use the recipient's name in every paragraph.

One of the best features of e-mail marketing is the ability to perform list segmentation or sub-lists. If you have a variety of e-mail lists for different product lines or for targeting different customer needs, you can use multiple lists within in a single account. This is ideal for companies that collected e-mail addresses only and do not possess the demographic data to allow for automated segmentation or targeting within their lists. They can continue to develop e-mail campaigns based on their targeted lists and maintain each list within one single account.

How to Write an Effective E-mail

The e-mail message is the heart and soul of an e-mail marketing campaign. The subject line is the first thing that a recipient will see, followed by your actual e-mail. Your e-mail blast is direct communication from your company to potential customers or clients; therefore, you want to ensure it is professional, effective, and error-free. You know what junk e-mail and spam look like — and no doubt receive some daily. Your e-mail must be designed so it does not look like amateur spam. A poorly designed e-mail will not inspire confidence in the recipient and will typically not result in a sale.

The subject line

The importance of the subject line cannot be stressed enough. This is the first thing your e-mail recipient will see, and it can be the single determining factor in whether they will open your e-mail or delete it. Additionally, it is one of the primary flags for spam filtering software. You should put as much thought and analysis into the subject line as you do for your actual e-mail creation. Take a quick look through your "junk" folder or "trash" bin — chances are you will find a variety of subjects that immediately trigger you or your spam filter to send the e-mail to the junk folder. Avoid using such words or phrases in your subject lines.

Obviously, the content of your e-mail will drive the construction of your e-mail subject line. There is a fairly simple formula to follow when creating an e-mail subject line, depending on your e-mail content. If your e-mail subject is entirely different than your e-mail creative content, your e-mail will head to the junk bin quickly, along with any chance of establishing a positive relationship with the recipient. Your e-mail subject line should:

- Describe an announcement, newsletter, publication, or article. Typically, the subject line is the title of the article, publication, newsletter, or the month/issue of a publication. For example:

  ◊ The Food Service Professional Issue #124

  ◊ Developer Shed Weekly News for 2007-01-04

- Entice the recipient with an intriguing offer. For example:

  ◊ DEAL ALERT: 2 new deals including Dell 20" Widescreen LCD Display for $279

◊   Southwest Airlines: Special Offers and News You Can Use

- Entice the recipient with something that may benefit them. For example:

    ◊   E-mail Marketer Monthly News: "How to write an effective e-mail"

    ◊   Jogging Daily: "How to choose the best running shoes"

Put it in perspective — you read e-mails everyday. What e-mail subjects entice you or make you curious? Write your e-mail subjects professionally and to the point. Subject lines that emphasize and promote cost-savings, opportunities for learning, or new and beneficial products or services are the most likely to succeed. Keep your subject short so your message is delivered clearly.

If you are producing newsletters or other recurring e-mail blasts, it is important that you maintain consistency in both your subject and the sender e-mail address. Stick to your company name or newsletter title. If you publish a series of e-mail newsletters, you should use a consistent format for the subject so your recipient recognizes it.

Here are some other do's and don'ts to keep in mind when writing an e-mail subject line:

- **Do not** use subject lines that shout. All caps is considered Internet "shouting." You will have much better success with "Improve Your E-mail Marketing Campaign" than with "IMPROVE YOUR E-MAIL MARKETING CAMPAIGN."

- **Do not** overuse the word "free." It is okay to use it if you are truly promoting something that is free, but do not make it the first word in the subject or spam filters will file it away quickly.

- **Do not** mislead your recipients with false claims, offers, or misinformation. Make sure your e-mail subject matches the content.

- **Do not** overuse punctuation, and avoid exclamation points in your subject lines.

- **Do not** forget to spell check. Yes, it sounds very obvious, but there are plenty of poor spellers out there. This will make you look unprofessional.

- **Do** emphasize urgency in an e-mail. If you have a deadline or some other form of compelling action, you will achieve better results.

- **Do** keep the subject short, simple, and to the point.

- **Do** incorporate your brand name or company name where possible. This increases brand recognition and builds trust and confidence with recipients.

- **Do** avoid using the dollar symbol in the subject line. This is commonly used by and associated with spammers.

When to E-mail, How Often, and What Time

Now that you created your e-mail masterpiece, you must address the issue of when to send it, how often to send it, and what time of the day is best to send out your e-mail blast. There is no cut and dry answer to any of these questions, but there are general rules you can follow to determine what will work best for you, based on the type of e-mails you are sending.

Traditionally, Mondays and Fridays are the worst days to e-mail. The reasons are fairly obvious — Monday is the traditional first day back to work after the weekend and typically a busy day for meetings, catching up from the previous week, planning the week ahead, and clearing out e-mails from the weekend. Your e-mails may fall victim to overload. Fridays have long been considered the worst day to e-mail simply because it is the end of the work week, and people are looking forward to the weekend and cleaning out their e-mails.

It is recommended that you start your e-mail campaign on a Tuesday or Thursday and then test the waters from there. Once your campaign is established, try a weekend and compare it to your other results. Try a Friday, check your open rates, and compare them to your averages on Thursdays. Depending on your target audience, you may have better luck on Mondays or weekends. Do not discount the weekends, but avoid scheduling e-mail blasts on holidays and holiday weekends.

There is no golden rule to follow, but research shows the best time to send an e-mail blast is between 7 a.m. and 10:30 a.m. Keep in mind that time zones may wreak havoc on an e-mail campaign unless you segment the delivery schedule by zones. A 7 a.m. delivery on the East Coast is a 4 a.m. delivery on the West Coast. Be aware that e-mail may take seconds to hours to deliver to all of your recipients — they will not all receive it at the exact same time. If you are delivering articles or newsletters, you may want to ask your subscribers what day of the week and time they prefer to receive your e-mail blasts. By making the time convenient for them, you will increase the likelihood of achieving positive open rates.

E-mail frequency should be established by the type of e-mail you are sending. Do not overload your subscribers with e-mails. Once as week is a good general rule to follow. Exceed that, and you may quickly annoy your subscribers and find them removing themselves from your list. Use segmentation to avoid saturating your list with e-mails that are not relevant to the recipients. The bottom line with frequency is to establish what works best for you and your customers. Creating e-mail campaigns can be time-consuming. Do not commit to sending weekly e-mails if you do not have the time and resources to produce them. As with when to send your e-mails, you will have to experiment and test your e-mail frequency to balance optimal results with workload to ensure that the ROI is maximized.

Harnessing the power of e-mail through targeted e-mail marketing campaigns and newsletters is one of the most effective and cost-effective methods to advertise and market your business. With e-mail marketing, you get direct and immediate communication with thousands of current and potential customers.

CHAPTER 8

Pay-Per-Click Advertising and Google AdWords

The key concept to understand pay-per-click advertising is that unlike other paid advertising campaigns where you pay for the campaign in hopes of generating customers and revenues, you are not paying for any guarantees or promises of sales, website traffic, or increased revenues. You are no longer paying out money in print advertising or other online marketing techniques hoping for a return on your significant investment. Google makes pay-per-click advertising easy, effective, and profitable with Google AdWords.

Banner advertising used to be the largest type of advertising on the Internet, and it still holds a small market share, but the main disadvantage of banner advertising is that the ads are embedded within pages. You have to rely on a Web designer to put your banner ad on a page that has similar or complementary content and, of course, it is useless unless someone clicks on it. With pay-per-click advertising, you do not pay to have your advertisement loaded on a Web page or to have your advertisement listed at the top of search engines, you *only* pay for results. In other words, pay-per-click advertising is entirely no cost (minus potential setup costs), even if your advertisement is viewed by millions of website visitors. You pay when your ad is clicked, thus the term pay-per-click.

When someone clicks on your AdWords advertisement, Google charges your account, based on a formula price. Bear in mind that the "click" in no way guarantees sales; it merely means that someone clicked on your advertisement and will be routed in the browser to the pre-determined Web page you specified when you created your advertisement. Do not underestimate the importance of having a user-friendly, information-rich website to capture the attention of the site visitor and close the deal. Not all pay-per-click campaigns must result in a purchase — many advertisers use pay-per-click advertising to sell products, but many more use them to sell services, promotional material, news releases, and other media, all intended to build business or disseminate information.

Pay-per-click advertising began in 1998 by a company called Goto.com, which eventually become Overture.com and was then purchased by Yahoo.com. The original concept was that anyone with a brick-and-mortar or online business could manage and determine their own search engine ranking based on pre-selected keywords and how much money they were willing to pay for the resultant "click" on their advertisement. Pay-per-click advertising is the fastest growing form of online marketing today. Google is the industry leader in terms of market share and offers advertisers a feature-rich application called Google AdWords.

You will likely admire the simplicity and functionality of pay-per-click advertising, which allows you to have significant control over your campaign. Before you forge the path toward implementing a Google AdWords pay-per-click marketing plan, it is critical to understand pay-per-click advertising and develop strategies to design an effective campaign, optimize and monitor overall ad performance, and employ sound business principles in the overall management and financial investment of your campaign. One of the success factors in creating and managing a Google AdWords pay-per-click campaign is the effective selection and use of keywords, key phrases in the creation of an effective ad using advanced statistical reporting tools from Google, as well as your Web hosting company. To ensure the potential for success of a Google AdWords pay-per-click campaign, you must choose the most effective keywords, design an effective and captivating advertisement, and, as we mentioned earlier, have a well-designed, information-rich website with easy navigation.

Pay-Per-Click Advertising Walkthrough

You pay a rate that you specify for every visitor who clicks through from the search engine site to your website. Every keyword has a "bid" price, depending on the popularity of the keyword in search engines. You set your own budget and financial limitations, and you are done. Here is a step-by-step walkthrough:

- You join Google AdWords, and, with a credit card, put money on your account to get started

- You create your ad as you want it to appear with your own selected keywords you wish to target

- Based on the keyword value, you set how much you are willing to spend on each keyword. More popular keywords are more costly per click than others

- Upon completion, your ad is ready to appear in the Google Search Engine

- When someone searches through Google, by using one of your keywords, the advertisement is matched to the keyword query, and the ad is displayed in the Google Search Engine results

- If the person "clicks" on your advertisement, they are navigated to your website, and you are "charged" for the click

The search engine will return a rank-ordered list of the most popular websites matching your search criteria, and may display your advertisement if it also matches the search criteria and keyword. One of the benefits of Google AdWords pay-per-click advertising is that your advertisement will be placed right up there with the top-ranked websites in your search category.

The rules for most pay-per-click search engine applications operate on the same principles: the advertiser with the highest bidder gets top billing in the search engine return. It is a combination of experience, knowledge of the market, and some trial and error which lets you balance keywords and phrases to delivery optimal results, and the tools provided by Google AdWords help you achieve that goal.

Google AdWords Pay-Per-Click Benefits

- It is easy to implement

- The results are clearly measurable

- It is cost-effective in comparison to other types of traditional and online advertising programs

- It is for both large and small businesses

- It is ideal for testing out market response to new products or services

- It gives you full control over your budget — you can set systematic budgetary limits to minimize your overall financial risk and investment

- It is more effective than banner advertising

- It delivers a higher click-through rate than banner advertising

- Ads are ideally placed with top search engine results on the world's most popular search engine

- It is only delivered to your potential customers when they are searching on keywords related to your products or services contained in your pay-per-click ad

- Ads are delivered based on keyword searches, and delivered immediately — meaning the chances of turning one of those potential customers into an actual customer is dramatically increased

- It allows you to design your ad, which is strategically placed in a prominent location on the website

- Ads can be delivered in search engine results or within the content of a Web page

Below is an example of a Google AdWords pay-per-click advertisement in a Google Search Results page. The ads are located at the top of the search results, known as "sponsored links," as well as in the column along the right side of the page:

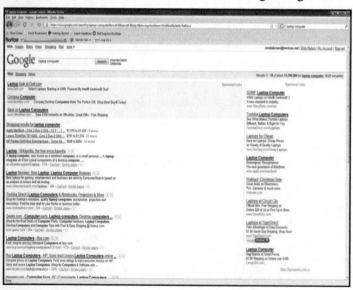

Google screenshots © Google Inc. Used with permission.

In the "Sponsored Links" section on the top, right-hand side of the page, you will see the pay-per-click results based on the query "laptop computer." As you can see, Sony is top shelf, with Toshiba second. Notice TigerDirect has "Google Checkout," which we will discuss in a later chapter of the book. There is no cost to any of these advertisers to have their sponsored links shown in your search engine results. If you were to click on one of those links, say the link for Sony, you would be taken to their site, and they would be charged a

Google screenshots © Google Inc. Used with permission.

Another primary benefit of a Google AdWords pay-per-click campaign is that you have fully customizable advertising solutions in your toolbox. You can create dozens of separate pay-per-click ads, with different wording, and based on different keywords, all within a single advertising campaign. This gives you tremendous flexibility to target a wide array of potential customer segments. Having a wide variety of advertisements available is a critical component of Google AdWords, where you are delivered pay-per-click advertisements based on a variety of keywords.

Cost of Google AdWords Pay-Per-Click Advertising

Google AdWords pay-per-click advertising is, of course, limited by the size of your advertising budget. You will know in advance how much you will pay per click, and most start out with a minimum price per click, such as .10 cents, and can quickly escalate to significantly more money, even as much as $100 per click, depending on the keyword. Essentially, you "bid" with your competitors with the amount you are willing to pay for each click on your advertisement based on the keywords you choose. It may be cost-prohibitive to be the top bidder, as your advertising budget will be consumed much quicker than if you were a No. 2 or No.3 bidder, but there are also times when it is more critical to be the No. 1 bidder, regardless of the financial impact. Your bid is the maximum amount you are willing to pay for the website visitor to click on your advertisement, so be careful what amount you are willing to bid per click, as you may have to pay it.

Tips, Tricks, & Secrets for Google AdWords Pay-Per-Click Advertising

- Design Google AdWords ads so they target potential customers who are ready to buy.

- Ensure your Google AdWords ad is specific in nature.

- Target one product for each Google AdWords ad, instead of a generic ad that targets a large market segment.

- Link the ad directly to the product page with a link to buy the product on that page, instead of a generic page or the website home page.

- If your Google AdWords ad targets a specific product, you may see a reduction in clicks, but those clicks are most likely extremely profitable, since you are only getting clicks from individuals seeking information on your specific product.

- Be willing to bid for a good position.

- Bid enough to gain the exposure you need, but balance exposure to stretch your advertising budget. It is typically not worth the cost to have the No.1 bid, and it is often significantly less costly if you are in positions 2-10.

- The top listing is the one that is clicked the most often, but it also has the worst percentage of converting clicks into sales. Many "click happy" people click on the top listing without ever converting a sale. Those "clicks" will quickly eat up your advertising budget. You may have better luck by being below the No.1 listing, since the potential for better qualified clicks exists as potential customers screen all the advertisements, instead of just clicking on the first one.

- Use Google AdWords Tools to monitor performance and adjust keywords/bidding as necessary.

- Choose specific keyword phrases, and you will lower your overall costs.

- Do not serve your advertisement to countries where you will not do business. Save your money and concentrate in your primary market areas.

- Use capital letters for each word in the Title and Description fields of your pay-per-click ad.

- Use Google AdWords Ad Targeting if you are trying to reach a specific geographic area.

- Use the Google Keyword Suggestion Tool to help you determine which keywords are most effective for your campaign.

- Keep an eye out for fraud.

- Check the spelling in your Google AdWords ad to ensure it is correct.

- Embed keywords within your actual Google AdWords pay-per-click advertisement.

An In-Depth Look at Google AdWords

Google AdWords is a user-friendly, quick, and simple way to purchase highly targeted cost-per-click (CPC) or cost-per-impression (CPM) advertising. Ad-Words ads are displayed along with search results on Google, as well as on search and content sites in the growing Google network, including AOL®, EarthLink®, Ask.com®, and Blogger™. When you create an AdWords keyword-targeted ad, you choose keywords for which your ad will appear and specify the maximum amount you are willing to pay for each click; you only pay when someone clicks on your ad.

When you create an AdWords site-targeted ad, you choose the exact Google network content sites where your ad will run and specify the maximum amount you are willing to pay for each thousand page views on that site. You pay whenever someone views your ad, whether the viewer clicks or not. It is recommended that you start out with a Google AdWords keyword-targeted ad and do not allow content matching. There is no minimum monthly charge with Google AdWords, but there is a one-time activation fee for your account. Although your campaign can start in minutes, it is highly recommended that you invest the time to identify the best keywords possible. Hundreds of thousands of high-quality websites, news pages, and blogs partner with Google to display AdWords ads. The Google content network reaches across the entire Web.

Using the keywords you specify when you create your ad, Google's contextual targeting technology automatically matches your ads to websites that are the most relevant in content to your business — this means your ads are displayed only on relevant content sites in relevant content searches. For example, an ad for a laptop hard drive may show up next to an article reviewing the latest notebook computers.

By using the Google Placement Performance report, you can monitor where your ads appear and their performance based on impression, click, cost, and conversion data. You can use this in-depth analysis tool to adjust your campaigns, change content, and remove underperforming ads from your campaign. There is no minimum spending threshold, and you can set your maximum monthly budget for each ad. Google provides you with a wealth of tools and information that will help you choose keywords and stretch your budget to its fullest potential.

Google lets you specify country, state, city, or region as you create your ads so they are only served in the markets you choose. This will save your budget from clicks in markets where you have no presence. Your business location will show up on Google Maps™ along with contact information.

To work with Google AdWords, perform these three simple steps:

1. **Create your ads**: Create ads based on your keywords and key phrases, which are words that are relevant to your product or business.

2. **Ads are displayed on Google**: When users search using matching keywords or key phrases, your ad may be displayed in the search results. Since the user selected the keyword, your advertisement is a match for the products they are looking for.

Grow customers: Users simply click on the ad and are taken to the landing page you established for your campaign, increasing website traffic and creating a new customer.

How Google AdWords Ranks Ads

Ads are positioned in both search and content pages based on their Ad Rank; the ad with the highest Ad Rank appears in the first position, and so on down the page. If your ad achieves the fourth-highest Ad Rank, your ad will be positioned No. 4 in search engine results.

Here is where it starts to get confusing. While the Ad Rank determines where an ad is placed, the criteria Google uses to determine Ad Rank differs for keyword-targeted ads, depending on whether they appear on Google and the search network or just on the content network.

How Ad Rank is determined on Google and the search network

A keyword-based ad is ranked on a corresponding search engine result page based on the matched keyword's cost-per-click (CPC) bid and Quality Score.

Ad Rank = CPC bid × Quality Score

The Quality Score for Ad Rank on Google and the search network is determined by a number of factors, including:

- Historical click-through rate (CTR) of the keyword and the matched ad on Google

- Account history, measured by the CTR of all the ads and keywords in your Google AdWords account

- Historical CTR of the display URLs in the ad group

- Relevance of the keyword to the ads in its ad group

- Relevance of the keyword and the matched ad to the search query

- Your account's performance in the geographic region where the ad will be shown

Google allows up to three AdWords ads to appear above the search results, as opposed to on the side. It is important to note that only ads that exceed a certain Quality Score and CPC bid threshold may appear in these positions. If the three highest-ranked ads all surpass these thresholds, then they will appear in order above the search results.

The CPC bid threshold is determined by the matched keyword's Quality Score; the higher the Quality Score, the lower the CPC threshold.

How Ad Rank is determined on the content network

Your keyword-based ad is positioned on a content page based on the ad group's content bid and Quality Score:

Ad Rank = content bid × Quality Score

The Quality Score related to Ad Rank is determined by:

- The ad's past performance on the site and other similar sites

- Relevance of the ads and keywords to the site

- Landing page quality

How Ad Rank is determined for placement-targeted ads on the content network

If a placement-targeted ad wins a position on a content page, it uses up the entire ad space so no other ads can show on that page. To determine whether your placement-targeted ad will show, Google considers the bid you made for that ad group or for the individual placement, along with the ad group's Quality Score.

Ad Rank = bid × Quality Score

Google states that the Quality Score for determining whether a placement-targeted ad will appear on a particular site depends on the campaign's bidding option. If the campaign uses cost-per-thousand-impressions (CPM) bidding, Quality Score is based on the quality of your landing page. If the campaign uses cost-per-click (CPC) bidding, Quality Score is based on the historical CTR of the ad on this and similar sites and the quality of your landing page.

How to Improve Your Ranking

The bottom line is that relevant keywords, relevant text within your ads, a good CTR on Google, and a high keyword CPC bid all result in a higher position for your ad. The theory is that this system — which is not based entirely on the price you are willing to pay per click — uses well-targeted, relevant ads to ensure that the quality of your ads is factored into placement and helps ensure that your ads can get placed even if you are not the top keyword bidder. The AdWords Discounter monitors other ads and will automatically reduce the CPC for your ads so that you pay the lowest possible price for your ad's position on the search engine results page. One of the main advantages of this system is that you cannot be locked out of the top position, as you would be in a ranking system, based solely on price.

When you complete the account setup process, you will be required to activate your account through an opt-in e-mail, which is sent to your specified e-mail account. Once this is confirmed, your account is activated and you can log into your new Google AdWords account. At this point, you will be required to enter your billing information. Upon completion of this step, your ad often appears within minutes. Google AdWords is set up to operate with three distinct levels: account, campaign, and ad group. In summary:

- Your account is associated with a unique e-mail address, password, and billing information.

- At the campaign level, you choose your daily budget, geographic and language targeting, distribution preferences, and end dates.

- At the ad group level, you create ads and choose keywords. You can also select a maximum CPC for the ad group or for individual keywords.

- Within each ad group, you create one or more ads and select a set of keywords to trigger those ads. Each ad group runs on one set of key-words. If you create multiple ads in an ad group, the ads will rotate for those keywords.

- When you log into your account, you can see the CTRs listed below each of your ads. If a particular ad is not performing as well as the others, you can delete or refine it to improve the overall performance of your ad group.

How Much Google AdWords Will Cost

There are two versions of Google AdWords — the Starter Edition and the Standard Edition. Starter Edition is for those who want to advertise a single product or service and for those who are new to Internet advertising. You can upgrade from the Starter Edition to the Standard Edition at any time. You may pay a small set-up fee to set up your Google AdWords account. Each keyword has a minimum bid that is based on the quality of the keyword specific to your account, and if your keyword or ad group's maximum CPC meets the minimum bid, your ad will be displayed in response to search queries. The following are some key cost factors to remember:

- The position of an ad is based on the maximum CPC and quality.

- The higher the Quality Score, the lower the CPC required to trigger ads, and vice versa.

- There is no minimum spending requirement.

- You set the daily limit on how much you are willing to spend.

- You set how much you are willing to pay per click or per impression.

- You only pay for clicks on your keyword-targeted advertisement.

The Google Keyword Tool generates potential keywords for your PPC campaign and tells you their statistics, including search performance and seasonal trends. Your CPC will drive your total cost for AdWords, so knowing how much a keyword "costs" is critical in estimating your total monthly costs. Google provides a wide variety of tools to help you establish your account, choose keywords, and manage your budget and your account.

Establishing and Managing Your Google Account

Using the Starter Edition, this section will outline the AdWords process. The first step you must complete is to create a new Google AdWords campaign. To do this, click on the "Create a New Campaign" link on the Google AdWords Campaign Management screen.

Simply answer the questions and follow the steps to walk through the process of creating your account and your first ad. Note that if you do not have a website, Google will help create one for you. Make sure you select whether you currently have a website. The example below illustrates a user who already has a website:

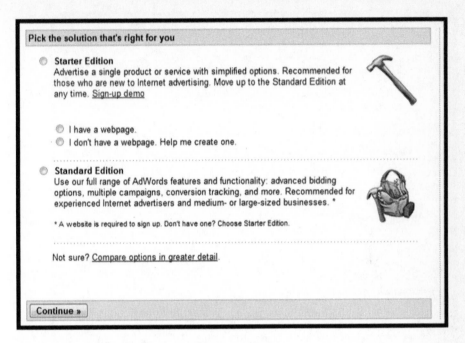

Google screenshots © Google Inc. Used with permission.

In Google AdWords Starter Edition, you choose your customer base, language, and the website your ad will direct them to.

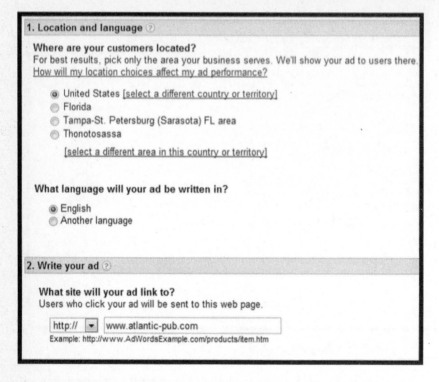

Google screenshots © Google Inc. Used with permission.

Next, you will create the actual advertisement that will be displayed in the search engine results page. Simply type in your advertisement as you want it to appear, and Google AdWords formats it for you as you type.

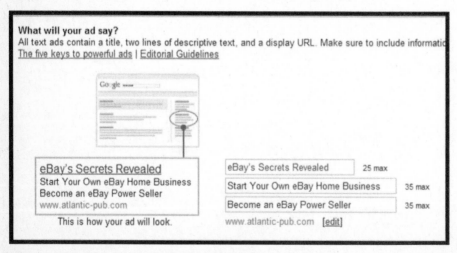

Google screenshots © Google Inc. Used with permission.

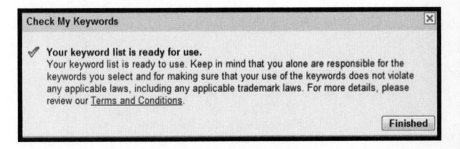

The next step is to choose your keywords. Do this using the Google Keyword Tool to ensure that your keywords are optimal for your advertising campaign. Simply enter your keywords one at a time, and then click "Check My Keywords" to see what Google thinks of your choices. Google also makes recommendations based on keywords or phrases it scans on your Web page as other recommended alternatives.

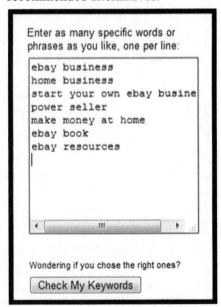

Google screenshots © Google Inc. Used with permission.

Google screenshots © Google Inc. Used with permission.

Next, choose your currency, set your monthly budget, and sign up for tips and newsletters from Google to improve your AdWords campaign. Set any monthly budget you want, and your ad will be served until you reach this dollar amount, or until it resets the following month or billing cycle.

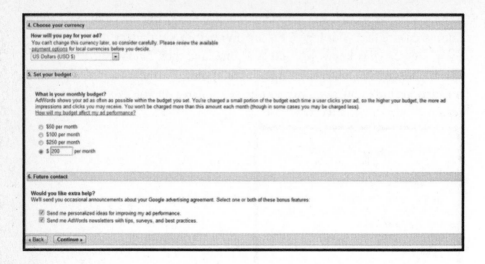

Google screenshots © Google Inc. Used with permission.

Follow the screen prompts to create your actual account and log into your newly created Google AdWords account. Your ad is not yet running and will not be until you enter your billing information and then activate the ad. After this, you are set. You can activate your ad; monitor your performance through impressions, clicks, or total cost; delete, edit, or add keywords or phrases; and manage your account.

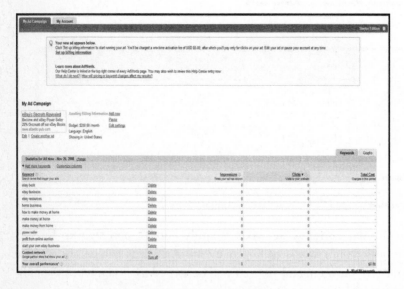

Google screenshots © Google Inc. Used with permission.

How to Graduate to Standard Edition Google AdWords

You can easily move from the Starter Edition to the Standard Edition. It does not cost anything to upgrade, and your account settings and ads will transfer over.

Below is a side-by-side comparison of the Starter and Standard editions:

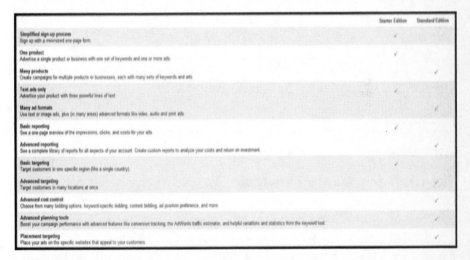

Google screenshots © Google Inc. Used with permission.

The Standard Edition offers significantly more features over the Starter Edition, including:

- Multiple ad campaigns

- Advanced location targeting

- Access to the complete Google content network and the ability to pick the sites your ad is placed on

- Powerful campaign planning and reporting tools

Creating a Standard Edition Google AdWords Account

The process for creating a Standard Edition account is quite similar to the Starter Edition, except that you do not create your single ad as you create your account; instead, you establish your account, and then all the tools and resources are available to you to create ads and manage your campaigns.

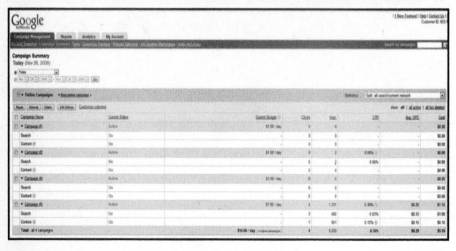

Google screenshots © Google Inc. Used with permission.

Within the Campaign Management module, you can create, edit, and monitor your campaigns and advertisements, as well as run reports, perform analyses, use the tools and the conversion tracking module, and optimize your website. This is your command center for Google AdWords. The screenshot above is a real, active Google AdWords account that will be used to modify and improve each of the under-performing ads.

Google Bidding Strategies

Google now offers a variety of bidding strategies to help you maximize your budget and maintain flexibility in how your ads are placed. The options you may choose are:

- **Manual bidding:** This option sets the highest price you are willing to pay for each click. Use this option if you need maximum control of each bid.

- **Conversion optimizer:** This option sets the highest price you are willing to pay for each conversion. Google will optimize your performance to aim for the best possible ROI. To use this feature, you must use Google Conversion Tracking.

- **Budget optimizer:** No bids needed, you set a 30-day budget, and Google will manage your bids, trying to earn you the most possible clicks within that budget. This is the best option for simplified bidding and the best choice for new users.

- **Preferred cost bidding:** This option sets the average price you want to pay for each click and lets Google manage your bids to give you a predictable average CPC.

Google AdWords Tools

Google provides you with a variety of tools to manage and optimize your campaigns with. These include:

- **Campaign optimizer:** Automatically creates a customized proposal for your campaign.

- **Keyword tool:** Builds a list of new keywords for your ad groups and reviews detailed keyword performance statistics, such as advertiser competition and search volume.

- **Edit campaign negative keywords:** Manages your negative keywords and reduces wasted clicks.

- **Site and category exclusion:** Prevents individual websites or categories of Web pages from showing your ads.

- **IP exclusion:** Prevents specific IP addresses from seeing your ads.

- **Traffic estimator:** Estimates how well a keyword might perform.

- **Ad creation marketplace:** Finds specialists to help you create multimedia ads.

- **Ads diagnostic tool:** Shows how and if your ads are showing up as a result of a search.

- **Ads preview tool:** Allows you to see your ad on Google without accruing impressions.

- **Disapproved ads:** Lets you review ads that have been disapproved.

- **Conversion tracking:** Shows which ads are your best performers.

- **Website optimizer:** Helps you to discover the best content for boosting your business.

- • **Download AdWords editor:** Enables you to make changes offline and then upload your revised campaigns.

Creating a New Campaign in Google AdWords

At this point, you created your Standard Google AdWords account, and you can now create a new campaign. From your Campaign Summary screen, click on "New Online Campaign," then choose "Start with Keywords."

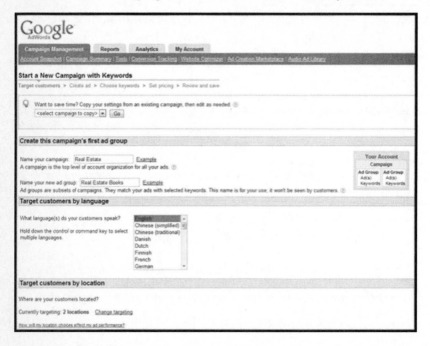

Google screenshots © Google Inc. Used with permission.

The first steps are to name your campaign and ad group, choose your target language, and target your location; then, create the actual ad. This is done in the same format as in the Starter Edition Google AdWords application.

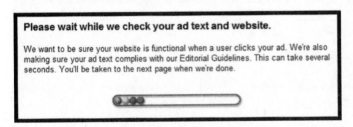

Google screenshots © Google Inc. Used with permission.

Once you complete your ad and click the "Continue" button, your advertisement is validated and checked by Google.

Please wait while we check your ad text and website.

We want to be sure your website is functional when a user clicks your ad. We're also making sure your ad text complies with our Editorial Guidelines. This can take several seconds. You'll be taken to the next page when we're done.

Google screenshots © Google Inc. Used with permission.

Enter your keywords and use the keyword checker to validate them. It will recommend removal of under-performing keywords or those that are too general in nature. Google will also scan your website and make recommendations for additional keywords to add.

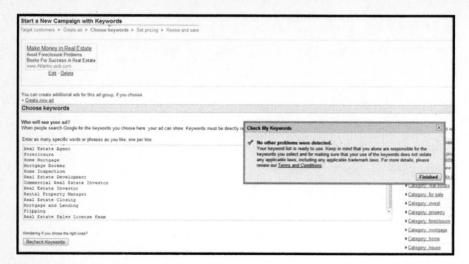

Google screenshots © Google Inc. Used with permission.

Now you must set your daily budget and bidding strategy.

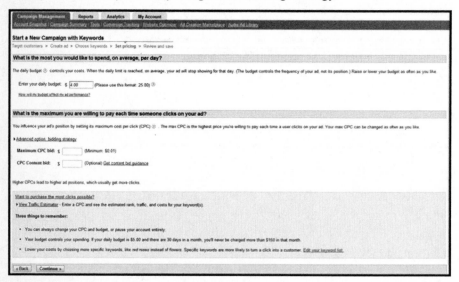

Google screenshots © Google Inc. Used with permission.

Google provides you with help each step of the way. There are always options for advice, detailed information, and guides to improve your campaign. One excellent tool is the Traffic Estimator, which you can use to enter a CPC and see the estimated rank, traffic, and costs for your keywords.

Traffic Estimates
View the ad performance estimates for your selected keywords on the Google Search Network below. Estimates are provided only as a guideline; your actual costs and ad positions for your keywords may vary. Learn more

Your keyword and CPC changes have not been saved.
You may continue making changes and re-calculating estimates below.
When satisfied, please save your changes

Without budget limitations:
At an average CPC of $0.69 - $1.00 these keywords could potentially generate 8,341 - 1
▸ Show total potential clicks in the table below

Keywords ▼	Max CPC	Search Volume	Estimated Avg. CPC
Search Network Total			$0.69 - $1.00
mortgage books (to be added)	$1.00		$0.09 - $0.88
Commercial Real Estate Investor	$1.00		$0.00
Overlaps with: commercial real estate, Real Estate Investor ⑦			
Flipping	$1.00		$0.55 - $0.82
Foreclosure	$1.00		$0.68 - $1.00
Home Inspection	$1.00		$0.65 - $0.98
Home Mortgage	$1.00		$0.66 - $0.99
Mortgage Broker	$1.00		$0.64 - $0.96
Mortgage and Lending	$1.00		$0.50 - $0.75
Real Estate Agent	$1.00		Not enough dat
Overlaps with: real estate agent ⑦			
Real Estate Closing	$1.00		$0.63 - $0.94
Real Estate Development	$1.00		$0.60 - $0.90
Real Estate Investor	$1.00		$0.67 - $1.00
Real Estate Sales License Exam	$1.00		Not enough dat
Rental Property	$1.00		$0.67 - $1.00
Rental Property Manager	$1.00		$0.00 - $0.97
Overlaps with: Rental Property ⑦			
commercial real estate	$1.00		$0.69 - $1.00
commercial real estate investing	$1.00		$0.00
Overlaps with: commercial real estate, real estate investing ⑦			
investing books	$1.00		$0.56 - $0.84
investment property	$1.00		$0.73 - $1.00
private mortgage investing	$1.00		$0.66 - $0.97
real estate agent	$1.00		$0.73 - $1.00
real estate books	$1.00		$0.67 - $1.00
real estate broker	$1.00		$0.66 - $0.99
real estate closing	$1.00		Not enough dat
Overlaps with: Real Estate Closing ⑦			
real estate financing	$1.00		$0.61 - $0.92
real estate investing	$1.00		$0.68 - $1.00
real estate investments	$1.00		$0.66 - $0.99
real estate listings	$1.00		$0.65 - $0.97
reverse mortgage	$1.00		$0.49 - $0.73
second mortgage	$1.00		$0.44 - $0.64

Google screenshots © Google Inc. Used with permission.

Google features multiple advertisement options, which include the following examples:

Text ad:

Luxury Cruise to Mars
Visit the Red Planet in style.
Low-gravity fun for everyone!
www.example.com

Google screenshots © Google Inc. Used with permission.

Image ad:

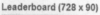

Leaderboard (728 x 90)

Banner (468 x 60)

Google screenshots © Google Inc. Used with permission.

Local business ad: Local business ads are AdWords ads associated with a specific Google Maps business listing. They show on Google Maps with an enhanced location marker. They also show in a text-only format on Google and other sites in the search network.

Mobile business text ad: Your ads will appear when someone uses Google Mobile Search™ on a mobile device.

Example Mobile Text Ad:

Google screenshots © Google Inc. Used with permission.

Video ad: A video ad is an ad format that appears on the Google content network as a static image until a user clicks on it and the video is played.

Video ads are a new ad format that will appear on the Google content network. Your video ad will appear as a static image until a user clicks on it and your video is played.

Opening Image - You supply us with a static image to display before a user interacts with your video.

Video - Add your video and select your display and destination URLs.

Video Ad - Preview an example When a user views your video ad and clicks the opening image, your video will play.

Step 1: Add your opening image [?]

The size of your image must be one of the following:		
Inline rectangle ad	300x225 or 300x250* Preview	
Square ad	250x225 or 250x250* Preview	
Large rectangle ad	336x252 or 336x280* Preview	
Small square ad	200x175 or 200x200* Preview	
*will be resized to fit dimensions of the ad		

Format: .gif, .jpg, or .png; maximum size: 50k

Google screenshots © Google Inc. Used with permission.

Display ad builder: This new feature lets you create display ads as easily as text ads. When you are done creating your new ad, it will run on Google partner sites based on the target settings you choose.

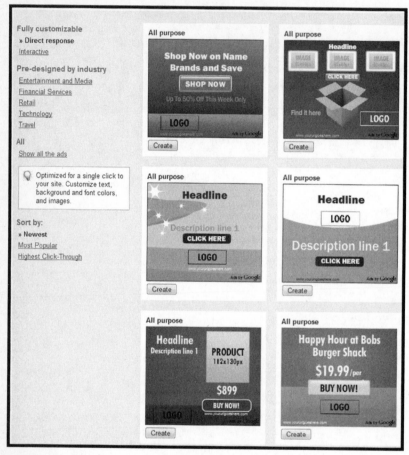

Google screenshots © Google Inc. Used with permission.

You should begin your campaign with a text ad. Google AdWords provides you with a simple form to create your text advertisement. As you enter data into the form, the example is updated with your data. In the following screenshot at the end of this section, notice that each keyword is capitalized in every line, and both the display URL and the actual destination URL are provided, as they may be different, depending on your campaign.

You will need to give some extra time and attention to the wording of your ad. Wording can be tricky because of the limited space you are given on each line of the ad, as well as the restrictions imposed by Google.

It is critical to load the title, or the first line of your ad, with keywords. Your goal is to capture the attention and interest of a potential customer. If you can do that, your ad will be successful. Test multiple versions of an ad to see which works best, and change keywords to help you analyze which is most effective. Review the ads of competitors; you may find they are outperforming you simply because their ad is more well-written, more captivating, or has more customer appeal. The use of words like "free," "rebate," "bonus," and "cash" are perfect for attracting the attention of website surfers. Other words that may encourage website visitors to click your ads should also be used as long as your ad message is concise and clear.

You should also consider the domain name listed in your advertisement, as it may have an effect on your ability to draw in potential customers. Your domain name should be directly related to your products or services, and it should be professional in nature. You will find an abundance of companies that offer search engine copywriting services, which is a good option if you are having problems developing successful ad campaigns.

Search engine copywriting is critical to a successful PPC advertising campaign. It is not overly difficult to achieve yourself if you apply some basic discipline and rules. While the insertion of keywords into an advertisement is stressed, simply cramming keyword after keyword into your PPC advertisements may be counterproductive. Successful SEO copywriting takes planning, discipline, analysis, and some degree of trial and error. Below are some guidelines for successful SEO copywriting:

- Use no more than four keywords per ad. Four keywords provide a variety without saturating the ad with keywords and losing meaning.

- Use all your allowed characters in each line of the advertisement. There is no incentive for white space.

- Write in natural language. "Natural language" is a popular term used extensively with copywriting. It simply means that the reader should not be able to — or should barely be able to — detect the keywords the ad is targeting. The best ads are written for an individual to read and understand, embedded with subtle keywords, and project a clear message; thus, they read "naturally." The opposite of this is a keyword-crammed ad that is nothing more than a collection of keywords, and is therefore entirely "unnatural" to read.

- Use keywords in the "Title" and "Description" lines, but use common sense so that you do not overload them with keywords.

- Test your ad and analyze your reports and results. Your ad may need tweaking or improvements, or it may be entirely ineffective and may need to be replaced.

Create an ad

Create Text Ad | Image Ad | Local Business Ad | Mobile Text Ad | Video Ad

Example short ad:

Restaurant Consulting
Reduce Costs + Increase Profits!
Discount Prices + Free Tech Support
www.restaurantprofits.com

Headline:	Restaurant Consulting	Max 25 characters
Description line 1:	Reduce Costs + Increase Profits!	Max 35 characters
Description line 2:	Discount Prices + Free Tech Support	Max 35 characters
Display URL: [?]	http:// www.restaurantprofits.com	Max 35 characters
Destination URL: [?]	http:// ▾ www.restaurantprofits.com/cheftec.html	Max 1024 characters

‹ Back   Reset Ad   Continue ›

Google screenshots © Google Inc. Used with permission.

You may discover that costs can escalate quickly if you do not set daily and monthly budget limitations. Keep in mind that limits on your daily/monthly budgets will also affect your ad performance, as your ad will not be displayed once you hit your budget limits. Google recognizes when your advertisement is bumping against its budget constraints and may suggest you increase your budget amount to increase visibility of your advertisement, as well as subsequent potential customers visiting your website, as shown below:

💡 **Campaign Budget Alert**
In the last 15 days, your ads missed 46% of impressions for which they were eligible. Increasing your budget could allow your ads to show more often and get more clicks.
Tell me more | Remove this message

Google screenshots © Google Inc. Used with permission.

The Google Campaign Summary

The Campaign Summary screen is where you will control all your Google AdWords campaigns. At this screen, you will be presented with an overview of each campaign, including campaign name, status, budget, clicks, impressions, CTR, average CPC, and total cost.

To delve further into each campaign, simply click on the campaign name to view a detailed status based on keywords and ad variation performance. This module will help you determine the effectiveness of each keyword and add or remove keywords. Your keywords may be marked "inactive for search" in the "Status" column and stop showing in search results if they do not have a high enough Quality Score and maximum CPC. This is another way of saying that your keyword or ad group's maximum CPC does not meet the minimum bid required to trigger ads on Google or its search network partners. This typically occurs when keywords are not as targeted as they could be, and the ads they deliver are not relevant enough to what a user is searching for — which ultimately means you need to refine your keywords or your ad.

Keywords marked "inactive for search" are inactive only for search. They may continue to trigger ads for content sites if you have the Google content network enabled for that campaign. Thus, a keyword marked as inactive for search may continue to generate clicks and charges on the content network. If your keyword is inactive for search, you may increase your keyword's Quality Score by optimizing for relevancy.

Optimization is a technique for improving the quality of your keywords, ad, and campaign to increase your keywords' performance — without raising costs. Try to combine each keyword with two to three other words to create a more specific keyword phrase. This will result in better targeting and, potentially, better performance. You may also increase your keyword's maximum CPC to the recommended minimum bid. Your keyword's minimum bid is the amount required to trigger ads on Google and is determined by your keyword's Quality Score. When your maximum CPC falls below the minimum bid, your keyword will be inactive for search. For this reason, you can simply increase your maximum CPC to the minimum bid to reactivate your keywords. You may also choose to delete all your keywords that are inactive for search.

The "Ad Variations" link allows you to review performance for each ad within a selected campaign. It is common to have multiple ads created for the same, or different, keyword combinations within the same campaign. In the following screenshot, it is clear by the percentages listed that the first ad is served considerably more than the second ad, which is rarely served. The reasons for this may vary, depending on the keywords chosen or campaign settings.

If you click on the "Edit" link, under the "Actions" column, you can tweak your campaign ads to improve your statistics.

Example short ad:

Restaurant Consulting
Cheftec Recipe Software Solutions
Discounts+ Free Technical Support
restaurantprofits.com

Headline:	Restaurant Consulting	Max 25 characters
Description line 1:	Cheftec Recipe Software Solutions	Max 35 characters
Description line 2:	Discounts+ Free Technical Support	Max 35 characters
Display URL: [?]	http:// restaurantprofits.com	Max 35 characters
Destination URL: [?]	http:// ▾ restaurantprofits.com	Max 1024 characters

Save Ad   Cancel

Restaurant Consulting
Cheftec Recipe Software Solutions
Discounts+ Free Technical Support
restaurantprofits.com
2 Clicks | 1.58% CTR | $0.85 CPC
Served - 0.7%

Restaurant Consulting
Increase Your Restaurant's Profit
Controls to Lower Food & Labor Cost
restaurantprofits.com
192 Clicks | 1.09% CTR | $0.78 CPC
Served - 99.3%

Google screenshots © Google Inc. Used with permission.

For each ad group you create, you can create up to 50 ad variations. The variations can be in any of the formats offered for AdWords, including text, image, and video. When you first sign up for an account, you will be offered the chance to create additional ad variations immediately after you create your first ad. You can also create ad variations later, after your account is running. Sign into your account and choose the ad group you want to work with. Click the "Ad Variations" tab, find the line reading "Create new ad," and select the type of ad you want to create. All ad variations in a single ad group are triggered by the same set of keywords. You may choose to have ads optimized, which would show better-performing ads more often, or rotate, which shows all ads equally. If you want different ads to appear for different keywords, you can create multiple ad groups or campaigns.

Editing Your Campaign Settings

In the "Edit Campaign Settings" menu, you have the ability to modify your campaign settings, including campaign name, budget options, ad scheduling, keyword bidding, network and bidding, and scheduling and serving.

Google screenshots © Google Inc. Used with permission.

Google AdWords will suggest the recommended budget amount for your campaign if you click on the "View Recommended Budget" link in the Edit Campaign Settings screen, as shown in the following screenshot:

Based on your current keywords, your recommended budget is $8.00 / day.

If the recommended amount is too high, try raising your budget to a comfortable amount. Or, to make the most of your budget, try refining your ads and keywords.

Google screenshots © Google Inc. Used with permission.

Ad scheduling lets you control the days and times your AdWords campaigns appear. Your AdWords ads normally are available to run 24 hours each day. Ad scheduling allows you to set your campaigns to appear only during certain hours or days of each week. For example, you might set your ads to run only on Tuesdays, or from 3 to 6 p.m. daily. With ad scheduling, a campaign can run all day, every day, or as few as 15 minutes per week.

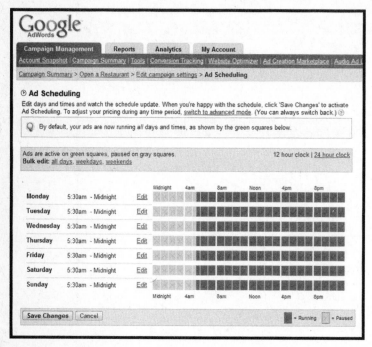

Google screenshots © Google Inc. Used with permission.

To determine when you want your ads to show, you may want to run an hourly report. Ad scheduling can be used with both keyword-targeted and site-targeted AdWords campaigns. If you select the advanced setting, the bid multiplier will apply to both CPC and CPM bids. Ad scheduling will not raise or lower your budget. The AdWords system will try to reach your usual daily budget in whatever number of hours your ad runs each day.

Position preference lets you tell Google where you would prefer your ad to show among all the AdWords ads on a given page. Whenever you run a keyword-targeted ad, your ad is assigned a position based on your CPC bid, your keyword's Quality Score, and other relevant factors. There may be dozens of positions available for a given keyword, spread over several pages of search results. If you find that your ad gets the best results when it is ranked third or fourth among all AdWords ads, you can set a position preference for those spots. AdWords will then try to show your ad whenever it is ranked third or fourth and avoid showing it when it is ranked higher or lower. If your ad is ranked higher than third for a given keyword, the system will automatically try to lower your bid to place your ad in your preferred position.

You can request that your ad be shown only when it is:

- Higher than a given position

- Lower than a given position

- Within a range of positions

- In a single, exact position

Position preference does not mean that your ad will always appear in the position you specify; the usual AdWords ranking and relevance rules apply. If your ad does not qualify for position No. 1, setting a position preference of No. 1 will not move it there. Position preference also does not affect the overall placement of AdWords ad units on the left, right, top, or bottom of a given page — it only affects your ranking relative to other ads across those units.

Google AdWords allows you to track and measure conversions and ultimately helps you identify how effective your AdWords ads and keywords are for you. It works by placing a cookie on a user's computer when he or she clicks on one of your AdWords ads. If the user reaches one of your conversion pages, the cookie is connected to your Web page. When a match is made, Google records a successful conversion for you. Please note that the cookie Google adds to a user's computer when he or she clicks on an ad expires in 30 days. This measure, and the fact that Google uses separate servers for conversion tracking and search results, protects the user's privacy.

Demographic bidding

Demographic bidding allows you to choose your audience by age and gender. Because some publishers on the Google content network know details about their users — such as social networking sites they partake in — they can serve ads based on age and gender. Google AdSense can display your AdWords ads to the demographic groups that you select or block them from groups you do not want to reach.

Google AdWords reports

Google provides full statistical, conversion, and financial reporting for the Google AdWords program. You can view all your account reports online 24 hours a day, and you can also have them set up to be e-mailed to you on a scheduled basis.

The AdWords Report Center allows you to easily create customized performance reports to help you track and manage multiple facets of your AdWords campaigns. There are dozens of highly customized options available for you to choose, all of which are simple and easy to generate.

Key features include:

- Quick report generation in categories such as site/keyword performance, URL performance, campaign performance, ad group performance, and account performance

- The ability to select individual campaigns and/or ad groups for report

- Customizable report columns to focus only on the data you need

- Performance filters to screen for the most relevant information in categories such as cost, impressions, clicks, and CTR

- Scheduling for automatic report generation and delivery

- E-mailing option for multiple recipients

- Saved templates for reusable reports

Google screenshots © Google Inc. Used with permission.

Google screenshots © Google Inc. Used with permission.

Google AdWords Ads Diagnostic Tool

One of the best features of Google AdWords is the Ads Diagnostic Tool, which helps you discover why your ads may not be showing on the first page of search results for a certain keyword.

Ads Diagnostic Tool
Choose one of the two options below to find out why your ads may not be showing on the first page of search results for a certain keyword.

Option 1: Search Terms and Parameters
Use this option if you're concerned about all ads within your account that should be appearing for a specific search term. For example, you could check your ad status for the phrase-matched keyword "Hawaiian cruises," targeted to California users.

Keyword:	
Google domain:	www.google.com << ex: froogle.google.com, www.google.co.uk
Display language:	English
User location:	◉ Geographic: United States / All regions within this country
	○ IP address: Format: xxx.xxx.xxx.xxx

Continue >>

Option 2: Search Results Page URL
Use this option if you're concerned about a particular search results page that you believe should be showing one of your ads. Copy and paste the URL from the address bar on the search results page where your ad should be showing.

Search results page URL:

Continue >>

Google screenshots © Google Inc. Used with permission.

Tips, Tricks, & Secrets for Using Google AdWords

Here are some tips that will help you develop and manage a highly effective Google AdWords Campaign, which in turn will generate higher CTRs, lower your CPC, and obtain conversions:

- Design ads so they target potential customers who are ready to buy. Rarely will banner ads or PPC ads draw in the curious website browser and result in a sale.

- Ensure your ad is specific in nature.

- Target one product for each ad if possible, instead of using a generic ad that targets a large market segment.

- Make your ad link directly to the product page with a link to buy the product on that page, instead of to a generic page or the website home page.

- If your ad targets a specific product, you may see a reduction in clicks because your advertising segment is narrow. However, those clicks are most profitable since you are only getting clicks from individuals seeking information on your specific product — this means your advertising costs may actually be reduced, while your sales go up.

- Be willing to bid for a good position. If you do not want to spend much money or are willing to settle for the bottom of the bids, no one is going to see your ad.

- Bid enough to gain the exposure you need, but balance exposure to stretch your advertising budget. It is rarely worth the cost to have the No. 1 bid.

- Being the No. 1 listing on search engines may not be all it is cracked up to be. The top listing is the one that is clicked the most often, but is also has the worst percentage of converting clicks into actual sales. Many "click-happy" people click on the top listing without ever making a purchase. Those clicks will quickly eat up your advertising budget. You may have better luck below the No. 1 listing, as you have the potential to garner better clicks.

- Use the provided tracking tools to monitor performance, and adjust keywords/bidding as necessary.

- Lower your overall costs while increasing the potential conversion rate by choosing multiple highly targeted words or phrases instead of generic terms.

- Use capital letters for each word in the "Title" and "Description" fields of your PPC ad.

- Use demographic and geographic targeting with your ad.

- Use the Google Keyword Suggestion Tool to help you determine which keywords are the most effective for your campaign.

- Keep an eye out for fraud. Although Google has fraud detection and prevention, if you suspect your competition is clicking on your ads, you may want to invest in additional protection. An example of this is the WhosClickingWho?™ Independent Auditing Service (**www. whosclickingwho.com**).

- Check the spelling in your ad to ensure it is correct.

- Embed keywords within your actual ad.

- Define your target audience and narrow the scope of your ad to potential customers.

- Develop multiple advertisements for each campaign, and run them at the same time. You will quickly determine which is effective and which is not. Do not be afraid to tweak advertisements or replace poorly performing advertisements.

- Monitor and use Google Reports by tracking your costs, ROI, and CTRs for each ad.

- Include targeted keywords in the "Headline" and "Description" lines of your ad. Keywords stand out in search engine results, help to attract the attention of potential customers, and increase your overall advertisement effectiveness. Be quite specific in your keywords.

- Include words that stand out and grab the attention of potential customers, such as "New" and "Limited Offer."

- Do not just link to the homepage of your website. Link directly to the relevant landing page for your specific product or service. This will help you convert the visit to a sale.

- Free may not be good for you. If your advertisement says "free," then you can expect considerable traffic from folks who just want the free products and will never buy anything, which will just increase your costs. Consider limiting the use of "free" to cut back on traffic that will never culminate in a sale.

Creating an Effective Google Pay-Per-Click Advertising Campaign

When choosing the keywords you will eventually bid on for your advertising campaign, you need to think like a potential customer, not as the seller or advertiser. You must determine which search terms a potential customer might use to find you through Google. Success is directly related to how competitive your chosen keywords are in relation to the terms used by individuals searching in the Google search engine.

You do not own any keywords or have exclusive rights to them, and chances are, your competitors are targeting the exact same keywords. The cost to buy a keyword in a Google AdWords PPC advertising campaign is primarily determined by how many other websites are competing for the same keyword or key phrases. Keywords are critical to your success in the Google search engine and in your Google AdWords campaigns. Keep them focused and specific to your products or services. Extremely general keywords, such as "real estate," are typically more expensive, since many people search on them, but for these same reasons, they are not as productive as specific keywords or phrases, such as "real estate foreclosure Miami." Using specific keywords to narrow the amount of times your ads are served will ensure that your advertisement is seen, and potentially clicked on, by those most interested; this will reduce your overall cost because you will not be paying for clicks that do not convert into sales.

Google's Exact Match is a good feature that serves your advertisement only when the search phrase is an "exact match," instead of just a close match. If your advertisement is on "private mortgage financing" and your settings are for an exact match, Google will not serve your ad when someone searches on "mortgage financing." However, if your keywords are not popular, generic terms, then this may not be the best option. For example, if you are selling ChefTec Software™, which is recipe costing software, the searcher may not know the brand name "ChefTec," and may be searching for "recipe costing software;" therefore, they would never see your ad.

Google recommends that you choose your keywords carefully by including specific keywords that are directly related to your ad group or landing page. You should include relevant keyword variations, along with singular and plural versions. The goal is to have your ad served often but drive your click rate up. Using keyword-matching options enables you to reach your target audience. Using negative keywords will reduce your ad impressions and increase your quality score with Google, which will ultimately save you money by avoiding clicks.

Use the Google Keyword Tool and Google Keyword Cost Calculator to help you determine what keywords to use and how much they may cost you. To do so, enter keywords into the appropriate fields — along with some optional entries, such as maximum CPC, daily budget limits, and targeted languages and locations — and click "Continue" to see the results. The results provide you with an average CPC, volume, estimated ad position, estimated number of clicks per day, and estimated cost per day.

Average CPC: **$8.19** (at a maximum CPC of $17.32)
Estimated clicks per day: **17 - 20** (at a daily budget of $150.00)

Estimates are based on your bid amount and geographical targeting selections. Because the Traffic Estimator does not consider your daily budget, your ad may receive fewer clicks than estimated.

Maximum CPC:	Daily budget:	Get New Estimates				
Keywords ▾	**Search Volume**	**Estimated Avg. CPC**	**Estimated Ad Positions**	**Estimated Clicks / Day**	**Estimated Cost / Day**
Search Total		$6.54 - $9.87	1 - 3	17 - 20	$80 - $150
chaltec		$0.71 - $0.89	1 - 3	0	$1
recipe software		$10.06 - $15.09	1 - 3	1	$6 - $20
restaurant consulting		$1.69 - $2.53	1 - 3	6	$10 - $20
restaurant management		$6.93 - $8.90	1 - 3	10 - 13	$70 - $120

Estimates for these keywords are based on clickthrough rates for current advertisers. Some of the keywords above are subject to review by Google and may not trigger your ads until they are approved. Please note that your traffic estimates assume your keywords are approved.

Google screenshots © Google Inc. Used with permission.

The primary factor in determining cost is the relationship of the keyword to top 10 rankings within a search engine. If your keywords are not competitive, then the cost of the keyword is relatively low, and it will yield high search engine rankings if used in a keyword search. If you are competing with hundreds or thousands of other companies for the same keywords, the cost of those keywords will escalate dramatically. Google AdWords's minimum CPC base rates depend on your location and currency settings. Your minimum CPC rates can fluctuate for each keyword based on its relevance. The quality is the most important factor in determining the cost of someone clicking on your ad. Your Quality Score sets the minimum bid you will need to pay in order for your keyword to trigger ads. If your maximum CPC is less than the minimum bid assigned to your keyword, you will need to either raise the CPC to the minimum bid listed or optimize your campaign for quality.

A key principle in selecting keywords is in the determination of how often someone will search the Web using that keyword or phrase. Logically, keywords that are less competitive will typically bring you less traffic simply because the keyword is not used often during a search. Conversely, you can expect more traffic with highly competitive keywords, but this may not always be the case, as the field of competitors often grows directly in proportion to the keyword competitiveness. When you begin your PPC campaign, you should be provided with in-depth analysis on a regular basis to help you monitor, adjust, and evaluate the performance of your marketing campaign. Google's reports will tell you exactly which keywords are being used in the search engines, which will help you to determine whether your chosen keywords are effective.

Keyword Research Tools

Another method to determine what keywords you should use is one of many keyword research tools provided on the Internet (please note that not all these tools are free). Some of the keyword research tools are:

WordTracker (**www.wordtracker.com**): Promises to find the best keywords for your Website. When you enter "restaurant consulting" into the generation tool, the application returns the following list of generated keyword suggestions:

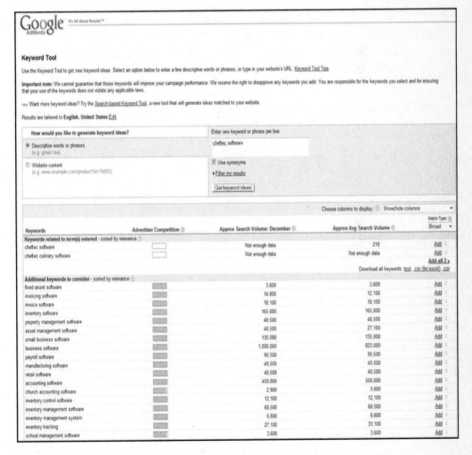

Google screenshots © Google Inc. Used with permission.

You choose the keywords you want to use and the application returns "count" and "prediction" reports. Count is the number of times a particular keyword has appeared in the WordTracker database, while prediction is the maximum total predicted traffic for all of the major search engines/pay per bids and directories today.

Google (https://adwords.google.com/select/KeywordToolExternal): The Google Keyword Tool generates potential keywords for your ad campaign and reports their Google statistics, including search performance and seasonal trends. The Google Keyword Tool can generate a variety of data, including keywords, key phrases, keyword popularity, cost and ad position estimates, global search, positive trends, and negative keywords. Of the tools listed, Google is by far the most user-friendly and comprehensive. There are also dozens of other keyword generation tools available on the Internet. The Google Search-based Keyword Tool provides keyword ideas based on actual Google search queries, matched to specific pages of your website with your ad. The Google Search-based Keyword tool is available at **http://www.google.com/sktool/**.

Google screenshots © Google Inc. Used with permission.

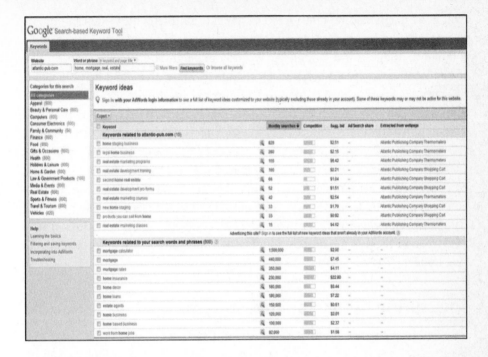

Google screenshots © Google Inc. Used with permission.

How to Establish a Budget for Your Google AdWords Campaign

Google AdWords advertising allows you to quickly pay to have your ad listed on Google and Google partners. Since they are considered "sponsored links," they are significantly different than standard search engine results you might see when you perform a search in a search engine, since these links will ultimately impact your advertising budget as you pay for each "click." Sponsored links, or pay-per-click ads, usually appear at the top, bottom, or right side of the results page following a search with any search engine.

You may see Google AdWords ads called Sponsored Links. Pay-per-click advertising allows you to have your ad listed on search engines with the agreement that you will pay for each "click" on your ad based on bids you have placed on your chosen keywords. When your ad is clicked, depending on the keyword used to perform the search and the value of that keyword, you pay a fee to Google for that click.

You need to give some considerable thought and planning to determining a manageable budget before starting your pay-per-click campaign. Establishing a monthly budget for a Google AdWords campaign is difficult because pricing is based on keyword bids, which change in value often, and may fluctuate over time. Most businesses tend to shift advertising funding from traditional marketing programs, such as print media and radio, toward pay-per-click advertising. An alternative method is to estimate your increased revenue based on your pay-per-click campaign and establishing a percentage-based budget (percent of anticipated or realized increased revenue due to the pay-per-click campaign). The advantage of this type of budget is that you can scale the percentage up or down based on your actual sales derived from the pay-per-click campaign. Google provides you with a Budget Optimizer for AdWords, which helps you to receive the highest number of clicks possible within your specified budget.

Measuring Return on Investment

You can measure the return on investment (ROI) for your Google AdWords campaign. Plus, if you exceed your budget, a pay-per-click campaign can be cancelled at any time. To determine what your starting budget should be, you will need to decide how much a pay-per-click conversion (this is when someone clicks on your advertisement and subsequently places an order) is worth in profit to your business, how many additional sales leads your company is ready to handle, your conversion rate (provided by your PPC company), and what your conversion goal is. The formulas below will help you to establish your pay-per-click budget:

- Number of conversions = sales leads per day x % of conversion x 20 work days in month

- PPC budget maximum = $ in profits per conversion x number of conversions

- PPC profit = total profit from pay-per-click campaign - total budget for PPC

Increase Profits by Combating Fraud with Google AdWords

Google AdWords Pay-per-click advertising can be extraordinarily profitable and, if managed correctly, will dramatically increase your customer base and potential revenue by driving targeted visitors to your site. Once you master the techniques of pay-per-click advertising, in addition to managing and optimizing your campaigns, one of your biggest challenges will be recognizing and combating fraud.

In this discussion, pay-per-click fraud refers to a well-thought-out, targeted, technologically advanced, and highly destructive automated process of creating applications, scripts, robots, or even sometimes humans, which will continue to generate thousands upon thousands of clicks using ingenious techniques to disguise their identity with IP spoofing (and many others), all designed to cost you thousands of dollars in fraudulent clicks while hiding behind a false identity.

You need to recognize and understand that you will not sell a product with every click on your advertisement. If you have ten clicks today on your advertisement and sell two products as a direct result of those clicks, your conversion rate is 20 percent. Most PPC providers provide you with free tools to automate the tracking of your conversion rates. Not everyone who clicks on your pay-per-click ad will buy your products, some of these reasons may include:

- Lack of interest in your products
- Being turned off by your Web page or website
- Inability to find enough information about your product on your site
- Price
- Brand
- Availability
- Competition
- Technical problems, such as a malfunctioning shopping cart

What is Fraud in Relation to Pay-Per-Click Marketing?

As much as 70 percent of annual online advertising spending is wasted because of click fraud. Corrupt affiliates of ad networks, such as Google and Yahoo, account for 85 percent of all click fraud.

No Click Fraud (**www.noclickfraud.com**) is one of a growing number of companies that can assist you in combating pay-per-click fraud. Clickrisk offers

"Click Verification Service," a full-service, 12-month engagement that helps detect click fraud, guard against it in the future, and obtain refunds on your pay-per-click ad spending.

Pay-per-click fraud is typically the result of:

- Unscrupulous pay-per-click traffic and content partners of pay-per-click search engines (PPCs) and directories. These companies gain financially based upon the volume of referral traffic to their partner, and may resort to fraudulent methods to obtain it.

- Competitors who attempt to break your budget by "clicking" away on your ad, quickly consuming your budget with no sales conversion.

- WebBots, spiders, and crawlers designed to maliciously generate fraudulent clicks and consume your budget with no sales conversion.

You should know the following facts about pay-per-click fraud:

- Search engine companies, PPC providers, and advertisers agree that click fraud exists.

- Search engine companies and PPC providers agree that pay-per-click advertisers should not be billed for fraudulent click activity.

- Search engine companies state that they have effective "click fraud" protection built into major search engines.

Tips and Suggestions to Combat Fraud

Here are some tips and suggestions on how you can combat click fraud without breaking your budget:

- Keep current with published anti-click-fraud tips and suggestions.

- Do your research when selecting a pay-per-click provider. While there are many reputable providers, review their policies and tools for combating fraud before you sign up.

- Do not sign up with PPC companies that allow "incentive sites." An incentive site is one that offers free products, free competitions, or "junk" promotions (this applies to AdSense-type campaigns where you are allowing advertisement on your website).

- Monitor click-through rates.

- Review your website traffic reports.

- Place daily click limits in your campaign.

- Establish a daily budget to limit your total costs per day.

- Limit your ad to your target geographic audience.

- Review your IP referral logs (usually provided by your website hosting company or the PPC provider). If you have multiple clicks from the same IP address, you are likely the victim of fraud.

- Report potential fraud to your PPC provider.

- Consider an advanced fraud-detection or tracking tool.

Available fraud protection options

This list of recommended fraud protection providers will help you in your fight to combat fraud and protect your financial investment in your pay-per-click marketing campaign. All major pay-per-click providers have active fraud protection measures in place, but their degree of effectiveness is difficult for you to determine. If you want to provide an additional layer of protection for your investment, you may want to consider one of these companies:

- AdWatcher (**www.adwatcher.com**). AdWatcher is an all-in-one ad management, tracking, and fraud prevention tool focused on helping businesses automate and improve their online marketing efforts. It was developed by the team of advertising experts at MordComm, Inc. — a New York-based online marketing firm. Founded in 2003, the company gained early success providing practical tools to help business owners get more out of search marketing. It currently also operates AdScientist — Pay-Per-Click bid management and optimization software that helps you manage your keyword bids in *all* the major pay-per-click search engines.

- ClickDetective (**www.clickdetective.com**). ClickDetective™ gives you the power to track return visitors to your site and alerts you immediately if there is evidence that your site may be under attack. ClickDetective uses sophisticated tracking mechanisms to determine whether visitor behavior is normal or abnormal and provides you with the tools to do something about it. The ClickDetective reports show individual clicks in real time, unlike most search engine reports, which provide only a summary of click-throughs several hours after the event. You can also set up return visitor alerts that remind the innocent repeat clicker to bookmark your site as well as alerting those visitors with less innocent intent that their movements are being monitored.

- ClickForensics (**www.clickforensics.com**). The problem of unwanted clicks is real. Publications from the *Wall Street Journal* to *Inc. Magazine* to *Barron's* discussed and debated this issue in great detail over the last year. Click Forensics, Inc. was formed to address this issue at the highest level. Click Forensics is focused on developing an industry solution to this growing problem.

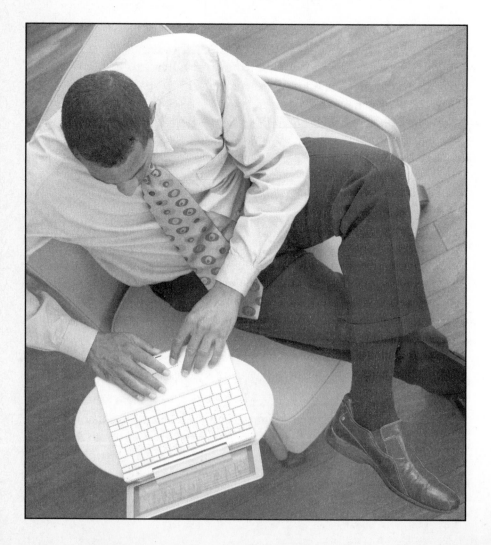

CHAPTER 9

Google AdSense

G oogle AdSense lets you place Google advertisements on *your* Web pages, earning money for each click by site visitors. While it is similar in concept to AdWords, you do not pay for it; instead, you give up some real estate on your website to "host" advertisements (relevant content to your website), which Google places onto this space. Instead of paying per click, you actually earn revenue per click, just for hosting the advertisements on your website. The bottom line is that AdSense is simple to use, costs nothing, and can generate significant amounts of residual monthly income for you. Google lets you generate revenue from advertisements you allow on your Web pages. The cost is free, and there is minimal effort to implement, you simply sign up and place a small bit of code on your Web page.

The concept of Google AdSense is simple: You earn revenue potential by displaying Google ads on your website. Essentially, you become the host site for someone else's pay-per-click advertising. Since Google puts relevant cost per click (CPC) and cost per impression (CPM) ads through the same auction and lets them compete against one another, the auction for the advertisement takes place instantaneously, and Google AdSense subsequently displays a text or image ad(s) that will generate the maximum revenue for you.

There are three basic types of AdSense products you can use.

1. **AdSense for Content:** Crawls the content of your Web pages and delivers text and image ads that are relevant to your audience and your site content

2. **AdSense for Search:** Enables website owners to provide Google Web and site search to their visitors and to earn money from clicks on Google ads on the search results pages

3. **AdSense for Mobile Content:** Earn money from your content with a simple, integrated solution for mobile-device-compatible websites

Becoming an AdSense publisher is simple. You must fill out a brief application form online at **www.google.com/AdSense**, which requires your website to be reviewed before your application is approved. Once approved, Google will e-mail you HTML code for you to place on your Web pages. Once the HTML code is saved onto your Web page, it activates, and targeted ads will be displayed on your website.

You must choose an advertisement category to ensure only relevant, targeted advertisements are portrayed on your website. Google has ads for all categories of businesses and for practically all types of content, no matter how broad or specialized. The AdSense program represents advertisers ranging from large global brands to small, local companies. Ads are also targeted by geography, so global businesses can display local advertising with no additional effort. Google AdSense also supports multiple languages.

You can also earn revenue for your business by placing a Google search box on your website — literally paying you for search results. This service may help keep traffic on your site longer since site visitors can search directly from your site; it is also available to you at no cost and is simple to implement.

Google states that their "ad review process ensures that the ads you serve are not only family-friendly, but also comply with our strict editorial guidelines. We combine sensitive language filters, your input, and a team of linguists with good hard common sense to automatically filter out ads that may be inappropriate for your content." Additionally, you can customize the appearance of your ads, choosing from a wide range of colors and templates. This is also the case with Google's search results page. To track your revenue, Google provides you with an arsenal of tools to track your advertising campaign and revenue.

How to Set up Your Google AdSense Campaign

The first step is to complete the simple application form, which is on the Web at **www.google.com/AdSense/g-app-single-1**. It is critical that you carefully review the terms of service. In particular, you must agree that you will:

- Not click on the Google ads you are serving through AdSense

- Not place ads on sites that include incentives to click on ads

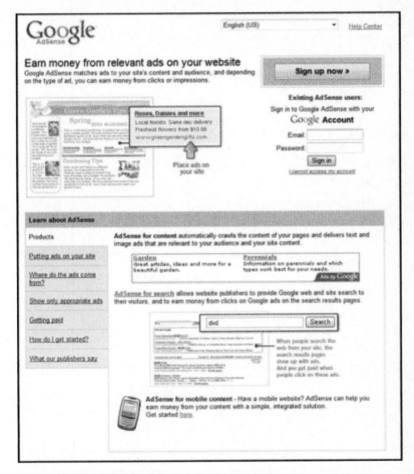

Google screenshots © Google Inc. Used with permission.

You cannot click on your ads, have others click on your ads, or place text on your website asking anyone to click on your advertisements. The reason for this is simple — you cannot click on (or have anyone else) click on your own advertisements to generate revenue.

Google screenshots © Google Inc. Used with permission.

Google AdSense Program Policies

Publishers participating in the AdSense program are required to adhere to the following policies. If you fail to comply with these policies, Google may disable ad serving to your site and/or disable your AdSense account.

Invalid clicks and impressions

Clicks on Google ads must result from genuine user interest. Any method that artificially generates clicks or impressions on your Google ads is strictly prohibited. These prohibited methods include but are not limited to repeated manual clicks or impressions; using robots; automated click and impression generating tools; third-party services that generate clicks or impressions, such as paid-to-click, paid-to-surf, autosurf, and click-exchange programs; or any deceptive software. **Please note that clicking on your own ads for any reason is prohibited.**

Encouraging clicks

In order to ensure a good experience for users and advertisers, publishers may not request that users click the ads on their sites or rely on deceptive implementation methods to obtain clicks. Publishers participating in the AdSense program:

- May not encourage users to click the Google ads by using phrases such as "click the ads," "support us," "visit these links," or other similar language

- May not direct user attention to the ads via arrows or other graphical gimmicks

- May not place misleading images alongside individual ads

- May not promote sites displaying ads through unsolicited mass e-mails or unwanted advertisements on third-party websites

- May not compensate users for viewing ads or performing searches, or promise compensation to a third party for such behavior

- May not place misleading labels above Google ad units — for instance, ads may be labeled "Sponsored Links" but not "Favorite Sites"

Site content

While Google offers broad access to a variety of content in the search index, publishers in the AdSense program may only place Google ads on sites that adhere to our content guidelines, and ads must not be displayed on any page with content primarily in an unsupported language.

Sites displaying Google ads may not include:

- Violent content, racial intolerance, or advocacy against any individual, group, or organization

- Pornography, adult, or mature content

- Hacking/cracking content

- Illicit drugs and drug paraphernalia

- Excessive profanity

- Gambling or casino-related content

- Content regarding programs that compensate users for clicking on ads or offers, performing searches, surfing websites, or reading e-mails

- Excessive, repetitive, or irrelevant keywords in the content or code of Web pages

- Deceptive or manipulative content or construction to improve your site's search engine ranking (PageRank)

- Sales or promotion of weapons or ammunition (e.g., firearms, fighting knives, or stun guns)

- Sales or promotion of beer or hard alcohol

- Sales or promotion of tobacco or tobacco-related products

- Sales or promotion of prescription drugs

- Sales or promotion of products that are replicas or imitations of designer goods

- Sales or distribution of term papers or student essays

- Any other content that is illegal, promotes illegal activity, or infringes on the legal rights of others

Copyrighted material

Website publishers may not display Google ads on Web pages with content protected by copyright law unless they have the necessary legal rights to display that content.

Webmaster guidelines

AdSense publishers are required to adhere to the webmaster quality guidelines posted at **www.google.com/Webmasters/guidelines.html**.

Site and ad behavior

Sites showing Google ads should be easy for users to navigate and should not contain excessive pop-ups. AdSense code may not be altered, nor may standard ad behavior be manipulated in any way that is not explicitly permitted by Google.

- Sites showing Google ads may not contain pop-ups or pop-unders that interfere with site navigation, change user preferences, or initiate downloads.

- Any AdSense code must be pasted directly into Web pages without modification. AdSense participants are not allowed to alter any portion of the code or change the behavior, targeting, or delivery of ads. For instance, clicks on Google ads may not result in a new browser window being launched.

- A site or third party cannot display your ads, search box, search results, or referral buttons as a result of the actions of any software application, such as a toolbar.

- No AdSense code may be integrated into a software application.

- Web pages containing AdSense code may not be loaded by any software that can trigger pop-ups, redirect users to unwanted websites, modify browser settings, or otherwise interfere with site navigation. It is your responsibility to ensure that no ad network or affiliate uses such methods to direct traffic to pages that contain your AdSense code.

- Referral offerings must be made without any obligation or requirement to end-users. Publishers may not solicit e-mail addresses from users in conjunction with AdSense referral units.

- Publishers using online advertising to drive traffic to pages showing Google ads must comply with the spirit of Google's Landing Page Quality Guidelines. For instance, if you advertise for sites participating in the AdSense program, the advertising should not be deceptive to users.

AdSense

AdSense offers a number of ad formats and advertising products. Publishers have a wide variety of placements, provided the following policies are followed:

- Up to three ad units may be displayed on each page.

- A maximum of two Google AdSense search boxes may be placed on a page.

- Up to three link units may also be placed on each page.

- Up to three referral units may be displayed on a page, in addition to the ad units, search boxes, and link units specified above.

- AdSense for search results pages may show only a single ad link unit in addition to the ads Google serves with the search results. No other ads may be displayed on your search results page.

- No Google ad or Google search box may be displayed in a pop-up, pop-under, or e-mail.

- Elements on a page must not obscure any portion of the ads.

- No Google ad may be placed on any non-content-based pages.

- No Google ad may be placed on pages published specifically for the purpose of showing ads, regardless of whether the page content is relevant.

Competitive ads and services

In order to prevent user confusion, Google does not permit Google ads or search boxes to be published on websites that also contain other ads or services formatted to use the same layout and colors as the Google ads or search boxes on that site. Although you may sell ads directly on your site, it is your responsibility to ensure these ads cannot be confused with Google ads.

Google advertising cookies

Google uses the DoubleClick DART cookie on publisher websites displaying AdSense for content ads. Subject to any applicable laws, rules, and regulations, you will have the sole and exclusive right to use all data derived from your use of the DoubleClick DART cookie for any purpose related to your business, provided that Google may use and disclose this data subject to the terms of Google's advertising privacy policies, and any applicable laws, rules, and regulations.

Landing Page and Site Quality Guidelines

The following Google site guidelines will help improve your landing page quality score. As a component of your keywords' overall quality scores, a high landing page quality score can affect your AdWords account in three ways:

1. By decreasing your keywords' CPCs

2. By increasing your keyword-targeted ads' positions on the content network

3. By improving the chances that your placement-targeted ads will win a position on your targeted placements

Relevant and original content

Relevance and originality are two characteristics that define high-quality site content. Here are some pointers on creating content that meets these standards:

Relevance

- Users should be able to easily find what your ad promises.

- Link to the page on your site that provides the most useful information about the product or service in your ad. For instance, direct users to the page where they can buy the advertised product, rather than to a page with a description of several products.

Originality

- Feature unique content that cannot be found on another site. This guideline is particularly applicable to affiliates that use the following types of pages:

   ◊ **Bridge pages**: Pages that act as an intermediary, whose sole purpose is to link or redirect traffic to the parent company.

   ◊ **Mirror pages**: Pages that replicate the look and feel of a parent site; your site should not mirror (be similar or nearly identical in appearance to) your parent company's or any other advertiser's site.

- Provide substantial information. If your ad does link to a page consisting mostly of ads or general search results, such as a directory or catalog page, provide additional, unique content.

Transparency

In order to build trust with users, your site should be explicit in three primary areas: the nature of your business; how your site interacts with a visitor's computer; and how you intend to use a visitor's personal information, if you request it. Here are tips on maximizing your site's transparency:

Regarding your business information:

- Openly share information about your business. Clearly define what your business is or does

- Honor the deals and offers you promote in your ad

- Deliver products and services as promised

- Only charge users for the products and services that they order and successfully receive

- Distinguish sponsored links from the rest of your site content

Regarding your site's interaction with a visitor's computer:

- Avoid altering users' browser behavior or settings, such as back button functionality or browser window size, without first getting their permission

- If your site automatically installs software, be upfront about the installation, and allow for easy removal

Visitors' personal information:

- Unless necessary for the product or service that you are offering, do not request personal information

- If you do request personal information, provide a privacy policy that discloses how the information will be used

- Give options to limit the use of a user's personal information, such as the ability to opt out of receiving newsletters

- Allow users to access your site's content without requiring them to register, or provide a preview of what users will get by registering

Navigability

The key to turning visitors into customers is making it easy for users to find what they are looking for. Here is how:

- Provide a short, easy path for users to purchase or receive the product or offer in your ad

- Avoid excessive use of pop-ups, pop-unders, and other obtrusive elements throughout your site

- Make sure that your landing page loads quickly

Setting up Google AdSense on Your Website

To set up your initial AdSense account, click on the "My Account" tab. Since Google will be paying you, you will be required to complete several steps before your account is activated, such as providing W-9 tax data and choosing your form of payment (electronic transfer or check payment).

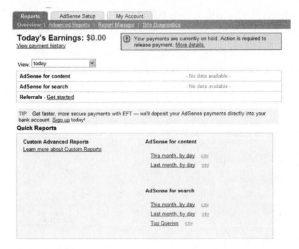

Google screenshots © Google Inc. Used with permission.

Click on the "Account Setup" to begin setting up your ads. The following screen will be displayed:

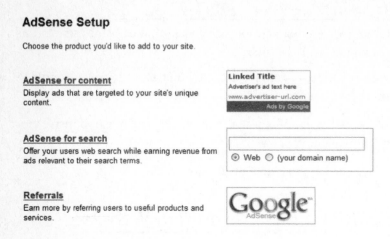

Google screenshots © Google Inc. Used with permission.

Choose which product you would like to add to your website. You may choose either AdSense for content, AdSense for search, or referrals. You will now choose your ad type. You may choose ad unit (use the drop down menu to choose text and image ads, text only, or image only ads). Ad unit with text and images is the default — and recommended — setting, or you may choose a link unit, which displays a list of topics relevant to your Web page. Then click on the ad unit to continue.

Google screenshots © Google Inc. Used with permission.

You will be presented with several options to choose from, including unit format and colors. Choose your desired options using the drop-down menus (note: this is not the actual ad that will be displayed on your website, but merely a sample of how it may appear). AdSense lets you customize the appearance of ads to match the look and feel of your website. You can also customize the style of your AdSense for search box and search results page.

AdSense for Content

Choose Ad Type > Choose Ad Format and Colors > Get Ad Code

Wizard | Single page

You can customize your ads to fit in with your pages. Use the options below to specify ad size, style, and more.

Format

Ad units come in a variety of sizes - view all the options on our Ad Formats page.

728 x 90 Leaderboard

Colors

Choose from one of our pre-designed color palettes, or create your own palette. Tips

* Some options apply to text ads only.

Sample
Linked Title
Advertiser's ad text here
www.advertiser-url.com

Ads by Google

Palettes | Default Google palette
Edit palettes

Border # FFFFFF
Title # 0000FF
Background # FFFFFF
Text # 000000
URL # 008000

More options

Custom channel
Specify a custom channel to track the performance of these ads. Learn more...

No channel selected
Add new channel | Manage channels...

Alternate ads or colors
Choose what to display if no relevant ads are available. Learn more...

◉ Show public service ads
○ Show ads from another URL
○ Fill space with a solid color

Google screenshots © Google Inc. Used with permission.

You may use "more options" to enable custom channels or elect to alternate ads or colors, including the option to show public service ads if there is no advertisement ready to be displayed on your website. After making your selections, you will be provided with HTML code, which simply needs to be placed in the HTML code on your website. You are free to place the code on one or many Web pages within your website.

AdSense for Content

Choose Ad Type > Choose Ad Format and Colors > Get Ad Code

Wizard | Single page

Click anywhere in this box to select all code.

You may paste this code into any web page or website that complies with our program policies.

For more help with implementing the AdSense code, please see our Code Implementation Guide. For tips on placing ads to maximize earnings, see our Optimization Tips.

Your AdSense code:

```
<script type="text/javascript"><!--
google_ad_client = "pub-2693250782343896";
google_ad_width = 120;
google_ad_height = 240;
google_ad_format = "120x240_as";
google_ad_type = "text_image";
google_ad_channel ="";
//--></script>
<script type="text/javascript"
   src="http://pagead2.googlesyndication.com/pagead/show_ads.js">
</script>
```

Google screenshots © Google Inc. Used with permission.

When you insert the HTML code into your website, your campaign is activated and advertisements are immediately served to your site. Since you cannot click on your advertisement at any time, even to "test" them, Google provides a preview mode for testing. Google's AdWords technology matches the most relevant, highest performing AdWords ads to your website. You can bid on ads on a per-click or per-impression basis. Depending on the type of ad appearing on your site, you will be paid for valid clicks and impressions. You also have the option of payment monthly via check or electronic fund transfer (EFT). How much you earn depends on a number of factors, including how much an advertiser bids on your site, but you will receive a portion of what the advertiser pays.

The following ad was created and set up on our website in under five minutes:

Google screenshots © Google Inc. Used with permission'

You can expand your AdSense account well beyond traditional Web pages. They can be implemented successfully into blogs and feeds. Last year, Google even implemented "AdSense for Feeds," which lets you place ads into RSS feeds, allowing you to increase the reach of your content while earning revenue.

How to Set up your Google Referrals

Google AdSense program policies allow you to place one referral per product, for a total of up to four referrals, on any page. You simply click on the referral link to choose your referrals.

Choose the product you'd like to refer.

Google referrals

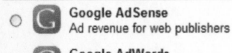 **Google AdSense**
Ad revenue for web publishers

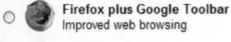 **Google AdWords**
Targeted online advertising

Firefox plus Google Toolbar
Improved web browsing

Google Pack
Collection of essential software

Picasa
Photo organization software

Google screenshots © Google Inc. Used with permission.

Google AdSense will generate the HTML code for your website. Once the code is placed on your Web pages, your referral will be activated and displayed on your website, as shown in the following screenshot. You have a variety of options in size, color, and wording to choose from and are free to change your referral ads at any time.

Generate revenue from your website with Google AdSense.

 **Professional Guide To...Book Series**
This new series from the editors of the Food Service Professional Magazine are the best and most co guides on a specific management subject are easy-to-read, easy to understand and will take the my the brim with up to date and pertinent information. These books cover all the bases, providing clear and web sites of all companies discussed.

In the Weeds Poster
This whimsical new poster, available exclusively from Atlantic Publishing, spoofs the madcap world of poster will boost the moral and tickle the funny bone of everyone who sees it. Available in two sizes.
24″ x 36″ Item # INWL-PS • $29.95 [ADD TO CART]
11″ x 17″ Item # INWS-PS • $14.95 [ADD TO CART]

Google screenshots © Google Inc. Used with permission.

Google AdSense is simple to implement, non-intrusive to your website, and allows you to open channels to earning potential revenue for your business.

Hints & Tips for Maximizing Google AdSense on Your Website

Google AdSense is an outstanding way to generate website traffic, attract advertisers, and create a revenue stream for your business. Use these hints and tips to maximize your earning potential:

- Always follow the Google AdSense Guidelines.

- Do not modify or change the Google AdSense HTML code you place on your website.

- Do not use colored backgrounds on the Google AdSense ads. If you have a website with a colored background, modify the advertisement to match your background.

- Place your ads so they are visible. If someone needs to scroll down to see your ads, you will likely not get any clicks on them. Play with the placement to maximize visibility.

- Do not place ads in pop-up windows.

- Do not buy an "AdSense Template Website," which is readily available on Ebay and other online marketplaces. These get-rich type "click" campaigns are against Google's policies and do not make money.

- Text ads tend to do better than image ads. If you insist on image ads, keep them reasonable; it is recommended to only use the 300 x 250 medium rectangle.

- You can modify the URL link color in the ad through the Google AdSense account panel to make it stand out among your ads and attract the eye of the site visitor.

- If you have a blog, use it to have others place ads in it. You will need to get Google approval for your blog.

- If your website has articles on it that you wish to embed ads in, use these guidelines:

    ◊ For short articles, place the ad above the article.

    ◊ For long articles, embed the ad within the content of the article.

- Wider-format ads are more successful. The paying ad format is the "large rectangle."

- Distribute ads on each Web page. Combine ads with referrals and search boxes so your website does not look like a giant billboard.

- Put the Google search box near the top right-hand corner of your Web page.

- If your ads are based on content, the first lines of the Web page determine your site content for ad serving purposes.

- Set the Google AdSense search box results window so that it opens in a new window, as this will keep your browser open and users will not navigate away from your website.

Google AdSense allows webmasters to customize their Google AdSense ads. Because of this, you can actually customize the links, borders, and color themes of your ads. Borderless AdSense Web banners tend to produce more clicks.

CHAPTER 10

Google Base and Google Product Search

G oogle Base and Google Product Search are two separate, but inter-relat-
ed, applications available from Google. Google Product Search replaced
Google Froogle (**www.froogle.com**), which is an online pricing comparison
of products — essentially, Google's online shopping search engine. Google
Product Search lets you search the Web for virtually any product and retrieve
relevant results, specifically intended to compare pricing and vendors and let
you shop for products. Google Base is a free service that simply lets you publish information or products online for inclusion into Google search results.
Items in Google Base will appear in either Google Base or Google Product
Search, depending on the type of submission. For your products to appear in
Google Product Search, you must submit your information to Google Base.
The Google Base database will be incorporated into other Google tool results,
such as the Google Search Engine and Google Maps. This is important be-
cause it means you can potentially load all your products into Google Base
and make them available for free on the Google Search Engine and in other
Google applications.

Google Base

Google Base is an online database offered by Google that allows you to add
your products to it in a preset format, and then your products are featured
on the Google Search Engine and through other Google searches, including
Google Product Search and Google Base. Google Base has been called the
"Google" version of "Craig's List" because you can use it to buy and sell
products, post resumes, search for jobs, find vacation rentals, and buy and sell
vehicles — even houses have appeared on Google Base.

Google Base is absolutely *free*. You can submit information about all types of
online and offline content to Google Base, by either the standard Web form
or, if you have more than ten items to submit, via Google's bulk upload op-

tions. When you submit information via the Web form, you can attach up to 15 digital files in the following formats: PDF (.pdf), Microsoft Excel (.xls), Text (.txt), HTML (.html), Rich Text Format (.rtf), Word Perfect (.wpd), ASCII, Unicode, and XML. Google is available in English and German interfaces. Items submitted to Google Base may be displayed on Google, Froogle, and Google Maps.

Google screenshots © Google Inc. Used with permission

By clicking on the "products" link, you can narrow your search to "product" listing only, where you are presented with a variety of sort options, including price, relevance, stores, brands, and links to view via Google Maps

Google screenshots © Google Inc. Used with permission.

Google screenshots © Google Inc. Used with permission.

A unique feature of Google Base is called attributes. Attributes is the ability for you to describe your item with detailed information, including characteristics and qualities, for any potential buyer. Google Base is not just about selling products — it lets you put *anything* online, for free. It can be products, inventory, books, resumes, jobs, poetry, letters, a diary, or reports. Many shopping carts, such as PDG Cart, automate the data export process for creating a Google Base data file based on your product inventory. Please remember that all items that are uploaded into Google Base must comply with Google Editorial and Program Policies, which are posted at **http://base.google.com/support/bin/answer.py?hl=en_US&answer=61118**.

How to Add Products to Google Base

To add products to Google Base, you must have a free Google Account, which gives you access to all Google services within your account management page. **www.google.com/accounts/NewAccount** to establish your Google account:

Google screenshots © Google Inc. Used with permission.

Google screenshots © Google Inc. Used with permission.

You can upload products one at a time or through a data feed or API. Detailed instructions for how to create your bulk upload file are located at **http://base. google.com/base/products.html**. Google even provides you with sample bulk load files to help you ensure your file is properly formatted.

To submit an item using the Google Base standard form, simply click on "Post your own item." On the "Post an Item" page, choose an item type from the drop-down menu or create your own item type in the text box below. Then click "Next" to add details, edit, review, and publish your item. In about 15 minutes, your item will have a unique Web address and be visible to the world.

If you have a website that you would like to lead searchers to, include an attribute as type "Web URL," which includes the page's full URL. If you would like to submit more than ten items, you will want to use a data feed. Following is a sample one-at-a-time entry form for adding products to Google Base:

Google screenshots © Google Inc. Used with permission.

To establish and use "data feeds," simply choose the "data feed" option to set up your account options to register and load your data file or data feed into the Google Base database. Google will process and validate your file to ensure it passes all edits and controls. After your file has been processed and approved, it will tell you the date and time it was uploaded, as well as the number of active items and when the listing will expire (they are good for 30 days), and then you must upload a new data file. Detailed instruction on how to create your data feed in .txt, XML, or other formats is available at **http://base.google. com/support/bin/answer.py?hl=en&answer=59461**.

Google screenshots © Google Inc. Used with permission.

Following is a sample properly formatted Google Base bulk upload file in .TXT format:

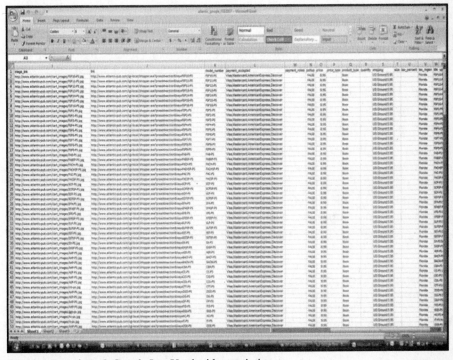

Google screenshots © Google Inc. Used with permission.

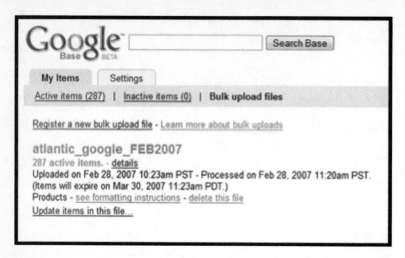

Google screenshots © Google Inc. Used with permission.

Google will perform edits and validations on your bulk upload file and notify you via your Base control panel if there are problems with your upload. You will also be notified via e-mail. Go to the "bulk upload" page to load your file into the Google Base database. Google will process and validate your file to ensure it passes all edits and controls. Initially, your upload will show as "pending approval," and then it will migrate to "Approved" or "Disapproved." Once your items are approved, they are visible in Google Base and Google searches. There are no commissions, fees, or other charges associated with Google Base, and it is simple to use. Once your bulk upload file is created (Google Base will accept feeds in TSV, RSS 1.0, RSS 2.0, Atom 0.3, and Atom 1.0 formats), content providers who already have RSS feeds can easily submit their content to Google Base. Google Base can essentially provide free promotion of your company, products, and services.

Detailed instructions on how to create and upload your Google Base items are contained in the comprehensive Google Base Help Center, located at **http://base.google.com/support/**. Additional resources about Google Base can be found on the official blog, at **http://googlebase.blogspot.com**.

Google Product Search

Google Product Search is Google's price comparison program. You can use it to drive business to your website and promote your products for free. Google Product Search helps shoppers find and buy products across the Web and provides you with pricing and seller comparisons so you can find the best deal on products, and you can use it to provide the best deals to your potential customers and drive traffic to your website. You can easily submit your products to Google Product Search, allowing shoppers worldwide to find your products, as well as your website, quickly and easily. Google Product Search allows you to:

- **Increase Website Traffic and Generate Sales:** Google Product Search connects your products to the shoppers searching for them. Products submitted to Google Product Search appear in Product Search results, and may also appear on **www.google.com**.

- **Submit Your Products to Google for Free:** Inclusion of your products is completely free. There are no charges for uploading your items or for the additional traffic you receive.

- **Find and Connect with Qualified Shoppers:** You will find potential buyers at the precise moment they are searching for your products.

Uploading products to Google Product Search is identical to the process used for Google Base, using the Google Base interface, Web forms, API, or data feeds exactly as you would for Google Base. Additionally, you may use the Store Connector, which is a free download that extracts and places products from your Yahoo, eBay, and osCommerce stores directly into Google Base. Additionally, it automatically formats items to align with the Google Base requirements. You can access Google Product Search through your Google.com account for adding products, establishing an account, and more. To access the user interface to search for products, go to **www.google.com/products**.

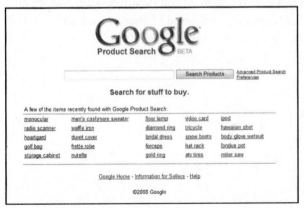

Google screenshots © Google Inc. Used with permission.

To search for products, simply type in your search criteria, and results are returned back to you in the browser.

Google screenshots © Google Inc. Used with permission.

Matching criteria is returned, including product description, images, pricing, and price comparison options for matching items. You may also use Product Search to generate a shopping list. Click on the "compare prices" button to compare pricing and vendor information for a particular product. Comparison data includes seller ratings, links to the products on their websites, and tax and shipping information, as well as pricing. Advanced features, such as "Preview this book on Google Book Search," may be available.

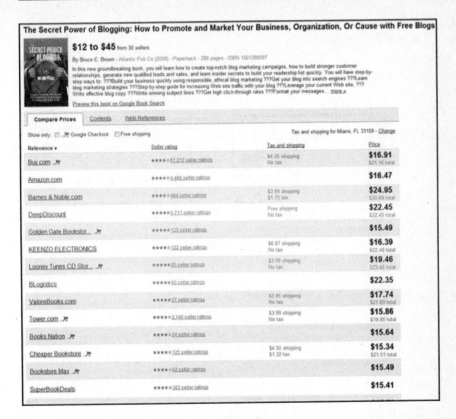

Google screenshots © Google Inc. Used with permission.

The "contents" link will show you the table of contents for books, and the "Web reference" link will do a search for the product on the Web and pull back exact match criteria, enabling you to do advanced research or reviews of the product. The following screenshot is a sample of Google Book Search, which enables you to preview books located in Google Product Search.

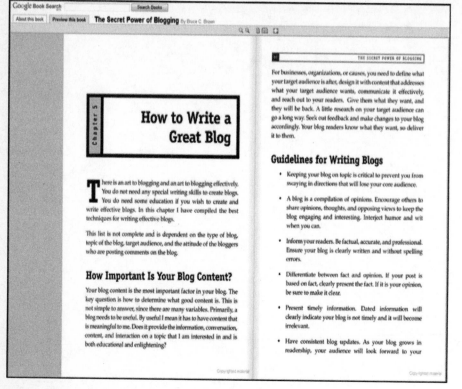

Google screenshots © Google Inc. Used with permission.

Google Product Search is simple to use and highly effective at promoting your products and website. Since you are going to do the work to upload your products via the Google Base interface, simplify and automate the process with a monthly or fresher data feed to ensure data accuracy is achieved while maintaining an active inventory at all times in Google Product Search.

CHAPTER 11

Blogs

A blog is an ideal alternative to a website or an ideal way to complement a blog and gain instant search engine visibility. You can set up a blog for free in minutes. Blogs offer a wide variety of pre-designed templates, the ability to customize to suit your needs, and are excellent for search engine visibility. Of course, you need to know and understand what a blog is, how it functions, what it does and does not do, and how it can help you achieve your personal or business goals.

What is a Blog?

The word "blog" is a combination of the words "Web" and "log." A blog is a website in which short entries or "postings" are made in an abbreviated style format, and they are displayed in reverse chronological order. Blogs can consist of numerous topics, personal to a political or business collaborative that discusses specific topics, products, or services. Blogs can also be used as a news-style of publication; this is something that a lot of journalists are beginning to utilize to publish their thoughts and perspectives on a variety of issues, or to get the word out instantly about a breaking news item of concern to a local community.

Blogs can be about any subject, including politics, news, world events, public opinion, and cooking. There are also many personal blogs from celebrities, world leaders, and aspiring political candidates. If you can think of a topic, there is most likely a blog related to it. Personal blogs are often considered online versions of a diary or journal. Although this is a pretty good comparison, they are far different from paper-based diaries or journals since they offer interactivity you cannot get with these more traditional forms, or even with a static HTML-based Web page diary or journal.

A blog uses a combination of text, images, and hyperlinks to other blogs, websites, and multimedia content such as movie or audio clips. One of the features associated with blogging is that blog visitors can leave comments on the blog, thus creating a collaborative dialogue between you and potential customers, donors, or others you may wish to interact with. A blog opens the door to two-way communications between yourself and millions of people on the Internet. A blog can be used as a website or in place of a Website.

Everything on a blog, especially if it is a news-oriented project, must be consistently and constantly updated, including the answers to your visitors' comments and questions. Unlike a website where visitors can post a comment on a news article and you can respond if you choose, blogs require a more in-depth commitment because your visitors expect you to answer their comments and questions, which can be time-consuming if you are trying to update your site several times a day to keep it active.

If you are going to build a blog, you also have to remember that blogs become outdated much faster than a regular website. The need to update is continuous because if you do not, visitors will disappear much quicker than if you were hosting a normal website. People visiting a website expect it to be updated regularly, but if you miss a day, you do not necessarily lose all of your visitors. In contrast, if you miss a day or two updating your blog, your visitors will move on to someone new who updates his or her blog more consistently.

A blog is an ongoing journal of events, news, or opinions offered for others to interact and respond to, creating an ongoing dialogue between the "blogger" and the reader. The key difference between a Web page and a blog is that the Web page is static content — you can read the page, but not interact with it — while the blog is interactive. Another major difference between static Web pages and blogs is that blogs can be syndicated using RSS or Atom feeds. Syndicated blogs allow subscribers to "join" the blog and receive updates automatically.

If you write a blog, you are a "blogger." There are millions of blogs, and thus millions of bloggers, and the numbers grow every day as blogging continues to gain popularity. The majority of blogs are personal blogs, but there is a growing trend for businesses and organizations to produce blogs for their company, products, and services. The exception is in news media and politics, where blogging is a part of the culture and an integral form of accepted communications.

Blogging is all about linking. As with websites, links can help raise visibility with search engines. Links to and from blogs to other blogs and websites are directly relevant to the popularity and overall visibility and ranking of blogs. A blog is an invitation for customers to look into your company and allows you to develop trust, two-way communication, and, ultimately, increased sales.

The Construction of a Blog

There are many tools available to help you write and publish blogs. Many are retail software, but there is also a wealth of free products to simplify the process. Before delving into a discussion about writing blogs, however, you first need to understand how a blog is constructed.

Every blog essentially consists of the following:

- **Title:** The title of the blog. This provides the blog reader an overall idea of what the blog is about.

- **Date:** The date of the blog's most recent update or post. Blogs are displayed in reverse chronological order, so the most recent post is at the top of the blog.

- **Post title:** The title of each blog post.

- **Blog text:** This is the actual text of each blog post.

- **Blog post information:** This is information about the individual or business who actually wrote the blog. Sometimes this contains contact information as well.

- **Blogger comments:** This is an area for the readers of a blog to place comments, responses, opinions, or reactions to a blog post. This is not a mandatory field; if your intent is only to push information via your blog, you do not have to accept comments.

- **Previous blog posts:** This is the reverse chronological listing of previous blog posts from most recent to oldest.

- **Archived posts:** Even the best blogs get unwieldy; it is not uncommon to archive old posts after a preset period of time.

- **Blogroll:** A list of links to other related sites.

- **Advertising:** This is a common sight in the world of blogging. Many advertisements are prominently featured, typically in free blogging applications. In some cases, you can generate revenue through the use of advertising, but often these are third-party advertisements you allow for the use of blogging software.

- **Feeds:** Feeds to push blogs posts automatically to subscribers, either in RSS or Atom form.

What Do I Need to Create My Own Blog?

You need two critical elements to create your own blog. These are blogging software and Web hosting.

Blog Software and Blog Hosting Options

Essentially, you have four choices when deciding how to publish your blog:

- **Free blog software with free blog hosting**: This option is of no cost to you. However, you must often allow paid advertisements to be placed within or on your blog pages. These paid advertisements are typically obtrusive and will not generate any residual income for you as they might through Google AdSense. Also, free blogging software typically has some reduced functionality compared to paid software. But there are two outstanding, advertisement-free options available to you. Both Blogger and WordPress produce professional blogs and are customizable through templates, powerful, and very easy to use. Blogger even lets you switch between a hosted application and publishing directly to your Web server via File Transfer Protocol (FTP).

- **Free blog software with paid blog hosting**: You pay for the domain name and/or hosting space with the hosting company, and the blog software is provided at no cost to you. This is very common with many Web hosting companies; as part of the hosting package, you get "free" blog software. While you do not have advertising on your blog, the software may have reduced functionality compared to commercial software. In most instances, this is an attractive option since your blog is usually hosted under your own domain name; however, some providers charge you an extra monthly fee for the blogging service. If this is the case, you will most likely do better to use Blogger or WordPress for free. However, if you wish to use your own domain name and want to use the blog software your hosting company provides, this may be an option to consider. Since your hosting company is providing the blog software, you are stuck with the brand they use. They take care of the installation and maintenance, which is one major plus.

- **Paid blog software with paid blog hosting**: This means you buy the full-featured software and also pay for the hosting service through a service provider. This is a great option if you need very powerful blog or CMS software and a very large hosting account under your own domain name.

- **Paid blog software hosted on your own web servers**: This means you buy the full-featured software and install and host it on your own servers — you must physically own or lease the servers; this is not just a shared hosting space. This is a good option if you do not want to use open source or free software but already have Web servers, meaning you do not need to pay for hosting commercially.

The free options may not offer all the functionality you desire, but both Blogger and WordPress will meet the needs of most small businesses and individuals, making this the perfect option for a small budget. Even with free blog hosting, do not forget the power of hyperlinks. You can easily establish a blog on a commercial hosting provider, and link or integrate that blog into your own website, even though it is not physically hosted on your own Web servers and does not use the same URL as your company's website. This practice is very common. Blogger allows you to host under your domain name as part of their built-in functionality, and WordPress allows you to export your blog if you wish to move it to a new domain. The only real factor in deciding whether you want to host your blog under your own name may appear years down the road if you outgrow the free products and want to move to a new domain name. Your audience will already know the old domain name, so it may be hard to move your blog without losing them. The following sections will provide a more detailed look at the five options.

Free Blog Software with Free Blog Hosting

While you may find this option to offer limited features — including limited functionality, limited access, and limited control over design, colors, and presentation — this option will cost you nothing. Blogger and WordPress are the recommended options because both offer advertisement-free, hosted blogging solutions, and both are customizable, rich in features, and easy to use.

One of the main advantages of having your own website is that you own the domain name, so you can choose a domain name that is directly related to your company or corporate image. With free hosting, you have no control over your domain name. In fact, you will most likely be hosted under another domain name and utilize a subdomain name. A subdomain is a domain name that is part of another domain name, such as **www.yourfreeblog.brucecbrown.com**. This might not be bad if your blog is hosted on your corporate website; however, if it is hosted by another free hosting provider, your blog domain name may be very lengthy and not at all related to your company name or profile.

The primary advantage to this option is that there is no cost involved. This is a great way to start blogging because you can try it out to see if it is something you will truly enjoy. If you find it is not your kind of hobby, you have not wasted any money. If you become an avid blogger, you can move to a better option in the future if you choose.

Free Blog Software with Paid Blog Hosting

This option may be the ideal solution if you already own a website and have it hosted with a provider that provides you with blog software for free on its servers. The main advantage is that you are ensuring that your blog is advertisement-free and is hosted under your domain name. The downside is that you are stuck with whatever blog software they provide, which may be subpar, and you often have to pay an extra fee to use the blogging features.

As in the first option, free software may have reduced features or functionality, which will limit your control over the look and feel of your blog and may not have all of the features you seek. In addition to free software, there are numerous "shareware" versions of blogging software that are both reliable and widely used. The primary disadvantage of this type of software is that many hosting services will not allow it to be installed on their servers. A common theme with Web hosts is the exclusion of third-party software on their sites to protect themselves from security breaches as well as performance hits by allowing you to run bandwidth-hungry software on their servers.

If your current Web hosting provider allows you to install third-party blog software on their servers, this is also a possible option, especially if you already have a website and domain name. Be sure to check with your current Web hosting provider; they most likely already offer free blog software to you as part of the hosting package.

Paid Blog Software with Paid Blog Hosting

This is a good option if you want to get feature-rich, fully functional software, do not want to hassle with hosting or software setup, and require reliable technical support for both hardware and software. The tradeoff is, obviously, you have to pay for it. In this case, the hosting is provided by the reseller of the blog software, sometimes on their domain, but typically hosted under your domain name. There is usually no installation fee, no setup, and one monthly payment; however, sometimes you pay for the software and hosting separately, depending on which software package you buy.

This is considered an all-in-one solution that provides the most feature-rich blog software with hosting services dedicated to support Web and blog servers. Software installation is not an issue since the service provider usually installs and configures the software and hosting. It is also one of the more expensive options. You may also be charged based on the volume of blog traffic, so as your blog popularity grows, so do your costs. One of the main advantages with this option is that you have full control over the look of your blog and can mimic your main website branding, unless the hosting provider limits your options. Typically, though, you have full design control.

One advantage of a dedicated blog hosting account is that the rates are typically flat, meaning they do not change based on the volume of blog traffic. From the technical support perspective, multiple accounts and multiple hosting providers typically equal multiple headaches when it comes to support and troubleshooting. Although the software and hosting is supported by the commercial provider, that does not mean you will not have a degree of tech support and troubleshooting headaches of your own if the service is unreliable.

Paid Blog Software Hosted on Your Own Web Servers

This is an ideal solution if you want to get feature-rich, fully functional software, and you already own or lease your owner-dedicated Web servers. If you own them, or lease them, you might as well use them if you can install the blog software and configure it to operate on your Web server under your own domain name.

One of the main advantages with this option is that you have full control over the look of your blog and can mimic your main website branding, and since you own the servers, the cost for hosting is non-existent. Additionally, you have full control over your hardware and server maintenance. With leased servers, although you are leasing a dedicated machine, you will still rely on the service provider to perform installations and hardware maintenance, so you will need to check to be sure that your provider will support the blog software installation and other requirements.

Who Blogs?

Obviously, a critical component to the success of any blog is who will participate in the blog. A blog is nothing without participation from subscribers, readers, customers, and potential customers. Whether you are a business, organization, or cause will determine your target blog audience.

Bloggers come from every walk of life, including professionals, executives, blue-collar workers, housewives, and technology geeks. Blogging exploded in popularity and is considered a communications method of the future. Blogging is much more than simply a journal, as it was when it was first invented. Blogging is a marketing tool allowing you to communicate and interact directly with your readers. The beauty of blogging is that it is very simple to do. Not only is it easy to establish a blog site, it is very easy to become an active blogger. You do not need any technical knowledge, special skills, or training to establish a highly effective blog site or become an expert blogger.

Instead of publishing static information, you are engaging your visitors in an online conversation on a blog. You want bloggers to talk to you and with each other, discussing your company and products and/or services. Ultimately, if you can engage current and potential customers through conversation, you will successfully promote your products and services through blogs. Since anyone on the Internet can read and join your blogs, and they are searchable, you will quickly discover that your blogs are a primary source for promotion, marketing, and building brand-name reputation and recognition.

Blog Versus Content Management Systems

Blogs and CMS software are distinctly different, although related. Blog software simply provides you with the features and functionality to create, maintain, and manage your blog. A CMS typically has a built-in blogging module, but it provides significantly more features and functionality across all spectrums of content management than blog publishing software.

Understanding Pings and Trackbacks

The most unique feature of blogging is comments. Comments create the two-way communication between you and your blog readers. Bloggers read your blog and post comments, questions, opinions, and concerns. This dialogue is what makes blogging unique. Your readers can also link directly to your blog posts and recommend your blog to others. This is known as trackbacks and pingbacks.

Trackbacks are simply a notification method between blogs. It allows a blog reader to send a notice to someone else that the blog might be something they would have an interest in reading. Here is an example:

- You publish something in your blog.

- One of your blog readers sees this blog post and decides to leave a comment. In addition to having other blog readers see what they posted, the commenter also wants to allow any fellow readers to comment on his or her blog.

- The blog reader posts something on his or her own blog and sends a trackback to your blog.

- You receive the trackback and display it in the form of a comment on your blog along with the link back to the blog reader's post.

- Anyone who reads this blog can follow the trackback to your blog, and vice versa.

This illustrates how blogging is unique from websites and discussion forums. The theory is that blog readers from both your blog and the commenting reader's blog can read the blog posts, and ultimately more people will join in the blog discussion. The idea is to encourage blog readers to click on the trackback link and visit the other blog. As you can see, the number of blog posts and trackback links can grow exponentially. The problem with trackbacks is that they can be spammed easily, and there is no real authentication process to ensure that a trackback is valid.

Pingbacks are a method for Web authors to request notification when somebody links to one of their documents. Typically, Web publishing software will automatically inform the relevant parties on behalf of the user, allowing for the possibility of automatically creating links to referring documents. Here is an example:

- You publish something in your blog.

- One of your blog readers sees this blog post and decides to leave a comment. In addition to having other blog readers see what they posted, the commenter also wants to allow any fellow readers to comment on his or her blog.

- The blog reader posts something on his or her blog and links back to your blog.

- The blog reader's blogging software automatically sends a notification telling you that your blog is linked to and automatically includes this information about the link in your blog.

Although they are very similar, there are differences between trackbacks and pingbacks, including:

- They use different technologies to communicate.

- Pingbacks are automated, while trackbacks are manual; pingbacks will automatically find hyperlinks within a blog posting and try to communicate with those URLs, whereas trackbacks require you to manually enter the URL that the trackback needs to be sent to.

- Trackbacks send the comments while pingbacks do not. Trackbacks typically send only part of your comments to entice the reader into following the actual links to read the entire blog or blog entries.

- Pingbacks appear as links only. Trackbacks appear as links with content or comments.

- Trackbacks can be faked, spoofed, and spammed. Pingbacks are not easily faked.

- Trackbacks provide the reader with a preview of the content on the blog, whereas pingbacks do not.

Blogging & Spam

Just as spam is a huge problem for e-mail, it is a growing problem for blogs. There are two major categories of blog spam. They are:

- **Bogus blogs, or spam blogs**. These are designed purely for spamming purposes by launching spam attacks through viral methods.

- **Comment spam**. This occurs when spam comments are inserted into legitimate blogs.

Spam blogs are also referred to as splogs, a combination of the two words. According to Blogger's help pages, spam blogs "cause various problems, beyond simply wasting a few seconds of your time when you happen to come across one. They can clog up search engines, making it difficult to find real content on the subjects that interest you. They may scrape content from other sites on the Web, using other people's writing to make it look as though they have useful information of their own. And if an automated system is creating spam posts at an extremely high rate, it can impact the speed and quality of the service for other, legitimate users." The spam blog problem continues to grow despite efforts to stop it through IP blocking and word verification fields.

Comment spam contains links to one or more websites, which are usually also irrelevant, inappropriate, or purely spam-centric websites. Combating spam blog entries is time-consuming, frustrating, and a growing problem. While most blog software has built-in tools to combat comment spam, they are not foolproof. Spammers use automated software applications, robots, auto-responders, and other techniques to spread spam throughout the blogosphere. The secret to defeating — or at least minimizing — spam in your blog is to employ the tools of your blog software and host to their fullest potential. Just like with e-mail, you may not stop all content spam, but you can certainly minimize it. Spam is not a reason to quit blogging; it is simply an annoyance you will have to deal with.

Free Blog Software

There are two major players who offer free blogging software. They are Blogger and WordPress. Here is a close look at each:

Blogger (www.blogger.com)

Blogger is entirely free. It is a very basic but effective way to start a blog. Blogger is simple to use and works nicely for a basic blog. Blogger, which was started in 1999, was recently bought by Google, so you can assume it will continue to be supported and improved upon.

Blogger uses standard templates to get you started with an attractive site right away without the need to learn HTML. It also allows you to edit your blog's HTML code whenever you want, and you can use custom colors and fonts to modify the appearance of your blog. The simple drag-and-drop system lets you easily decide exactly where your posts, profiles, archives, and other parts of your blog should live on the page. Blogger also allows you to upload photos and embed them in your blog.

Blogger Mobile lets you send photos and text straight to your blog while you are on the go. All you need to do is send a message to **go@blogger.com** from your phone. You do not even need a Blogger account. The message itself is enough to create a brand new blog and post whatever photo and text you sent.

An example of how to use Blogger to create your own blog is included later in the book. You will not find a simpler free option for creating a blog than Blogger. It is perfect for casual bloggers or personal blogs; however, if you want to use your blog for business, you may wish to choose WordPress or invest in blog software that you can host on your site.

WordPress (www.wordpress.org)

WordPress is a free, open source blogging application. It is fully featured and fairly simple to install. If you prefer, you can have your blog hosted on the WordPress servers for free. WordPress boasts outstanding features that will give you control over most aspects of your blog without being overcomplicated and difficult to use.

WordPress has features for user management, dynamic page generation, RSS and Atom feeds, customizable templates and themes, password protection, the availability of plugins to enhance functionality, scheduled postings, multi-page posts, file and picture uploads, categories, and e-mail blog updates. It is as powerful and feature-rich as most commercially available blogging applications. You should install it on your existing Web servers if they can support it, but as an alternative, you can host it free on WordPress.

How to Write a Great Blog

There is an art to blogging effectively. You really do not need to have any special skills to write blogs. However, you do need some education if you wish to create and write *effective* blogs. You are not writing the next great novel, but it also is not an e-mail. Lose your audience, and your blog is useless. This list is certainly not complete, and is in fact dynamic, based on the type of blog, topic of the blog, target audience, and the "attitude" of the bloggers who are posting comments on the blog. That said, this is a helpful compilation of the best techniques to help you write effective blogs and become a master blogger.

How important is your blog content?

Your blog content is the most important factor in your blog. Of course, the key question is, how do you determine what good content is? There is not a simple answer, since it depends on the type of blog, the intention of the blog, the target audience, and the experience of the bloggers. A good blog entertains, enlightens, captures interest, fascinates, sparks debate, and inspires conversation. A blog needs to be unique, invigorating, and useful. There are many, many blogs in the blogosphere. You need to be unique or create your own market niche in order to gain an audience.

You need to define what your target audience is after, design it with content that addresses what your target audience wants, communicate it effectively, and reach out to your readers. Give them what they want, and they will come back. A little research on your target audience can go a long way. Seek feedback and make changes to your blog accordingly. Your readers know what they want, so deliver it to them. One of your challenges will be to establish a unique blog when using free blog software such as Blogger, since it is not as customizable as some of the higher-end commercial products.

Guidelines for writing blogs

Your blog needs to be relevant and on topic. Keeping your blog on topic is critical in preventing you from going in directions that may cause you to lose your core audience. Keep your main blog intact, and keep it lively and interesting.

A blog is a compilation of opinions. What draws in the audience initially is the topic. Keep the topic on track, and encourage others to share opinions, thoughts, and opposing views where possible to keep the blog engaging and interesting. Interject humor and wit when you can.

Here are some guidelines to help you establish your blog:

- Inform your readers. You must convey knowledge about what you are posting. Be factual, accurate, and professional. Ensure that your blog is clearly written and there are no spelling or grammar errors.

- Differentiate between fact and opinion. If your post is based on fact, then clearly present the fact. If it is your opinion, be sure to make it clear that it is your opinion only, and is not based entirely on fact or corporate policy.

- Be timely. Blogging can be time-consuming, but you need to present timely information for it to be of value. Dated information will indicate that your blog is not timely, and it will ultimately become irrelevant.

- Punctuality is important. You need to have periodic blog updates, and you need to stick to that schedule. As your blog grows in readership, your audience will look forward to your scheduled blog posts. Do not disappoint them by failing to stick to your schedule. Be realistic with that schedule; do not announce daily updates if you cannot stick to it. Do not lose your audience because your communication is lacking.

- Be straightforward and simplistic in your blog entries. Keep them clear, easy to read, and easy to understand.

- Keywords drive search engine rankings, so if you want to have your blog visible, you need to insert keywords into your blog posts. Include related keywords in both the title and content post of your blog entries. Do not overload your keywords to the point that your blog post becomes nothing more than a string of unreadable keywords. Use them in natural sentences.

- To increase your visibility, you need to develop thorough content that is keyword-enriched and captures the both the reader and the search engines.

- The frequency of your blog posts also affects search engine rankings and visibility. Update your blog on a regular, frequent basis. This not only develops and increases your audience, but it also helps you with search engine rankings.

- Spelling counts. It reflects professionalism and attention to detail. Make sure you read what you post before you publish.

- RSS expands your blog like a spiderweb by pushing your blog out to your subscribers as you post entries.

- Be patient. You may think your blog is exciting, but it takes time for people to find it, and even more time to cultivate your audience.

- Blogging is all about opinions. Although you do need to be careful about posting your blog opinions, your audience wants your personality, thoughts, and feelings — so express them.

- Links are critical. Link where possible to other Web pages that are relevant to your blog post. Link to websites, other blogs, books, articles, and news.

- Keep it brief, but not too brief. Get your point across quickly using a minimal number of words. Long posts can lose your readers and get off-topic. Short blog posts may not contain enough information to be of value. Learn the magic length for your blog and try to stick to it. You may have more success keeping your blog posts shorter and breaking them into multiple posts to capture increased readership through your RSS feeds and in search engines.

- Titles attract attention. Make them capture the essence of your blog post. Good titles also drive your overall readership. Most people scan Web pages and only stop when something catches their eyes. If your titles do not attract attention, you will lose potential blog readership.

- Organize your posts for clear readability. Keep sentences short, and use spacing or bullets to organize thoughts. Use bullets and white space to maintain easy readability.

- Consistency is important, especially as you win over audiences by adding your unique personality or interjections into your blog posts. Keeping your posts consistent is important in sustaining audiences.

- Blogging is not an art form. It does not require a graduate level education. Try not to overthink it; keep a sense of humor and do not patronize your readers.

- Write something that you would actually want to read. If your blog is boring and contains no useful or interesting information, do not write it. No one will read it, anyway.

- You are not writing a term paper. Do not get hung up on grammar rules. Yes, spell correctly. Beyond that, keep it simple and clear, but do not spend hours worrying about perfect grammar. You will not be receiving a grade on it.

- Bullets are great for organization. Use them in your blogs to help with readability and to present key topics/ideas.

- Bold and italics are good for emphasizing key words, phrases, and ideas.

- Jargon and acronyms are bad. Do not use them. You may understand them, but others may not.

- Write in clear, captivating, and descriptive tones. While following the length rules, give enough verbal signals in your descriptive words to "paint the picture" in the readers' minds. By providing enough detail to capture the imagination, you draw in interest and avoid monotone, colorless one-line entries.

- Take a risk. Write outside of your comfort zone about topics you have an interest in, want more information about, want to learn about, or want to offer your opinion on. If you only write about your specialty, you will get bored, and your blogs will get boring and one dimensional.

- Be humorous or witty when you can. It makes for a fun read, and captures audience attention.

- Give readers the details they crave. Nothing is worse than headlines that capture your interest only to find the blog posts have no substance and are boring.

- Be tough. Your opinions and blog posts may be your opinion, or your company position on issues, but there will be opposing thoughts and opinions. Do not take them personally, and do not worry about negativity. It comes with the territory.

- Topic and content are what make or break a blog. You have to have a topic someone is interested in, and the content needs to support the topic.

Blog Comments

The best bloggers out there are known by reputation for their blogs and blog comments, and several have written articles on blogging. There are some specific guidelines you can follow when posting comments that will help you build a reputation and improve your professionalism as a blogger. Write respectfully and intelligently, and support your comments. In the blogosphere, reputation is everything.

Your blogs will be read by a wide variety of individuals. Some will seek you out for potential partnerships, to purchase products, and for marketing ventures. You never know who will read your blog, so follow the guidelines of professionalism. This is critical for corporate blogging.

The key is to provide useful, factual information so that, over time, it becomes clear to other readers of the blogs to which you post that you know what you are talking about. In general, it is a good idea to keep your posts short and on point.

Guidelines for blog comments

- Keep your comments short and simple.

- Keep your comments relevant, professional, and on topic. Blog administrators will purge offensive material, personal flames, and other inappropriate content. When using someone else's material, give them the appropriate attribution.

- Sign your comments. Include your e-mail address, website URL, and blog URL.

- Provide quality comments that add substance and meaning. Fluff or generalized two-word entries are of no value.

- Promote your blog, business, and website in your blog posts by either providing a URL and brief description or embed it naturally into the blog comment so readers can have the option to follow your link if they wish to visit your site and obtain more information relative to your blog comment.

- If you have nothing useful to add to a blog, do not add anything.

Getting Started on Blogger

As stated earlier, Blogger started out as a small independent company in the late 1990s. In 2002, Blogger was bought out by Google. While you go to Blogger to create your blog, you will be using your Google account login information to access your blog.

The following example will show you how to create a blog using Blogger. As shown below, navigate in your browser to **www.blogger.com**:

Click on the "Create Your Blog Now" arrow to continue. If you already have a blog with Blogger, you simply log in to access your account.

Since Blogger is owned by Google, you must have a Google account to access your blog or create a new blog. Follow the instructions to create a blog, or log in if you already have an account.

After you log in or create an account, you will see the "Sign up for Blogger" screen. You must specify your display name, which is the name you will use to sign your blog posts, and you must check that you accept the terms of service. Click the "Continue" button to continue.

Enter the desired title of your blog. This example will create a blog for this book. You have the option to choose which blog address, or URL, you want to use. Note that your chosen title may already be in use, so you must click on "Check Availability" to ensure it is available; it will either tell you that the blog address is available or recommend alternatives if it is already in use. The first example will use the basic setup; the advanced setup will be shown in a later example.

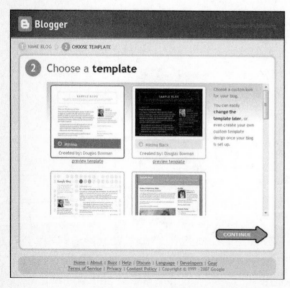

Choose one of multiple template formats for your blog. With blogger, although it is free, you do lose some control over the look and feel of your blog. Blogger does compensate for this by offering a multitude of attractive templates to choose from. Click the "Continue" button after you choose your template.

You are done. Your blog is ready for you to start posting. Click the "Start Posting" button to navigate to your blog.

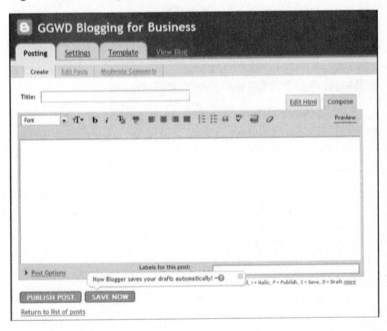

In this screen, you can create and publish new blog posts, edit your posts, moderate comments, and compose and save draft blog posts. You can also edit your settings and template design.

On the top right-hand side of each page, you will see a link to the "Dashboard." This is the central control panel for your blog. It is also where you edit your settings and profile, manage your blog, and read news and features from Blogger.

Now you will edit the settings of your blog. Click on the "Settings" link and go through each section to customize your preferences:

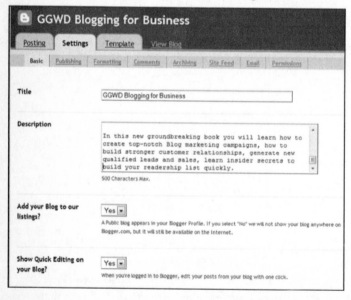

Most of the setting features are self-explanatory and are based on your personal preferences. The "BlogSend Address" is an e-mail address to send your blog when it is published, and the "Mail-to-Blogger Address" is an address you can use to e-mail posts directly to your blog without having to access it.

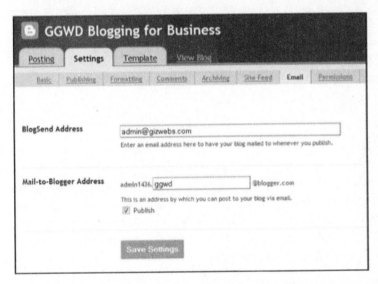

The permissions page lets you specify blog authors and who can read your blog.

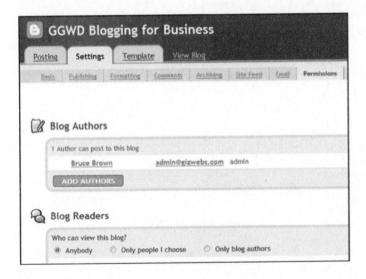

The "Template" link lets you edit and format your template. Although you

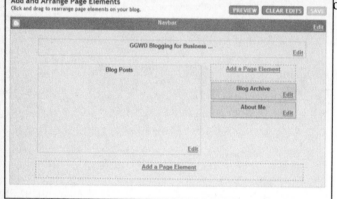

You can customize quite a few elements and add page elements, images, links, and text. Blogger is configured to add page elements automatically by clicking the "Add a Page Element" link. Page elements are things such as Google AdSense accounts, labels, pictures, and text, as well as a profile of yourself, which can easily be plugged into your blog.

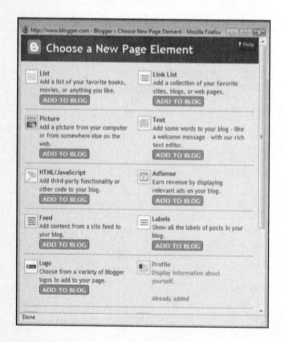

You can also change your template with the click of a button.

You have now completed your blog and customized it. You are ready to publish your first post.

Navigate back to the "Posting" tab of your Blogger site to create your first blog post. Simply type in the title and post content, and you are ready to publish.

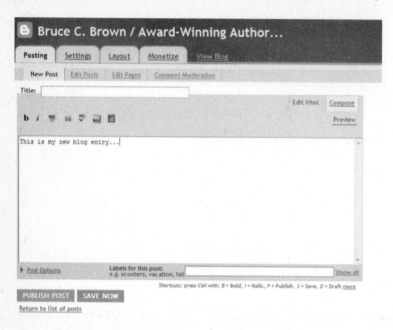

Click the "Publish Post" button to publish your new post, or click the "Save Now" button if you wish to save it for editing or posting at a later time. Once you publish your post, you will receive a confirmation from Blogger.

You may now view your blog. Since Blogger automates the ping process for you, the notification service is kicked off each time a blog post occurs.

Since you have enabled e-mail notification of each post in the "Settings" section, you will receive an e-mail after each blog post is published. You can also e-mail blog posts to Blogger. You are provided with the e-mail address. Simply create the e-mail and send it; your post will automatically publish to your blog.

The e-mail blog entry is created within seconds of receipt at Blogger, and you will receive an e-mail confirmation of the published blog.

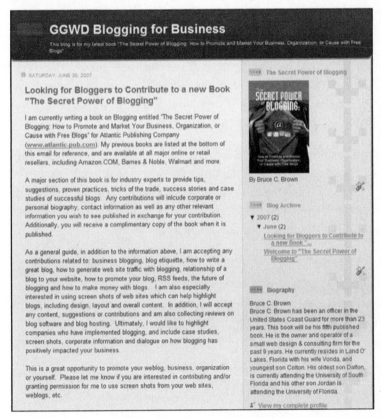

At this point, you have created a blog, published several posts, and have customized your blog. Blogger is completely free, easy to use, and does not include any advertising on your blog pages. You have dozens of templates to choose from, and although you do not have total control over your blog, it is a great way to get started. Make sure to link your blog to your website and place the URL on your business cards, e-mail signatures, company literature, and e-mail newsletters.

Blogger supports syndication feeds for your website. Syndication means that when you publish your blog, Blogger automatically generates a machine-readable representation of your blog that can be picked up and displayed on other websites and information aggregation tools. The setup within Blogger is very simple; you should click on the "Site Feed" link to specify your feed parameters. You can specify "full" or "short" to syndicate the full blog text, or truncate the first 255 characters.

Blogger supports Atom, which is a syndication format or "feed" for your blog. When a regularly updated site such as a blog has a feed, people can subscribe to it using software for reading syndicated content called a "newsreader." People like using readers for blogs because it allows them to catch up on all their favorites at once and avoid navigating to multiple websites, and it is delivered spam free. There are many newsreaders that support Atom, including News Monster, NewzCrawler, NewsGator™, NetNewsWire™, Shrook, RSSOwl, and BottomFeeder.

Spend the time to customize your blog through the settings control panel. Some features you will want to turn on and customize may be under the "Comments" tab, which lets you specify whether to turn backlinks and word verification on or off. Allowing word verification is a critical step in preventing spam posts from hitting your blog through automated blog systems.

Help is readily available by clicking the "Help" link in the upper right-hand corner of any page.

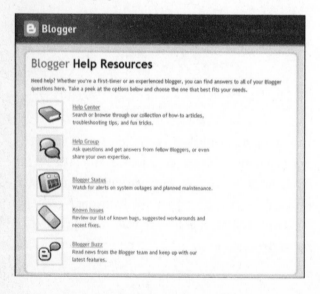

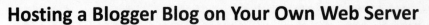

Hosting a Blogger Blog on Your Own Web Server

The next example will show you how to configure Blogger using the advanced setup to host the blog on your own Web servers or hosted Web account.

With an existing blog at Blogger, you may switch, at any time, from the hosted blogging website to your own website. To do this, click on the "Publishing" link and switch to a custom domain link.

Simply enter the URL for your blog, and blog readers will be re-directed to your hosted URL. The "missing files host" allows Blogger to redirect to your original blog URL in the event it cannot find files at your hosted site.

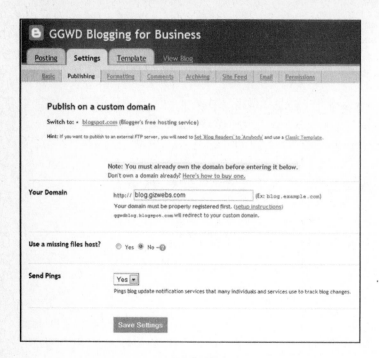

To set up a blog from scratch and host it on your own website, navigate in your browser to **www.blogger.com** and either create your account or log in with your existing account.

Instead of choosing the basic setup option, this time click on the "Advanced Blog Setup" link to access the advanced setup screen. At this screen, you will enter your blog title, listing options, and detailed server information. You will also need to enter your FTP server information, blog filename, and FTP access information.

Once this is completed, you are ready to customize any other settings and publish your blog.

You will be given a confirmation if your FTP publishing update is successful, and you can click the "View Blog" link to view your blog. All of the other features are available to you, giving you control over the template, style, and settings, as well as the ability to publish posts via e-mail to your own Web server. The best part is you do not need to have a new website or domain name for your blog; you can host it right alongside your main website.

In the image below, you will see that the sample blog was created via the FTP publishing feature and is hosted on the main domain URL. For businesses or organizations who wish to maintain a professional website, it is best to host the blog on the company's URL instead of on Blogger or another free hosting service. Since you own the domain name and Web server/hosting, you have ultimate control over access to the data. You may have multiple blogs with Blogger; some may be hosted on Blogger, and some may be hosted by yourself, but all are managed within the main control panel.

WordPress

WordPress is immensely popular within the blogging community. It is by far the most powerful and customizable application with many available plug-ins. Just as with Blogger, WordPress is simple to set up.

Features of WordPress

As mentioned previously, WordPress is by far the most powerful and popular free blog software application available. It has a wide variety of built-in features. This includes pre-designed blog templates that let you change the look of your blog with dozens of professionally designed themes. You can switch between themes instantly with just a click of a button, as with Blogger. WordPress also lets you customize your blog code using CSS, and it includes a system that allows you to categorize and tag your posts while you write them — this is another feature shared with Blogger.

WordPress also includes a spell check option, previews, autosave, photos, and videos. You can upload your own photos or easily include images from other services such as Flickr® or Photobucket®. You can also embed videos from places like YouTube or Google. An inline spell checker makes it easy to proof your posts. As with Blogger, you have the ability to preview your blog post before you publish it, and your draft posts are automatically backed up while you write.

Just as with Blogger, WordPress allows you to have a completely public blog, a blog that is public but not included in search engines, or a private blog only members can access. WordPress also provides you with an integrated stats system that gives you up-to-the-minute stats on how many people are visiting your blog, where they are coming from, which posts are most popular, and which search engine terms are sending people to your blog. This is a feature that is not available in Blogger.

You will find that automatic spam protection is one of the best features of WordPress. WordPress uses Akismet™, the world's best comment and track-back spam technology, to block spammers from leaving spam comments on your blog.

If you grow tired of using Blogger or are ready for more features, you can actually import your entire blog from sites like Blogger, TypePad, and Live-Journal™. You can also easily track follow-ups to your comments — Word-Press created a special page that notifies you so you can track these follow-up comments, even if they are on other blogs. What sets WordPress apart from Blogger and most other blog applications is the availability and ease of adding widgets to your site. WordPress defines widgets as "tools or content that you can add, arrange, and remove from the sidebars of your blog." You can add widgets to your sidebar by simply dragging and dropping. Widgets add functionality, design, and interactivity. With WordPress, you can also create Web pages, not just blog pages. You can even create an entire website, using your blog as one of the pages on your site.

All WordPress blogs support RSS, while Blogger supports Atom. WordPress creates feeds in RSS format and allows people to subscribe to updates on your blog using services like My Yahoo! or Bloglines™.

Establishing a WordPress account

The following example will guide you through the process of setting up a WordPress Blog. This example will use Atlantic Publishing Company, which uses a blog to promote its new book releases and publish related news and information. To start, navigate to **www.wordpress.com** and click on the "Start Your Free WordPress Blog" link.

You will need to establish a username, enter your e-mail address, comply with the terms and conditions, and then click the "Next" button.

WordPress will use your user name as part of your domain name; in the example, this would be **http://atlanticpub.worldpress.com**. Enter your blog title and language; then click the "Privacy" box to allow your blog to be publicized to search engines such as Google and Technorati™. You will be directed to the confirmation screen, which tells you that an e-mail has been sent to you to confirm your account.

Once you confirm your login through the e-mail activation process, you may use the provided password and your username to log into the blog site. Your basic blog is now completed and published.

You will receive a confirmation e-mail that contains your account information along with helpful links, frequently asked questions, and other information to help you access, update, and publish to your blog.

Begin by clicking on the "My Account" link and the "Edit Profile" option to start customizing your account. Update the basic information such as name, profile, and password. You are now ready to start customizing your blog. Although it takes only a few minutes to actually create the blog, it most likely does not yet have the look and feel you desire.

Customizing your WordPress blog

Begin by clicking on the "Options" link in your WordPress account to begin customizing your blog. This allows you to update your general settings and customize most other publishing options.

Under the "Privacy" link, you will want to ensure that you have selected the options for your blog to appear in search engines and public listings in Word-Press to ensure maximum visibility. Click on the "Presentation" tab to begin the process of selecting a site template and adding widgets and extras to your blog.

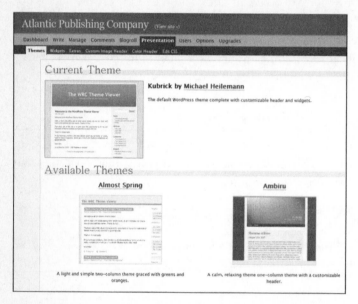

Go through each tab to customize your blog to your desired settings. You have a great degree of flexibility in choosing the final appearance of your blog. Simply drag and drop your desired widgets into the sidebar of your blog. For widgets that require customization, click on the blue customization tab within the widget in your sidebar to modify the settings and preferences.

The "Write" link is where you will post your blog entries. The "Manage" link lets you manage your blogs, uploads, imports, and exports, and delete individual posts. The "Comments" tab allows you to search, view, edit, and delete comments from your blog.

The blogroll is where you can add your favorite blogs or relevant blogs that have content your audience may be interested in. Maintaining your blogroll is a great way to increase your audience. As you can see below, this process is very simple.

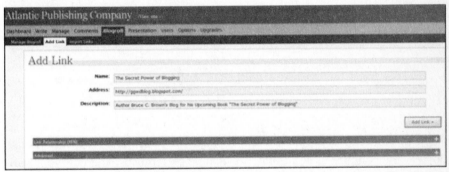

You can also create and indicate which specific categories each blogroll listing should be listed under by selecting it when you add the new blog listing. If you need to change anything later, just click the "Edit" link to change any of your information, links, or category selections.

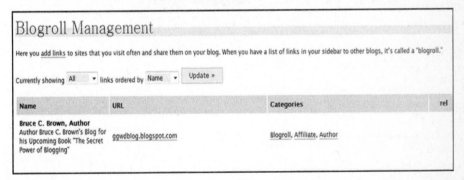

The "Write" feature is what you will use to publish blog posts. This is much more robust in features than Blogger. You can use pre-edited HTML formatted text or format on the fly in the entry form. You can attach images, include trackbacks, and upload files, slideshows, or videos. WordPress saves every 60 seconds, and you can also save drafts for later publishing to the blog.

The "Dashboard" is the main control panel for your blog. You can publish posts, view comments, edit your site, change preferences, and edit your template, layout, widgets, and extras.

You should always turn on the RSS syndication feature. You will then want to clearly publicize the link for readers to subscribe to your feed on both your blog and your Web page. To do this, grab the RSS image icon and save it to your Web server or Web host. Drag a text widget to your sidebar and open it by clicking the blue lines. Type in the following code:

```
<a href=http://atlanticpub.wordpress.com/feed> <img
src="http://www.atlantic-pub.com/rss.png">
```

Save the changes and your RSS subscription feed will appear on your blog. You can use the same HTML code on your website. RSS feeds will be covered in greater detail later on.

It is recommended that you spend some time on the discussion forums, help files, and other readily available resources for WordPress. There is a wealth of information available, as well as an abundance of widgets you can use to customize and enhance your blog. At this point, your blog has been published, and several posts have been published. All that is needed now is to link the blog with the website and start promoting it.

Office 2007 and Blog Posts

If you use Office 2007, you will find that Word 2007 has built-in support for blogging, and it supports most major blog products on the market. To use this feature, simply open Word 2007, click on "New," then click on "Blog Post."

Click on the icon labeled "New Blog Post." You will be given a drop-down menu of options to configure the first time you use this feature in Word 2007:

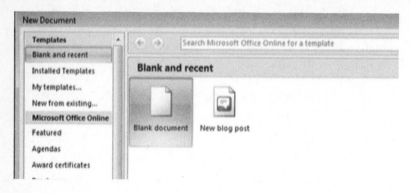

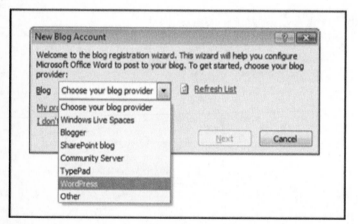

As you can see, Word supports Blogger, Windows Live, TypePad, WordPress, and others. You will need to set up your account information, user name, and password; you can then publish to your blog directly from Word:

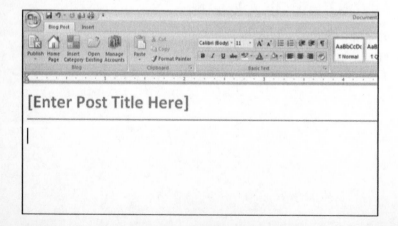

Other Free Blogging Applications

There are many other free blogging applications you can use as an alternative to Blogger and WordPad. A detailed listing is available at **http://asymptomatic.net/blogbreakdown.htm**. The following list contains some of the best in the blogosphere:

Movable Type (www.movabletype.org)

Movable Type is powerful blogging software that is free to download and install on your own Web servers. The advantage of Movable Type is that you have full control over the design of your blog; however, you provide the support since you are hosting it. Extensive documentation is available, and there is significant user-based support.

LiveJournal (www.livejournal.com)

You can use LiveJournal in many different ways: as a private journal, a blog, a discussion forum, and a social network. It is not recommended in use for a business, organization, or cause.

ClearBlogs (http://clearblogs.com)

This is free, but you will have advertising on your blogs.

SoulCast™ (www.soulcast.com)

At SoulCast, you can blog about anything without the constraints of society, friends, or family. It is great for personal use, but not so much for business use.

Blog.com (http://blog.com)

This is also free and supported by advertisements.

ExpressionEngine (http://expressionengine.com)

You will also find this listed under the "commercial" section below. ExpressionEngine is an outstanding and robust product, and a free version with reduced capabilities is available for personal use only.

TeamPage5 (www.tractionsoftware.com)

Traction® TeamPage5™ is a free version of Traction's TeamPage™ software. TeamPage5 supports up to five projects and five named user accounts. Your personal account will allow you to download software updates, read customer and product FAQs, and participate in the customer forum. For the free download, visit **https://tractionserver.com/traction/post?type=newprofile**.

TeamPage5 is easy to download, install, and manage. All TeamPage products are pure Java standalone server applications. Full requirements and an extensive list of features are listed at **www.tractionsoftware.com**. TeamPage is fully featured, and the free download is an incredible deal. There is also a more robust version available for purchase. To use this product, you must have your own Web server to host it.

Introduction to RSS Feeds, Atom, and Syndication

RSS and Atom are XML-based file formats that provide you with an easy way to syndicate your blogs to your readers. These feeds provide your readers with all recent content posted to your blog, with links to each content page. By subscribing to feeds, your customers are automatically notified whenever new content is posted. They can also use newsreaders to read your updated content along with any other feeds they may subscribe to, all in one place.

RSS- and Atom-powered blogs are the most effective way to keep the lines of communication open with your audience and site visitors. They will support all of your goals, such as customer interaction, acquiring new customers, improving customer relations, selling products, and promoting your goods, services, or business/organizational philosophy.

E-mail can be time-consuming, ineffective, and challenging due to spam blockers and filters that prevent even legitimate subscriber e-mails from reaching their intended targets. Syndication helps generate new business by effectively marketing directly to your subscribers. It is free and simple to use. Both of the free blog applications featured in this book, Blogger and WordPress, automatically include the capability to create RSS or Atom feeds.

The concept is very simple. You publish blog posts on a regular basis, and people want to read your blog posts. It may be time-consuming for individuals to navigate to blog after blog to read the latest post. To simplify things for your readers, you can syndicate your blog posts to everyone who has subscribed.

As you publish blog posts, they appear on your blog and are also sent out in an XML formatted file — either RSS or Atom — to your subscriber or syndication list, and they are automatically delivered to your subscribers' "readers."

Typically, the reader is an e-mail application, or it is built into the Web browser. To find a free reader to download, peruse the list at **http://blogspace.com/ rss/readers**. As you publish new posts, they are automatically sent to the subscribers. The subscribers then open your feed in their reader and browse your new blog posts. They do not even need to be online to do this. A perfect example is for individuals who travel often for work or pleasure. They subscribe to various blog RSS or Atom feeds, and the information is delivered to them as soon as it is published. They can then browse, read, and reply to these new blog posts offline and maximize the use of their time when they do not have Internet connectivity, such as during air travel.

Web feeds eliminate all of the concern with e-mail subscription-based delivery. With RSS or Atom, there is no spam, no viruses, no phishing, no identity theft, and no opt-out process. They are safe and simple to establish, send, and receive.

You must have a reader in order to subscribe to a feed. Bloglines, located at **www.bloglines.com**, is a great free source for blogs, feeds, and podcasts, and it includes a reader. Both Internet Explorer and Firefox include the ability to accept feeds. Google Blog Search, found at **http://blogsearch.google.com**, is a great tool for searching blogs, and since it is Google, it is the most widely known.

There are many free RSS or Atom feeds you can subscribe to. Think of a topic, and it has an RSS or Atom feed. Since your blog software creates the feed for you, there is no reason not to have your own RSS feed. While there are dozens of readers and syndication services to choose from, stick with what you know, and use either your e-mail client or your browser as your reader.

When you subscribe to feeds, you are usually asked how you want them delivered, such as in the example below, where you can choose from Mozilla Firefox "Live Bookmarks," Outlook, Yahoo!, and Bloglines. In this example, "Live Bookmarks" is chosen.

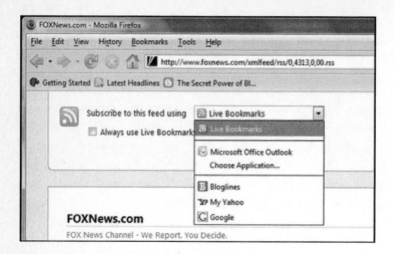

You are asked how you want to store the data from the subscription:

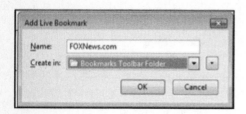

Your subscription to the feed is effective immediately, and it brings in all the recent posts you have subscribed to for you to review. You simply pick which ones are of interest, and you can view them. In this example, there is a subscription to the headline stories from FOXNews.com. You would click on this "Live Bookmark" to obtain the latest top news stories from this site.

You can find RSS or Atom feeds in directories and search listings and through search engines. You can even specify parameters in your subscriptions to deliver only content that has relative keywords to your search parameters.

Creating an RSS Feed in WordPress

Establishing an RSS feed with WordPress is simple. Navigate to your dashboard, click on the "Presentation" link, and then click on the "Widgets" tab. Drag one of the "Text" widgets to your sidebar and double-click on the blue lines in the text box to open the parameters feature.

In the parameters, enter your title and RSS link in the format below. Replace **yourblog.wordpress.com** with your actual blog address, such as **atlanticpub. wordpress.com**, and replace **imagelocation.com** with the location of your RSS image icon:

```
<a href="http://yourblog.wordpress.com/feed"> <img
src="http://www.imagelocation.com/rss.png">
```

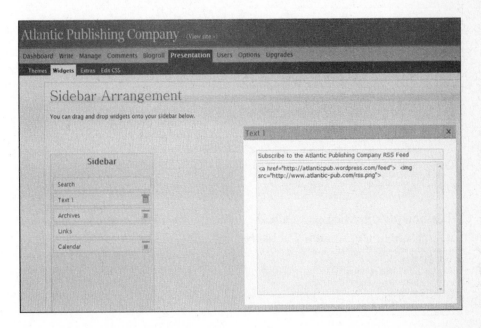

When it is saved, your RSS syndication feed is then displayed on your blog, as shown in the image below:

When a visitor clicks on this link, he or she will be presented with the subscription form, options on how to subscribe to the feed, and a listing of recent blog posts. In the example, Microsoft Outlook is used.

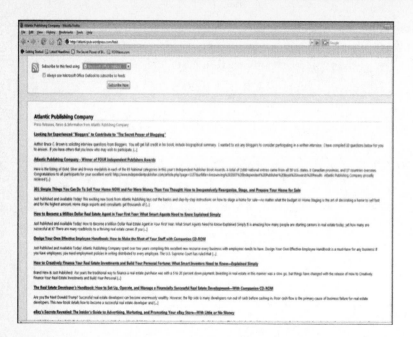

When you look in Microsoft Outlook under the RSS Feeds, you can now see your subscription to Atlantic Publishing, including nine new entries.

You can look in the preview pane of Outlook to read each item, or you can double-click it to open it, as if it were an e-mail.

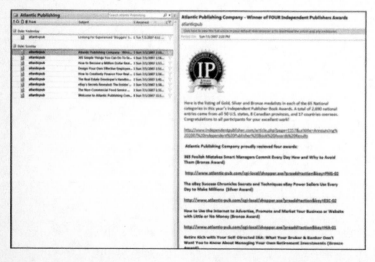

The last thing you will want to do is add your RSS feed image and link to your website to allow individuals to subscribe from both your blog and your website.

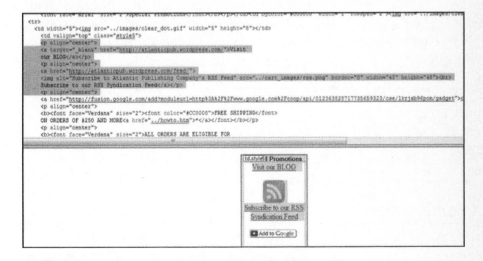

Creating an Atom Feed in Blogger

To create the Atom feed in Blogger, simply log into your Blogger dashboard. Click on "Settings," then "Site Feed." Here you can turn your site feed settings to off, short, or full. With new Blogger accounts and templates, your feed is automatically displayed on your blog unless you turn it off. If you have turned it on, but are not seeing it displayed in your blog, follow the manual procedures located at **http://help.blogger.com/bin/answer.py?answer=42663**.

Microsoft provides a nice guide to setting up an RSS feed in Outlook, which is available at **http://office.microsoft.com/en-us/outlook/HA101595391033. asp**. Also, if you are using Microsoft Internet Explorer 7 or Firefox 2.0, the browser will automatically detect and notify you of any feeds available on the Web pages you are browsing. If you want to offer your RSS feed through a variety of free readers, visit **www.toprankblog.com/tools/rss-buttons**, which creates buttons automatically for you to place on your website.

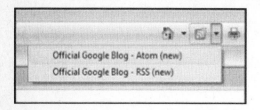

Feedburner™

As you read the expert advice at the end of this book, you will notice that Feedburner is often recommended. Feedburner, a service of Google, is the leading provider of syndication services for blogs and RSS feeds. There is a free version of Feedburner and a professional version which you must pay for.

To use Feedburner, you simply type in your blog URL and follow the on-screen prompts. You set up your feed, and it provides you with your Feedburner URL. You can enable tracking and statistics options on your feed. A step-by-step walkthrough is provided to insert the code on your Blogger blog, and you can add the code as a text widget in WordPress. If you upgrade to the full self-hosted version of WordPress, a plug-in is available to simplify the process.

One of the nice features of Feedburner is the statistics it provides. It also presents the subscriber with a variety of options to choose from.

There is no reason not to create an RSS or Atom feed; it will help you increase your audience base and allow you to consistently send all blog posts to your subscribers. Best of all, the process is completely automated, seamless, and free.

CHAPTER 12

Social Networking

Social networking focuses on building online communities of people who share similar interests and/or activities. Most social network services are Web-based and provide a variety of ways for users to interact. Social networking has become tremendously popular, and its membership grows daily at an exponential rate. The potential marketing and networking power of using social networks to promote your business and products cannot be understated, and in many cases, it is the perfect substitute for personal Web pages or blogs.

Here are some of the benefits to using a social networking service:

- **Meet new people** — With just a few clicks, you can meet new people from all over the world or focus on making certain types of friends.

- **Find old friends** — You can find friends with whom you have lost contact. These could be friends from high school or people you used to work with.

- **Join interest groups** — Many social networking services offer specific groups called "communities." These groups can be on anything. If there is not a group you like, you are permitted to create your own and invite others to join and share.

- **Create photo albums and share photos** — Not all social networking sites offer photo albums, but many do. You can create photo albums to share with friends and relatives.

- **Add videos** — Some social networking sites will allow you to add your own videos to the network, while others only let you upload your video to your profile.

- **Get advice and help others** — Whether on forums or in interest groups or communities, you can always find and give advice.

- **No cost** — These services are absolutely free.

Social networking has grown tremendously in popularity in the last few years and is an incredibly powerful marketing and networking tool. Do not assume that social networking is just for teenagers. Social networking sites not only aid in keeping in touch with relatives and friends, but they also help to find new friends and establish new networking opportunities. These services allow people to be close even if separated by continents, and the viral effect of social networking means that you can build large "networks" effortlessly and quickly.

With the ever increasing number of people who use the Internet on a regular basis, these social websites have become a must, as this is the best and the easiest way for people to get connected with each other and stay in touch.

Social Networking Sites

Orkut is a popular social networking site owned by Google. This social networking site has millions of users; 63 percent of Orkut traffic originates from Brazil, followed by India with 19.2 percent. Like other sites such as Facebook, Orkut permits the creation of groups known as "communities" based on a designated subject and allows other people to join the communities. Orkut is an online community designed to make your social life more active and stimulating. Unlike other social networking websites that prevent users from viewing your profile if they are not on your "Friends" list, Orkut has no such restriction. Anyone can view anyone else's profile. However, there is also an "Ignore List," where members can list people they want to restrict from viewing their profile or sending them messages.

Facebook is the leading social networking site, with over 250 million active users at the time of publication. Initially, Facebook was developed to connect university students, but over time, the site became available publicly and its popularity exploded. The majority of users on Facebook are college and high school students, but this trend is shifting rapidly to people of all ages and backgrounds. On Facebook, it is extremely easy to add friends, send messages, and create communities or event invitations. To discover Facebook, you must create a free account. Once you create an account and answer a few questions about where you work, where you went to school, and where you live, Facebook will generate a profile for you. A great feature of Facebook that makes it unique among other social networking sites is the "Photos" application, where users can upload unlimited numbers of photos. Facebook is a great place to share information and stay in contact with friends, family, and co-workers.

MySpace is a social networking website that offers an interactive platform for all its users. It allows the sharing of files, pictures, and even music videos. You can view the profiles of your friends, relatives, and other users; you can also create and share blogs with each other. Users often compare Facebook to MySpace, but one major difference between the two websites is the level of customization. MySpace is a large social networking site that allows users to decorate their profiles using HTML and CSS, while Facebook only allows plain text. The most prominent feature that makes MySpace unique among other sites is its affiliate program. If the affiliate product you are selling has a broad appeal, you may want consider using MySpace to market your product, as you will be able to reach the largest crowd quickly.

YouTube is another social networking site owned by Google. To become a member of YouTube, go to the "Signup" page, choose a username and password, enter your information, and click the "Signup" button. YouTube is the largest video sharing network site in the world, and it is a great place to do video marketing.

Digg™ is a place to discover and share content from around the Web, from the smallest blog to major news outlets. Digg is unique compared to other social networking sites because it allows you to directly network with people and directly sell products. Once a post is submitted, it appears on a list in the selected category. From there, it will either fall in ranking or rise in ranking, depending on how people vote. Digg is actually what is known as a "social bookmarking" site. You submit your content to Digg, and other Digg users — known as Diggers — will review and rate it. Once it is rated high enough, your content may get posted on the homepage of Digg, which gets thousands of visitors a day, potentially driving tons of traffic to your website or blog.

Twitter is different from other social networking sites, and the popularity of Twitter has grown at an amazing rate. Instead of having to sit down at the computer to update your status such as with MySpace, with Twitter, you can let your friends know what you are doing throughout the day right from your phone. When you sign up with Twitter, you can use the service to post and receive messages with your Twitter account, and the service distributes it to your friends and subscribers. In turn, you receive all the messages sent from those you wish to follow, including friends, family, and even celebrities. In essence, Twitter is a cell phone texting-based social network.

Flickr is a photo and video sharing website that lets you organize and store your photos online. You can upload from your desktop, send by e-mail, or use your camera phone. It has features to get rid of red eye, crop a photo, or get creative with fonts and effects. Google Picasa™ is another great photo sharing and storing application.

Friendster had 110 million members worldwide at the time of publication and is a place where you can set up dates and develop new friendships or business contacts. This site is a leading global online social network. Friendster is focused on helping people stay in touch with friends and discover new people and things that are important to them.

Using Social Networks to Expand Your Web Presence

The main objective of social networks is to allow members who have the same interest to interact and exchange information. Members of social networking sites are numerous, which creates an excellent opportunity for an individual to expand and promote their business without having to pay for advertising. With social networking, you can build an image and develop your customer base. To increase their website traffic, many site owners are quickly realizing the value social networking sites have in drawing new customers. Here are some ideas on how to use social networking site to generate website traffic:

- Link from your website to your social network profile.

- Use social bookmarking to increase your website's exposure on social networking sites.

- Create and share videos and photos on Flickr and YouTube describing your business, products, and services.

- Use social networking forums to promote your business, website, and blog.

- Promote your business through your profile, with links to your homepage.

You can use the power of social networking sites to promote your website by sending messages, leaving notes, and creating communities. You can establish yourself as an industry expert and promote your business services or products through the established networks. Once you gain credibility, you gain popularity; once you gain these, you can increase website traffic.

Social networking sites can be fun for personal use, but they can also be beneficial for your website. It may surprise you how many people who visit your website will take the time to take a peek at your Facebook site and ask to be your friend so they can look at your Facebook content and share information. As your network grows, you will quickly find that you have established a powerful business network that will help you maintain relationships and increase your website traffic dramatically. Spend some time researching and using social bookmark sites; they can generate a great deal of website traffic for you. The focus of your social networking activities are to increase the popularity of your website or blog, so target those communities that have mutual interests.

CHAPTER 13

eBay Storefront and Unlocking the Secrets of eBay

Do not make the mistake of overlooking the potential of eBay sales and how they can dramatically improve the visibility and sales of your products. There are many advantages to advertising and selling products on eBay, and low cost is one of the main reasons. eBay is one advertising opportunity that you might not want to miss so that you can maximize your business exposure on the Internet through a variety of targeted and auction-style sales. When you open and operate an eBay Storefront (or eBay Store), you can connect with millions of people every day who shop on eBay and gain significant search engine visibility for your website.

By opening an eBay store, you can promote your products online through eBay. To assist you with the process, eBay provides you with an array of tools and wizards to facilitate the process. You can typically have your storefront operating in less than an hour. eBay provides you with a wide range of management tools and, most importantly, provides you with the eBay turbo loader software, which manages your inventory, controls pricing, and allows you to easily list any or all products on eBay with just a few simple mouse clicks.

It costs very little for you to open an eBay Store. For as little as $15.95 per month you can start to boost your Internet presence, increase your sales, and add to your customer database. When you start an eBay Store, you will have these tools at your disposal:

- An online storefront that is completely yours to develop and create to fit your business needs

- Easy tools to manage the running of your eBay Store

- Tracking methods and a way to analyze how your business is doing within the eBay community

- Tools at hand for marketing and merchandising your product

Benefits of an eBay Storefront

When you open an eBay Storefront, you will find that there are many benefits to you and your business. An eBay Storefront gives you the opportunity to reach thousands of people each day and increase the exposure that you need to obtain more customers. One of the big benefits of having an eBay Storefront is that it gives your website a look of professionalism that is going to give you the credibility that you need to reach customers that are looking for a particular product or service on the Internet. It takes only a few minutes to start your eBay Store, which means that you will be up and running in no time and ready for customers to find you. Many businesses that already have their own website still use eBay Storefronts as a tool to reach even more sales customers on a daily basis.

You are able to customize your storefront to the exact design that you feel best stylizes the products that you are selling. There are dozens of different design categories from which you can choose when you sign up with eBay Storefront, or you can simply design your own (even based on your current website design). One of the most overlooked benefits, aside from the increased visibility and generated Web sales, is that when you operate an eBay Storefront, you are given a unique website address or URL on the Internet so that customers can find you fast and easily, bookmarking your storefront website so that they can return again later for repeat sales and to find out what is new in your store. Of even more significance is the fact that this website URL can be submitted to all search engines, dramatically increasing your overall sales visibility within the search engines and on the World Wide Web.

You will have access to a variety of reports that will let you know exactly how your product sales are doing. Some of the data information that you will receive each month includes (1) a traffic report so that you know how many Web visitors are stopping by your eBay Storefront, (2) sales reports, to let you know how many sales your storefront has generated, and (3) accounting information that you can use to export your PayPal and eBay sales transactions into accounting software programs such as QuickBooks or your own Excel spreadsheet.

eBay Storefront Promotion

When it comes to the promotion of your eBay Storefront, you will not be left in the cold since eBay will give you all the help that you need to bring customers to your eBay Store. eBay will list your storefront on all the appropriate listings within their website pages as well as send out marketing correspondence to your customers.

When you sign up with eBay Storefront, you will have a search engine in the content of your store. This means that your customers will be able to use this search tool to find the products, or services, that you are selling. You will save a lot of time using the eBay Storefront to sell your products and spend more time concentrating on your business and other marketing strategies. When you sign up with eBay Storefront, you will see a definite increase in your sales and profits as well as watch your customer database grow and turn into repeat sales. You should consider linking your main website to your eBay Storefront, offering the opportunity for customers to shop in the "auction"-style storefront setting of eBay as an alternative to fixed prices.

How to get started with eBay sales

To get started, all you really need is a good computer, preferably with a broadband Internet connection and a good digital camera. Good digital imagery of products greatly increases your product sales. You must have a good e-mail address, and it is highly recommend to create one just for your eBay sales traffic. You will need a bank account or PayPal — or both. Some recommend you establish a PayPal account and make this your preferred method of payment since payment is instantaneous and secure. You will need some photo editing software to crop, resize, and touch up your digital photographs. Although not required, it is highly recommended that you design your storefront and product descriptions using HTML code with a program like Microsoft Expression Web 3. If you want to display more than one photograph of your product (eBay lets you display one image at no cost), then you will have to have access to a Web server to import your digital images and then insert the HTML links to those images into your eBay Storefront, or you can also simply pay the fee and upload them to eBay's servers.

eBay tips, tricks, and secrets to generate sales

- eBay sales are predominantly auction based, and therefore the more bids you receive, the more likely your product will sell at a higher price. Start your listings at a low price to encourage interest and bids. Products with multiple bids tend to sell more frequently and at a higher cost than similar items with a high initial listing price.

- It is all about feedback. This is what your customers say about their shopping experience with you. Feedback can be given on any transaction, and savvy eBay shoppers check the feedback quality of the prospective seller before they bid. 100 percent positive feedback is simple to attain — just follow through with the sale and quickly package and ship the products and you will always have satisfied customers. As your number of positive feedback grows, so does your status as a reputable seller within the eBay community.

- To create listings from your eBay Storefront, here are some simple rules to follow:

  ◊ Do not use ALL CAPITAL LETTERS.

  ◊ Be descriptive, and provide lots of detail on your products. You can expand to include much more than just the product details. This is a great opportunity to tell the prospective bidder why they should have the product, benefits, and more.

  ◊ Always include one or more digital images. You get one free with eBay, but we recommend more for certain products where multiple-angle views may enhance sales.

  ◊ Use HTML code to create your descriptions. If you just type into the eBay description block, your paragraphs will not be broken up properly and will be difficult to read. To create your description in Frontpage, go to the HTML view, and cut/paste the HTML code into the description block in eBay. Although this is not readable, when displayed in the browser, the HTML code is interpreted and displayed with proper formatting, coloring, tables, etc. Keep your coding simple and classy. Do not overdo it with flashing icons, images, and text that distracts the viewer. A clean, simple interface is best to sell your products. We also recommend you only use white backgrounds for any descriptions or Web pages.

  ◊ Include shipping costs and methods (first class, media mail, priority mail, UPS). We recommend you only include flat rate shipping, which covers your costs for the packaging and shipping costs. You can also pay for shipping and print USPS shipping labels directly from PayPal after the completion of the sale. Shipping estimates or unknown shipping costs will lose potential bidders who are wary of unknown shipping costs. You should figure high for shipping costs, but be reasonable. $20 to ship a 1 pound book is not reasonable; however, $5 may be reasonable. As a side bonus, you can ship books media mail for under $3, making a profit off the excess shipping costs. This is a great way to offset the costs for your eBay and PayPal fees. You should also give some thought to packing materials, which can be expensive. By using USPS priority mail services, you can get free boxes and packing tape. Don't forget about USPS flat rate boxes and envelopes, which are also free packing material plus have the benefit of flat fee shipping costs, regardless of the envelope or box weight.

◊ Ensure that your description and title are relevant to what the user will be searching for.

◊ If you have multiple items to sell, space them out over time; do not list one after the other. Turbolister from eBay simplifies this process, and you can also use delayed listings to specific auction listing start times.

◊ Highlight the unique features of your products in the title.

◊ You can list items for 3, 5, 7, or 10 days. You do pay a 10 cent premium per listing for 10 day listings. There is much debate on what length of time items should be listed and when the best time of day is to start a listing. Seven-day auctions are the standard, and often recommended, unless you must sell products quickly and opt for the 3 or 5 day options. As an experienced eBay seller, you will soon discover that the last 60 seconds or so of all auctions are when most of the bidding action takes place.

◊ Auctions should start at the lowest amount possible. Bidders are looking for bargains, and starting bids of a few dollars or less are more likely to attract interest than bids that start at or near full retail value. In most cases, bids for low starting amounts produce significantly more interest (and thus more bids) and typically sell above the expected final bid amount.

◊ As discussed earlier, the flat shipping fee should cover your shipping costs (including packaging) and, potentially, some of your eBay and/or PayPal fees. Under no circumstances should you ever have a case where the shipping charges do not cover the actual shipping costs.

◊ Do not use a reserve price. The main reason is that people are looking for a deal, and they know that if you have a reserve price, you are not willing to part with the item at a lower price and let them get a great deal. Most bidders will ignore anyone who puts a reserve price, and you should never put a reserve on your products. You do take a risk that they may sell for less than your desired profit.

◊ Make sure you follow up with the winning bidder via e-mail. Typically, there is no reason to use the telephone as all eBay communication is Web/e-mail based. eBay accounts should be checked daily at a minimum, or more often for storefronts. You should review the "My Messages" folder for any questions or comments from sellers. We highly recommend that you create template e-mails that are generated by eBay when an item you are selling has been won. These e-mails validate the sale, confirm payment information, act as an invoice, and tell the auction winner that you value and appreciate their business and will ensure that they are satisfied with the transaction.

◊ You should also send out a template e-mail when an auction is paid for. This confirms that payment was received and the order will be processed, and you can tell them how the item will ship.

◊ We highly recommend using PayPal to generate shipping labels for all your products. In addition to being very simple, it also includes free delivery confirmation from the U.S. Postal Service and automatically notifies the winner that their item has been shipped; it will also provide the date and delivery tracking information via e-mail.

CHAPTER 14

Banner Advertising

A Web banner or banner ad is simply a form of advertising on the World Wide Web. Banner advertising involves embedding an advertisement into a Web page. Banner ads are designed to draw traffic to a website by linking them back to the website of the advertiser. The advertisement is typically comprised of an image (GIF, JPEG), but can come in Flash or other technologies. Banner ads are typically placed on pages with relevant content. When the banner is loaded into a site visitor's browser, this is what is known as an "impression." When the site visitor then clicks on the banner, the visitor is directed through a hyperlink embedded in the banner ad to the website advertised in the banner. This is what is commonly known as a "click-through." Banner ads are commonly "served" through a centralized ad server, however, they may also be embedded directly in the Web pages. Even if they are embedded, they can be rotated by using scripting to rotate multiple image files, or by creating an animated GIF file, which automatically changes the displayed images on a preset timer.

Most banner ads operate under a "pay-per-click" system or under an affiliate system. With pay-per-click, such as Microsoft AdWords, you create your banner ads on-the-fly within the AdWords application. With affiliate software, you typically either create an array of banner ads (if you are hosting the affiliate program), or simply have a choice banners to choose from if you are joining an affiliate network or becoming an affiliate of someone else. Software tracks the number of "clicks," and each click will generate revenue to the content provider of the banner ad (not the advertiser). The advertiser typically does not make any commission on the "click-throughs;" instead, they get the direct sales if a customer buys from them. Banner ads are very similar to traditional road-side banners or billboard advertisements. They notify potential consumers of the product or service and strive to create enough interest to get you to click the banner and travel to their website and buy their products or services. Banner ads also allow you to be much more dynamic when it comes to your advertising techniques because you can change the way the image looks at any time by adding unique forms of animation to the banner ad.

There are several reasons why online or brick-and-mortar businesses may choose to use banner ads to promote their products and services. Some of the reasons include:

- To increase the amount of traffic to your website

- To increase the sales of your products and services

- To let your customers know about any special deals that you are offering or any new products or services that you are selling

- To get your name out onto the Internet so that potential customers know who you are

How Do Banner Ads Work?

Banner ads are essentially an image with embedded HTML code which launches a hyperlink. The HTML code tells the Web browser, or server, to pull up a certain Web page when someone clicks on that particular hypertext, which is displayed in the banner as text or as graphics or a combination of both. Typically, a third-tier server is utilized to track the impression and click-throughs. Obviously, banner ads are an integral part of an effective affiliate program, which we will discuss in detail later. Overall, traditional banner advertising success continues on a downhill trend, while pay-per-click advertising grows. The models for both are different and clearly the dynamically generated pay-per-click ads are much less obtrusive than larger, traditional banner ads. That said, particularly when used as part of a PPC or affiliate marketing campaign, they are still an effective, low-cost form of advertising, and many companies still use banner ads in their marketing and advertising portfolio.

Understanding Banner Advertising

Banner advertising is simply a form of online advertising where Web developers embed an advertisement into the HTML code of a Web page. The idea is that the banner advertisement will catch the attention of website visitors and they will click on the ad to get more information about the products or services advertised. When clicked, the banner ad will take the Web browser to the website operated by the advertiser. A banner ad can be created in a variety of formats such as .GIF, .JPG, or .PNG. Banner ads can be static images or employ a variety of scripting code, Java, or other advanced techniques such as animated GIFs or rollover images to create rotating banner advertisements which change every few seconds. Over the past five years Shockwave and Adobe Flash technology have become increasingly popular by incorporating animation, sound, and action into banner advertisements. Banner ads are created in a variety of shapes and sizes depending on the site content and design and are designed to be placed unobtrusively in the "white" space available in a traditionally designed Web page.

When a page is loaded into a Web browser such as Microsoft Internet Explorer or Mozilla's Firefox, the banner is loaded onto the page, creating what is called an "impression." An impression simply means that the Web page containing the advertisement was loaded and potentially viewed by someone who is browsing that website. Impressions are important to advertisers to track how many visitors loaded that particular page (and banner ad) in a set period of time. If the impression count is low, it is logical that the click-through rate and subsequent sales will also be extremely low. When the website visitor clicks on the banner advertisement, the browser is navigated to the website that is linked to the banner ad and the website is loaded into the browser. The process of a site visitor clicking on a banner ad with their mouse is commonly called a "click-through." Click-throughs are important to advertisers because they track how many visitors actually clicked on a particular banner ad and how many resultant sales were generated by the banner ad in a set period of time. Unfortunately, a high click-through rate does not necessarily guarantee high sales. Banner ads can be static (embedded within the actual HTML page) by the Webmaster or may be "served" through a central server, which enables advertisers to display a wide variety of banner ads on thousands of websites with minimal effort.

As already discussed, most banner ads currently work on a per-click system, where the advertiser pays for each click on the banner ad, regardless of whether that click results in a sale. Originally, advertisers simply paid for the ad space on a website, usually for a preset period of time, such as a week or month and hoped that someone would see the banner ad and click on it to visit their website. Banner advertising is typically a very low-cost investment per click (usually under ten cents per click), and the banner provider or hosting company then bills the advertiser on a pre-determined basis.

The key difference between banner advertising and pay-per-click advertising is that banner advertisements are placed within the content of Web pages, while pay-per-click advertising is not image-based and may be dynamically generated based on a search result. Banner advertising is designed to inform potential customers or consumers about the products or services offered by the advertiser, just like traditional print advertising, but they offer the advantage of allowing advertisers to track individual statistics and performance at a level not possible with print media advertising.

Different Types of Banner Ads

Using banner ads does not mean that you are limited to one kind of ad to use to advertise your product or service. In fact, there are many different types of banner ads from which you can choose, including altering the shape and size of the banner ad to suit your purposes. There are eight different unique sizes of banner ads from which you can choose, as indicated by the IAB (Internet Advertising Bureau). Each of these banner ad sizes is based on a pixel, which is the unit, or section, of color that creates the images that you see on your computer or on a television. The standard specific sizes for banners, as dictated by the Internet Advertising Bureau, are as follows.

- A full banner: 486 by 60 pixels

- A vertical navigation bar on a full banner: 392 by 72 pixels

- A half banner: 234 by 60 pixels

- A vertical banner: 120 by 240 pixels

- A square button banner: 125 by 125 pixels

- Button size, number 1: 120 by 90 pixels

- Button size, number 2: 120 by 60 pixels

- A small, or micro-size, button: 88 by 31 pixels

The most commonly used banner size is the full banner, at 486 by 60 pixels. However, you will find all sizes of banner ads in all areas of the Internet, with many variations of the standard sizes. The above banner sizes of pixels are not the only banner sizes that you need to stick to, but they are by far the most common, and you should stick to the standards whenever possible. Keep in mind that banner size is also dictated by the amount of memory size that can be given to the banner.

When you look at the already existing banner ads on the Internet, you will notice that there are many different varieties of graphic and other animated creativity to be found among banner ads. Some of the most simplistic banner ads will have only one JPEG or GIF image on them that link the banner ad to the main website of the company doing the advertising. By far, the most popular of all the banner ads is an animated ad that uses a GIF animation tool. GIF animation allows the banner ad to change over a few minutes, showing various GIF images one after the other, and many times in a flowing sequence. These ads instantly grab the attention of visitors to the Internet and are sure to make people notice your banner ad. There are many programs available that help you create animated GIF images, many are free and can be found with a quick Web search.

Reasons for Using Banner Ads

When you decide to use banner ads for the advertising of your website and business, you want to entice the visitor to click the ad so that they go directly to your Web page. The visitor to your website would not be at your site if it were not for the banner ad. This means that the person may not have been searching for the product or service that you are selling, so you need to keep that in mind when designing the ad as it may or may not generate a sale from the banner ad click. Statistics show that banner ads do amount to a certain percentage of Internet sales. If you are going to host ads on your website, there is no cost to doing so, and you will get paid for the "click-throughs" generated, regardless of whether it results in a sale or not. Including a small amount of tasteful, low-bandwidth banner ads on your site is a good idea. If you wish to use banner ads as an advertising campaign, there are many services which offer banner ad hosting, exchanges, and marketing.

How to Make Banner Ads

Even if you have minimal knowledge about computers, you will be able to make a simple banner ad for your website. Making a banner ad is simply a matter of coding and imaging with HTML hyperlink tags that are going to link back to your website. You will be able to develop the graphics for your banner ad with the use of software such as Paint Shop Pro or most other graphics programs such as Microsoft Digital Image Suite. The following is the simple coding that is used for a banner ad:

```
<a href="http://www.YourWebSiteHere.com"> <img
src="http://static.YourWebSiteHere.com/gif/banner-ad-
static.gif"> </a>
```

You can make simple banner ads on your own without too much computer knowledge, and keep in mind that GIF-animated banner ads are not that much more difficult to make yourself than any other banner ads. If you want to use banner ads that are filled with media, such as Shockwave programming, Java programming, audio techniques, or video techniques, you might want to hire someone to do the banner coding for you, however, this is typically not cost effective for emerging online businesses. You want your banner ads to look as professional as possible so that you keep up with your competition.

If you really want your banner ads to stand out in the crowd, you may want to hire a professional designer for banner ads. You would want to hire a professional who is able to create a banner ad that promotes your product or service as well as quickly grabs the attention of Web visitors so that they want to click on your banner ad. The price that you pay for your professionally designed banner ad will vary from as low as $75 to as much as $1200, depending on what type of banner ad you choose.

Successful Banner Ads

When it comes to creating and designing your banner ads, there are no strict guidelines that you need to follow. Different banner ads are successful for different reasons, and it is up to you to find out what works for you and your business. You may have to try a particular type of banner ad for a while and track how well it does before making changes and modifications. There are no rules to what works in Internet advertising and what does not work. There are, however, some things that you should know about banner ads so that you stand a fighting chance when it comes to designing your first ad.

One definite formula for success is to place your ads on Web pages that have some type of content that has a relationship to the product or service that you are selling. If you are selling chocolate, your banner ads might not be too successful if they appear on websites that are focused on diet-related information. Internet advertising studies show that the more relationship there is between banner ads and the websites on which they appear, the greater the number of clicks that take place. When you are creating your banner ads, you may want to make sure that the ad promotes your product or services and not your website, as the appeal is in the products, not necessarily your website. When Web visitors see a banner ad advertising a website, they are less likely to click and find out more than if the banner ad advertises a certain product that they are interested in. Banner ads should be a reflection of the things that you are selling and not about your website alone. Banner ads should take Web visitors directly to the portion of your website where that product or service is sold or promoted, rather than to the home page. Banner ads are designed to get you the sale, not to find potential customers who have time to browse your website.

If you have the choice and the option, you will want to put your banner ads at the top of a Web page and not at the bottom. The farther down on a Web page your banner ad is displayed, the less likely it will be noticed. Web visitors are usually browsing through websites at a fast rate, and you need to have your banner ad in a location where it can be seen and clicked quickly. The main point of your banner ad should be simple and easy to understand. Studies show that the more complicated your banner ad is, the less likely Web visitors are to read it long enough to want to click. You want the statement on your banner ad to be catchy, simple, and accurate. Internet advertising studies also show that animated banner ads do better than those ads that are stationary. Animated ads grab the attention of Web visitors long enough to make them read the message and for you to get the click-through. Another thing that you should pay attention to when it comes to the design of your banner ads is that the graphics you display on your ads should reflect your product or service in a way that people can understand without having to guess. Web visitors are less likely to click on banner ads if they have no idea what the graphic is trying to tell them than if they have some idea of what you are advertising.

You want to make sure that the Web page on which your banner ad is displayed loads quickly, or Web visitors will give up and continue browsing to another website. The smaller your banner ad is, the faster the Web page it is on will load. Large banner ads are not only slow to load, they are also too big and intimidating and often deter Web visitors from clicking on them. The types of banner ads that do well on the Internet are ads that are attractive and interesting to look at. Banner ads also need to be placed on a Web page so that they make sense and are aligned in an order that is easy to understand. You will have to experiment and try different things when it comes to the design and layout of your banner ads. As the Internet continues to grow, advertising techniques also continue to change to adapt to the needs of Web shoppers who are faced with more choices than ever as they search the Web for deals and unique products.

One of the key elements of using banner ads is to make sure that you target the right Web visitors. "Targeting" is a technique that focuses on the type of Internet browsing that a person does when they are on the computer. Web visitors who are searching for a specific item are presented with website results that match their keyword search. If your banner advertisements match these keywords, your ad is more likely to be found by people, and you increase your page views and click-through totals.

Advertising and Banners

When you take the steps necessary to implement banner ads for advertising your product or service, there are options that can simplify the process for you.

- You can pay certain websites to be a host for your banner ads.

- You can do an exchange program, where you post banner ads for another advertiser, and they post your banner ads on their website.

- You can pay a fee to what is called a "banner network," where you then can post your banner ads on a certain number of host sites according to the amount of money that you pay. An example of a successful "banner network" is DoubleClick (**www.doubleclick.com/ us**).

- You can use pay-per-click marketing, as described earlier in this book.

- You can take advantage of affiliate marketing.

You will need to decide which of the above options are best for you and your business. You may want to choose the exchange program option with another advertiser if you do not have the budget to post your banner ads on other websites for a fee to eliminate any costs. If you decide to exchange banner ads, there are two methods that you can use. The first is to establish working relationships with advertisers on other websites so that you can both exchange your banner ads and host them on your site. This way, you will be able to put your banner ads on those websites that closely match your own or where you know potential customers might see your banner ad and be interested enough to link back to your Web pages. The only disadvantage to this method is that you need to spend a lot of time looking for banner exchange partners for you to have a significant number of banner ads on the Internet.

The second method of getting your banner ads online is to use what are called "banner exchange" programs. You will become part of huge network of Internet advertisers that each host a variety of banner ads on their websites, whether or not there is a similarity between the websites or even any relevant content on the site. Banner exchange programs are discussed further in the next section. No matter what method you choose to use, when it comes to getting your banner ads on the Internet, you will be giving your website and business that cutting edge that you need to stay on top of your competitors.

Banner exchange programs

A banner exchange program is a great way for you to get your banner ads onto the Internet without spending any money. The exchange program works like this: when you host banner ads on your website, the exchange program will host the same number of your banner ads on other websites. In most cases you will be hosting more banner ads than you are posting elsewhere, but this is the way that the banner exchange program makes its own profits. This means that the banner exchange program can sell the extra banner ads that they do not use on your site to their paying customers so that they can stay in business and make a profit. This arrangement allows you to have your banner ads on many websites, while at the same time allowing the banner program to make a profit from those extra banner ads.

The main advantage of using a banner exchange program is that it does not cost you anything, which is great if you have a small budget for advertising. You get to post your banner ads on various websites so that you maximize the amount of exposure that your website gets on the Internet. There is one main disadvantage to using a banner exchange program: You lose most of the decision making about where your banner ads are placed and about which banner ads you display on your own website, plus these banner ads may overwhelm your site visitors. Most banner exchange programs control the decision making about where your banner ads are hosted, and there may be many times when you disapprove of where your banner ads appear. In most cases these banner programs will try to make some logical choice about banner ad placement, but there will be times when you wonder about the logic that placed your banner ad where it appears or the type of banner ad that you are required to host on your website.

How to buy advertising space

One way that you can increase the effectiveness of your banner ads is by buying advertising space on the Internet. There are several ways that you can buy advertising. They are

- Join an affiliate program

- Join a banner exchange program

- Contact websites on your own to buy advertising space

- Start a pay-per-click campaign

- Hire an agency that specializes in Internet advertising.

You will find that there are benefits and disadvantages to using each of the above methods for buying advertising.

Use an affiliate program

Using affiliate programs is a very effective way to place your banner ads on other websites as well as save you time and money. You can join other affiliate programs, or you can start your own affiliate program that will enable you to pay those sites that are hosting your banner ads only when there are results to show for the click of your ad or when a customer actually makes a purchase that is a direct result of the banner ad. The nice thing about using affiliate programs is that you will not have to buy a large number of page views or click-throughs. Instead, you will be paying only a certain amount of the profits that you generate from obtaining a new customer, which amounts to a minor percentage of your overall profits.

Join a banner exchange program

As discussed previously in this chapter, a banner exchange program is a great way to get your banner ads out onto the Internet on many other websites, although you will find banner exchanges to be quickly replaced by more modern pay-per-click applications such as Google AdWords. When you use an exchange program, you will not have to do the legwork and contact other websites about hosting your banner ads. Essentially, a banner exchange program is a system of brokers, where the program acts on your behalf to place your banner ads on appropriate websites on the Internet. A network of banner ad programs is much the same as a banner exchange program, but there is one drawback to using a banner ad network: You are giving up most of the final decision making power about where your banner ads are going to be placed as well as what banners ads you will be hosting on your own website.

Contact websites on your own

You can approach websites on your own to see if they will place your banner ads on their Web pages. Although this can take up much valuable time, it has several benefits of which you might be able to take advantage. One of the biggest advantages is that you will be in charge of the final decisions about on which type of Internet websites you place your banner ads. You will be able to determine what websites will most benefit and relate to the products and services that you are selling. You have the ability to target websites that do not have a lot of other banner ads on them so that your own banner ads become more effective. Many times, being choosy about where you place your banner ads can result in a big payoff when you target those sites that have a certain appeal to those same people who are interested in your products.

Hire an agency that specializes in Internet advertising

This method can be effective, and the most costly. If you hire an advertising agency that offers all the available services, you will have very little to do when it comes to your banner ads. These advertising agencies will help you to find the best websites on which to place your banner ads as well as find the best price for your advertising budget. You can also hire an agency that will help you create your banner ads as well as manage all of the advertising for your online or brick-and-mortar business. Many times, you will find that large advertising agencies are able to get a more competitive price than if you were looking for websites yourself on which to place your banner ads. This is because agencies are able to buy page views in large quantities.

Although there are many advantages when it comes to using advertising agencies, there are some disadvantages that you will need to consider before making your final decision about whether to use an agency or not. One of the most significant advantages is that many advertising agencies will not deal with small websites that are looking for help with their banner advertising. Each advertising agency will have different services that they offer, and this may include what is called an "account minimum." If you have a small website as well as a small advertising budget, you may not find an advertising agency that is going to start an account with you and your website.

Make sure that you shop around before making your final decision about which advertising agency you want to use to help you with your banner ads and other advertising needs. The questions to ask yourself are:

- How much experience does the agency have?

- What are the rate costs associated with the different services that the advertising agency offers?

- What services do they offer?

- Are customer referrals or client testimonials available?

If you have a large Internet-based or brick-and-mortar business, it may be worthwhile to hire an advertising agency since they will be able to give you the knowledge that you need to stay in competition with your competitors and their banner ads. Even if you are a smaller company, with a smaller website to promote, you may want to consider hiring an agency so that you gain the Web presence that you need on the Internet to reach your customers and potential customers. Internet advertising can be tricky if you do not understand all the elements that go into successful advertising. You want to have as much of an advantage as you can when it comes to getting your company name out there so that you can increase your profits as well as your customer database.

How to sell advertising

When you have a website on the Internet, you not only can buy advertising, you can also sell it. When you sell space on your website, you will be able to receive some revenue that you can turn around and put back into your own website or business. However, selling banner ad space on your own website can be a bit cumbersome, so it is recommended you use Google AdSense to make it easy and potentially profitable.

Become part of a banner ad network

One easy way to sell advertising on your website is to become part of a banner ad network so that you do not have to be in charge of the advertising that you have on your site. The banner network will allow you to keep track of the amount of money that you earn from selling advertising space as well as take charge of the banner ads that are placed on your website. The only thing that you need to keep in mind if you are going to be using a banner ad program to sell Web space for advertising is that they will take a certain percentage of the profits that you see from selling this advertising.

There will always be more websites selling space for advertising than there will be websites that are interested in buying the space. It is for this reason alone that banner ad programs will be a bit particular about the advertisers they list. You will find that most of the banner ad networks have monthly website traffic minimums that they require to participate in banner ad programs. For instance, there are some banner ad networks that set the minimum of at least 250,000 website visitors before you can join the banner network. Some other banner ad networks have a set of tiers that determine how much you pay based on the amount of traffic that hits your website each month. A tier system works well for smaller websites so that you can choose a banner ad program that your advertising budget can handle.

If you have a website that gets a large amount of traffic each month, such as more than 90,000 page views (or impressions) each month, you will have no problem joining a banner ad network that uses this CPM method of calculating website traffic. However, if your website generates less Web traffic each month, you will most likely need to look at those banner ad programs that calculate Web traffic using the click-through method. Do not forget, though, that the click-through method of Web traffic calculation means that you will not be making much money on the banner ads that you host on your website. This is because you will not actually be paid until a Web visitor clicks on the banner ad and links to the website that is being advertised. The average click rate is less than 1 percent, so your revenue from the click-through method will not amount to much at the end of each month.

CHAPTER 15

Business Directories

When you are trying to promote your online or traditional brick-and-mortar business on the Internet, you will want to ensure that your business is listed in as many places as possible so that you have a better chance of reaching as many people as you can, and even more importantly, provide all possible resource avenues for them to reach you. You need to connect with many potential customers before they become actual customers and you generate sales revenue from them. As discussed earlier in the book, as you gain customers, your goal is to retain repeat customers, developing a strong relationship and growing a loyalty in your customers toward your products and services. Word of mouth advertising is incredibly important and can only be gained through sustained loyalty and customer satisfaction among your existing and new customers.

Business directories can be found all over the Internet; in a sense they are typically nothing more than search engines combined with Web-based white and yellow page services. The primary purpose of business directories is simple. They exist to help you find:

- Products

- Services

- Companies

- Jobs

- People

There is really no reason not to have your business and websites listed with all of the business directories, and typically, the listing is free. Business directories, such as SuperPages.com and YellowPages.com on the Internet, can help send traffic to your Web pages, no matter what type of business you have. Directories place a listing of your business, product categories, website address, and other pertinent information into a consolidated listing that many people browse each day. Oftentimes, people are looking for exactly what you are selling or the services you are offering, and they can locate you through a business directory. You can find Web business directories that are specific to location, products, or services, or by random selection. It is highly recommend that you have your business listing in a variety of business directories so that you increase your chances of being noticed by Web visitors.

The following is a list of some of the more popular business directories that you can find on the Internet:

- **www.yellowpages.com**

- **www.business.com**

- **www.europages.com**

- **www.business-directory-uk.co.uk**

- **www.hoovers.com/free**

- **www.volta.com**

- **www.dir.yahoo.com**

There are many more online business directories from which you can choose. An Internet search using any search engine will yield you many results; however, the business directories can provide more detailed information about a particular company or organization.

B2B Web Communities

The Internet is a vast network where anyone can do business, exchange information, get an education, or search for any kind of data imaginable. With so much potential at your fingertips it is important that you take advantage of being part of business to business (B2B) Web communities or, in some cases, business to consumer (B2C) Web communities.

There are many different B2B Web communities on the Internet in which you can take part, and if you can not find the right community for you and your business, you can build your own community. B2B is often used to describe websites that sell goods or services to other businesses. Therefore these businesses are serving other businesses as opposed to consumers. The difference between a business to business e-commerce website and a B2B Web community is in the type of information and degree of functionality that is offered. A B2B Web community is a full-service centralized clearing house of data, which presents content such as news, industry analysis, e-mail, purchasing, an industry-indexed search engine, trading exchanges, electronic storefronts, and career information, just to name a few.

A B2B Web community is a community that exists on the Internet much like a big virtual marketplace that centers around a specific topic, product, service, or other bits of information. Other functions that the B2B Web community can provide for you and your business are

- A search engine within your product or service category

- A place to trade industry information

- A place to join discussion groups about your specific business

- A way for you to find out what the market value is of the products and services that you are selling

All of these elements combined are ways that you can improve your knowledge of the business, or industry, in which you are involved so that you can become more successful as a merchant.

Summary

The Internet is the future, and it has been for the past ten years or more. Consumer confidence in using the Internet has grown dramatically, and the sales volume of commercial and personal purchases online has exploded. If you do not have a website or blog, you are missing out on a vast number of potential customers looking for your business, products, or services. Using the Internet to advertise for your online or traditional brick-and-mortar business is all about technique, confidence, and planning for success. Set clear, definitive goals, and strive to reach them. Promote your business through every avenue possible — most of them are free. You should have a website, a blog, a Facebook page, use Twitter, and actively embrace PPC marketing, Google AdSense, Google AdWords, affiliate marketing, and e-mail marketing.

Take an organized approach to your online promotion and marketing; slowly expand into blogs, social media, e-mail marketing, and PPC advertising. The great thing about each of these is that you can build over time on previous successes. Start out with a solid business plan and a well-designed website; ensure that you follow sound SEO techniques; make your website e-commerce enabled to sell products; create a social networking site on Facebook and link this site to your main website; create a blog and link it to your website; and consider PPC marketing or selling ad space on your website through Google AdSense. An organized, systematic approach will serve you well and yield tremendous results, all at little or no cost to you.

I hope this updated revision to my very first book helps to both educate you and arm you with the tools to grow your website and achieve unprecedented levels of success with your online ventures. I always look forward to hearing from my readers. If you have any comments or success stories you wish to share, feel free to contact me at bruce@brucecbrown.com.

APPENDIX A

Ten Reasons to Follow the Guidelines in this Book

One: You have a wide variety of online promotion and marketing solutions available to you; start out with a systematic approach and build upon each layer of success. You will see that the more you advertise and promote your business and websites, the higher the rankings you will achieve in major search engines.

Two: The Internet has an incredible audience of billions of people, some of them desperately searching for the products or services that you provide. The Internet makes it possible for them to find *you.*

Three: Your business image improves when you advertise on the Internet. Established businesses have websites, and people expect to find your website to research your company, products, and services. Without a Web presence, you stand to lose a large share of business. Even if you do not sell products online, having a Web presence will significantly help you to achieve success and credibility.

Four: Advertising on the Internet is one of most cost-effective methods of advertising available. This is because all the advertising is done electronically; therefore, you do not have the added expenses of postage, printing, and duplication.

Five: The Internet is interactive and allows you to make changes to your website, which are then implemented immediately. This means that you can see results instantly when you make changes to your website, and you can change your advertising techniques just as quickly.

Six: The Internet is becoming ever more diverse when it comes to the types and methods of advertising that can take place on the Web. PPC advertising, blogs, social media, and PPC or e-mail marketing are just some of the many options you have.

Seven: The Internet is available and accessible at all times, which means that you can reach potential customers 24 hours a day, seven days a week, 365 days of the year. Your website and other online marketing efforts work for you, even when you are not working.

Eight: You can specifically target the marketing areas that you want to target with little or no expense to your business, reducing costs and targeting those areas most likely to yield you the biggest return on investment.

Nine: Advertising on the Internet allows you and your business to do market testing on the Internet. This is because you can test different products or services with minimal risk to your investment.

Ten: Advertising on the Internet means that you will be able to keep one step ahead of your competition. Be aggressive and try a variety of online marketing and advertising techniques.

Here are some parting tips and tidbits of information that are sure to propel your website to success:

- Good website content is critical.

- Invest in e-mail marketing; it is cheap, easy, and reaches many customers instantly.

- Avoid spam at all costs.

- Target your market.

- Learn how to design and maintain your website and blog yourself. You can save thousands annually.

- Automate your site. Let it do the work for you.

- Use a robust, secure shopping cart that gives customers confidence to do business with you.

- Establish an affiliate program.

- Implement PPC marketing campaigns.

- Do promotions, and do them often.

- Consider giving away free items as an incentive.

- Collect as many leads as possible.

- Communicate effectively and provide superior customer service.

- Start an eBay storefront to sell products.

- Establish a social networking site.

- Build a network of followers through Twitter.

- Establish an up-sell or cross-promotion program.

APPENDIX B

Recommended Reference Library

I t is highly recommended that you build a quality reference library to assist you with your overall online promotion and marketing plans. While there are plenty of excellent books on the market, it is recommended that you add the following to your library. All are available through Atlantic Publishing Group, Inc. (**www.atlantic-pub.com**).

The Complete Guide to All Aspects of Google Advertising — Including Tips, Tricks, & Strategies to Create a Winning Advertising Plan

Are you one of the many who think Google is simply a search engine? Yes, it is true that Google is the most popular search engine on the Web today. More than 275 million times a day, people use Google and its related partner sites to find information on just about any subject. Many of those people are looking for your products and services. Consider this even if you do not have a website or product. There are tremendous opportunities on the Internet and money to be made using Google.

Google has created numerous marketing and advertising products that are fast and easy to implement in your business today, including AdSense, AdWords, and the Google APIs. This new book takes the confusion and mystery out of working with Google and its various advertising and marketing programs. You will learn the secrets of working with Google — without making costly mistakes. This book is an absolute must-have for anyone who wants to succeed with advertising on Google. This book teaches you the ins and outs of using all of Google's advertising and marketing tools. You will instantly start producing results — and profits.

Online Marketing Success Stories: Insider Secrets from the Experts Who Are Making Millions on the Internet Today

Standing out in the turmoil of today's Internet marketplace is a major challenge. There are many books and courses on Internet marketing; this is the only book that will provide you with insider secrets. We interviewed the marketing experts who make their living on the Internet every day — and they talked. This book will give you real-life examples of how successful businesses market their products online. The information is so useful that you can read a page and put the idea into action right away.

With e-commerce expected to reach $40 billion and online businesses anticipated to increase by 500 percent, your business needs guidance from today's successful Internet marketing veterans. Learn the most efficient ways to bring consumers to your site, get visitors to purchase, how to upsell, how to avoid oversights, and how to steer clear of years of disappointment.

The Ultimate Guide to Search Engine Marketing: Pay Per Click Advertising Secrets Revealed

Is your ultimate goal to have more customers come to your website? You can increase your website traffic by more than 1,000 percent through the expert execution of pay-per-click advertising. With PPC advertising, you will only draw highly qualified visitors to your website. PPC brings you fast results, and you can reach your target audience with the most cost-effective method on the Internet today.

Master the art and science behind PPC advertising in a matter of hours. By investing a few dollars, you can easily increase the number of visitors to your website — and sales. If you are looking to drive high-quality, targeted traffic to your site, there is no better way than to use PPC advertising.

The Complete Guide to E-mail Marketing: How to Create Successful, Spam-Free Campaigns to Reach Your Target Audience and Increase Sales

2008
Eric Hoffer Award
WINNER
Excellence in
Independent
Publishing

E-mail is a fast, inexpensive, and highly effective way to target and address your audience. Companies like Microsoft, Amazon, Yahoo!, and most Fortune 1000 firms are using responsible e-mail marketing for one simple reason: it works. It generates profits immediately and consistently.

In this book, you will learn how to create top-notch e-mail marketing campaigns, build stronger customer relationships, and generate new qualified leads and sales. If you are interested in learning hundreds of hints, strategies, and secrets on how to implement effective e-mail marketing campaigns and ultimately earn enormous profits, then this book is for you.

How to Open and Operate a Financially Successful Web-Based Business (With Companion CD-ROM)

With e-commerce expected to reach $40 billion and online businesses anticipated to increase by 500 percent, you need to be a part of this exploding area of Internet sales. If you want to learn about starting a Web business, how to transform your brick-and-mortar business to a Web business, or even if you are simply interested in making money online, this is the book for you.

You can operate your Web-based business from home and with very little startup money. The earning potential is limitless. This new book will teach you all you need to know about starting your own Web-based business in the minimum amount of time. This book is a comprehensive, detailed study of the business side of Internet retailing.

The Secret Power of Blogging: How to Promote and Market Your Business, Organization, or Cause with Free Blogs

If you have a product, service, brand, or cause that you want to market online inexpensively, then you need to look into starting a blog. Blogs are ideal marketing vehicles. You can use them to share your expertise, grow market share, spread your message, and establish yourself as an expert in your field, all for virtually no cost.

In this book, you will learn how to create top-notch blog marketing campaigns, build stronger customer relationships, and generate new qualified leads and sales. You will also learn insider secrets to build your readership list quickly.

Word of Mouth Advertising Online & Off: How to Spark Buzz, Excitement, and Free Publicity for Your Business or Organization with Little or No Money

Word-of-mouth marketing (WOMM) is the least expensive form of advertising — and often the most effective. People believe what their friends, neighbors, and online contacts say about you, your products, and your services — and they remember it for a long, long time. Word-of-mouth promotion is highly valued. There is no more powerful form of marketing than an endorsement from one of your current customers. A satisfied customer's recommendation has much greater value than traditional advertising because it comes from someone who is familiar with the quality of your work.

The best part is that initiating this form of advertising costs little or no money. For WOMM to increase your business, you need an active plan in place to create buzz. If your business is on the Web, there is a myriad of possibilities for starting a highly successful viral marketing campaign using the Internet, software, blogs, online activists, press releases, discussion forums and boards, affiliate marketing, and product sampling. Technology has dramatically changed traditional marketing programs. This book covers it all.

How to Open & Operate a Financially Successful Web Site Design Business (With Companion CD-ROM)

The Pricing & Ethical Guidelines Handbook published by the Graphic Arts Guild reports that the average cost of designing a website for a small corporation can range from $7,750 to $15,000. It is incredibly easy to see the enormous profit potential.

Here is the manual you need to cash in on this highly profitable segment of the industry. This book is a comprehensive and detailed study of the business side of website design. It should be studied by anyone investigating the opportunities of opening a Web design business and will arm you with everything you need, including sample business forms, contracts, worksheets, checklists, and dozens of other valuable, time-saving tools that no entrepreneur should be without.

The Complete Guide to Writing Web-Based Advertising Copy to Get the Sale: What You Need to Know Explained Simply

Since the advent of the Internet, and since more and more people are making purchases online, writers have had to adapt to composing copy for the Web. Contrary to what many people think, writing for the Web and writing for print are not the same and involve very different skill sets. Instead of struggling to find the right words, copywriters should read this book from cover to cover to discover how to write sales-generating copy.

This book will teach you how to make your copy readable and compelling, how to reach your target audience, how to structure the copy, how to visually format the copy, how to pull in visitors, how to convert prospects to paying customers, how to compose eye-catching headlines and much more.

Internet Marketing Revealed: The Complete Guide to Becoming an Internet Marketing Expert

This is a carefully tested, well-crafted, and complete tutorial on a subject vital to Web developers and marketers. This book teaches the fundamentals of online marketing implementation, including Internet strategy planning, the secrets of search engine optimization, successful techniques to be first in Google and Yahoo!, vertical portals, effective online advertisement, and innovative e-commerce development. This book will help you understand the e-business revolution as it provides strong evidence and practical direction in a friendly and easy-to-use self-study guide.

You will find a variety of teaching techniques to enhance your learning, such as notes, illustrations, conceptual guidance, checklists of learned topics, diagrams, advanced tips, and real-world examples to organize and prioritize related concepts. This book is appropriate for marketing professionals as well as Web developers and programmers who have the desire to better understand the principles of this fresh and extraordinary activity that represents the foundation of modern e-commerce.

The Complete Guide to Affiliate Marketing on the Web: How to Use and Profit from Affiliate Marketing Programs

Affiliate marketing is now viewed as a key component of a company's online marketing strategy. It is an advertising technique that originally was developed by Amazon. In this book, you will learn how to master the art and science behind affiliate marketing in a matter of hours. By investing a few dollars, you can easily increase the number of visitors to your website and significantly increase sales. If you want to drive high-quality, targeted traffic to your site, there is no better way than affiliate marketing. Since you only pay when a sale is made, your marketing dollars are being used more effectively and efficiently compared to any other advertising method.

This exhaustively researched book will provide everything you need to start generating high-volume, high-quality leads. If you are interested in learning hundreds of hints, tricks, and secrets on how to implement affiliate marketing, optimizing your website for maximum search engine effectiveness, developing a cost-effective marketing campaign, and ultimately earning enormous profits, this book is for you.

Amazon Income: How Anyone of Any Age, Location, and/or Background Can Build a Highly Profitable Online Business with Amazon

The Internet affiliate program industry is one of the largest and fastest growing digital revenue generators in the world. This is because of programs like Amazon's Associate program, which has been around for more than a decade and allows casual, everyday users of the Internet to install widgets and links on their websites that link back to Amazon products. Users like you can earn commissions of up to 15 percent on products that your website visitors purchase when they visit Amazon. With the world's largest online retailer as a potential source of income, you can generate endless streams of income as a result.

No matter where you are from, how old you are, and what your background is, you can build and run a highly profitable business with Amazon. This comprehensive book is written to show you exactly how to do so. You will learn every detail necessary to complete the transformation from casual Internet user to Amazon guru in just a matter of weeks, making unfathomable amounts of money by selling Amazon products, your own products, starting a store, promoting outside projects, and making referrals.

The Small Business Owner's Handbook to Search Engine Optimization: Increase Your Google Rankings, Double Your Site Traffic...In Just 15 Steps — Guaranteed

This book is ideal for small business owners who want to learn an efficient and effective process for dramatically improving their website's search engine rankings and doubling their site's monthly unique visitors.

A business owner does not need to know technical skills like Web programming to be successful at search engine optimization (SEO). Instead, business owners will rely on marketing skills and the ability to think like their customers and prospects. You will learn how to select keywords that are proven performers, blend the keywords into site content, boost site popularity, and more. This practical and tactical guide includes a free SEO toolkit and other valuable resources that will help business owners increase the return on investment generated by their websites.

Google Income: How Anyone of Any Age, Location, and/or Background Can Build a Highly Profitable Online Business with Google

Google is the largest Internet company in the world. More than 90 percent of its income is generated through the use of their advertising program AdWords. The opportunity to make money with Google is so great that entire companies have been built around working with the search and advertising giant, and if you are properly situated, you can tap into that market and start generating your own massive profits.

There are dozens of ways to start making money with Google, and because of its digital nature, anyone can do it from anywhere in the world. This book leaves absolutely no stone unturned in cataloging for you every possible method through which you can generate and maintain steady income streams through the world's largest search engine.

Marketing in a Web 2.0 World — Using Social Media, Webinars, Blogs, and More to Boost Your Small Business on a Budget

Social networking started as a small idea that was novel but not necessarily viable in regards to making money or promoting businesses. But since 2003, sites like Twitter and Facebook have exploded to become two of the biggest, most powerful social networking hubs on the Internet and the two single most powerful marketing tools at many business owners' fingertips. Providing unparalleled, technologically-enhanced means to reach demographics in ways that were never before possible, businesses small or large can reach their target audience quickly and effectively through social networks and sites — and yours can be part of the revolution with the right tips.

This book will act as a map to success in marketing and promoting your business. It will allow you to take your business to new heights — without requiring you to spend much money to do so. You will learn how the social Web has fundamentally altered how the Internet is used as a marketing tool, allowing businesses to reach out and touch their target demographics like never before. You will learn how to recognize those demographics and how to fundamentally understand how and why they use the social Web. For any business or individual with a big dream, this book is a must-have, showing you how to take advantage of the top new business technology in more than two decades.

eBay Income: How Anyone of Any Age, Location and/or Background Can Build a Highly Profitable Online Business with eBay

The website eBay has changed the way products and services are purchased all over the world. Daily, over 1.5 million online customers and providers log on to bid and sell virtually anything that can be bought or purchased. There are businesses earning $1 million a year selling products on eBay today. It is estimated that more than half a million people make full-time incomes just with their eBay business. This book will show you how to take advantage of this business phenomenon and arm you with the proper knowledge and insider secrets. Filled with actual examples and antidotes from real eBay entrepreneurs, this book is as engaging as it is informational.

There is a level playing field on eBay — it does not matter how old you are, what nationality or income level, whether you own a business now or not, what your background is, or where you are located. No matter your situation, you can start making money on eBay today — and this book will serve as your guide in doing so.

How to Build Your Own Website with Little or No Money: The Complete Guide for Business and Personal Use

Websites are an essential tool that every business must have in today's economy. Creating a website can be a great way to market a new product, promote your business plan, promote yourself, or simply share a few details about your life with the world. But the cost of creating a website has risen right alongside the number of websites created, and many people are nervous about being able to utilize this medium without breaking the bank. This book was created for such people, outlining everything you need to know to create a traffic-attracting website while spending little or no money at all. There are countless resources available, and when you put them all together, they provide a complete toolkit that can make anyone a top-notch website in no time flat.

You will learn how to buy a domain name and host your website for less than $15, with no additional fees charged to your account. You will learn how to use open source software like WordPress, Joomla!, and Mambo to create a platform on which you can build anything you want. You will learn how blogging has made website creation easier than ever and how sites like Squidoo, Facebook, and MySpace allow you more freedom to build traffic and draw more attention to what you are advertising at any given time. If you are now, or have ever, considered starting your own website, this book will map the way for you.

Glossary

Ad

For Web advertising, an ad is almost always a banner, a graphic image, or set of animated images of a designated pixel size and byte size limit. An ad, or set of ads, for a campaign is often referred to as "the creative." Banners and other special advertising that include an interactive or visual element beyond the usual are known as rich media.

Ad impression

An ad impression, or ad view, occurs when a user pulls up a Web page through a browser and sees an ad that is served on that page. Many websites sell advertising space by ad impressions.

Ad rotation

Ads are often rotated into ad spaces from a list. This is usually done automatically by software on the website or at a central site administered by an ad broker or server facility for a network of websites.

Ad space

An ad space is a space on a Web page that is reserved for ads. An ad space group is a group of spaces within a website that share the same characteristics so that an ad purchase can be made for the group of spaces.

Ad stream

The series of advertisements viewed by the user during a single visit to a site.

Ad view

A single ad that appears on a Web page when the page arrives at the viewer's display. Ad views are what most websites sell or prefer to sell. A Web page may offer space for a number of ad views. In general, the term impression is more commonly used.

Affiliate

The publisher/salesperson in an affiliate marketing relationship.

Affiliate directory

A categorized listing of affiliate programs.

Affiliate forum

An online community where visitors may read and post topics related to affiliate marketing.

Affiliate fraud
Bogus activity generated by an affiliate in an attempt to generate illegitimate, unearned revenue.

Affiliate marketing
Revenue sharing between online advertisers/merchants and online publishers/salespeople, whereby compensation is based on performance measures, typically in the form of sales, clicks, registrations, or a hybrid model. Affiliate marketing is the use of other websites to market products sold by another website. Amazon.com, the bookseller, created the first large-scale affiliate program, and hundreds of other companies have followed since.

Affiliate merchant
The advertiser in an affiliate marketing relationship.

Affiliate network
A value-added intermediary providing services, including aggregation, for affiliate merchants and affiliates.

Affiliate software
Software that, at a minimum, provides tracking and reporting of commission-triggering actions — such as sales, registrations, or clicks — from affiliate links.

Accessibility
The degree that a website can be accessed by people with disabilities.

Animated GIF
A GIF file that is animated or has motion.

Apache
A popular Web server.

Bandwidth
A measure of how fast data can be transferred between two computers.

Banner
A graphic image that typically runs across a Web page or is positioned in a margin or other space reserved for ads. Banner ads are usually GIF images. In addition to adhering to size, many websites limit the size of the file to a certain number of bytes so that the file will display quickly. Most ads are animated GIFs, since animation has been shown to attract a larger percentage of user clicks.

Beyond the banner
This is the idea that, in addition to banner ads, there are other ways to use the Internet to communicate a marketing message. These include sponsoring a website or a particular feature on it; advertising in e-mail newsletters; co-branding with another company and its website; contest promotion; and, in general, finding new ways to engage and interact with the desired audience.

Behaviorally targeted advertising
A method of compiling data on Web visitors — such as surfing history, gender, age, and personal preferences

— to later target them with tailored ads.

Blacklist
Lists of URLs identified as spam URLs and therefore eliminated from comments and trackbacks on a blog.

Blammer
Blog spammer.

Blaudience
The audience of a blog.

Blawg
A blog about the law.

Bleg
A blog or blog post consisting of a request to readers of the blog for ideas; a combination of "blog" and "beg."

Blego
The self-worth of a blogger, as measured by the popularity of their blog; a combination of "blog" and "ego."

Blog
Short form for Weblog. A blog is a public website with posts or entries ordered, most often, with the most recent first. Blogs generally represent the personality of the author or reflect the purpose of the website that hosts the blog. It also means to maintain a blog by posting text, links, images, or other content using blogging software.

Blog client
An application that allows a blogger to post, edit, format, and perform a variety of functions for a blog or blogs without launching a browser.

Blog digest
A blog whose purpose is to summarize other blogs.

Blog feed
The XML-based file into which blog hosting software embeds a machine-readable version of a blog to allow it to be syndicated for distribution, often through RSS and Atom.

Blog hopping
To jump from one blog to another.

Blog mute
Someone who only occasionally blogs.

Blog roach
A commenter who rudely disagrees with all posted content.

Blog site
The location of a blog online.

Blog troll
A blogger who wants attention.

Blogathy
I do not want to post today and I do not care about doing it; a combination of "blog" and "apathy."

Blogger
A person who creates and posts to a blog.

Blogger.com
A popular — and free — blog hosting website.

Blogger bash
A party for bloggers.

Bloggies
Annual blogging awards.

Blogging
The act of posting on blogs.

Blogiversary
The anniversary of a blog's founding.

Blogography
The profile section of a blog, usually containing a biography of the blogger.

Blogoholic
A blogger addicted to blogging.

Blogophobia
Fear of blogs and blogging.

Blogorrhea
An unusually high volume output of articles on a blog; a blog entry with no real purpose, only posted for the sake of posting a blog entry.

Blogosphere
The Internet blogging community. The collective content of all blogs worldwide.

Blogroll
A list of blogs, usually placed in the sidebar of a blog, that reads as a list

of recommendations by the blogger of other blogs.

Blogsit
To maintain a blog while the blog's original or primary author is not available; like house-sitting.

Blogsite
A website that combines blog feeds from a number of different sources, including non-blog sources.

Blogsnob
A blogger that is unwilling to acknowledge comments on a blog from anyone outside of his or her circle of friends.

Blogspot
Hosting service for blogs operated by Blogger.com.

Blogstipation
Writer's block for bloggers.

BlogThis!
Allows a blogger to blog the entry they are reading.

Blogvert
A blog ad.

Blogvertising
Advertising that appears on a blog.

Booked space
The number of ad views for an ad space that are currently sold out.

Brand, brand name, and branding

A brand is a product, service, or concept that is publicly distinguished from other products, services, or concepts so that it can be easily communicated and/or marketed. A brand name is the name of the distinctive product, service, or concept. Branding is the process of creating and disseminating the brand name.

Browser

Software used to view and locate websites on the World Wide Web.

Caching

In Internet advertising, the caching of pages in a cache server or the user's computer means that some ad views will not be known by the ad counting programs and is a source of concern. There are several techniques for telling the browser not to cache particular pages. On the other hand, specifying no caching for all pages may mean that users will find your site to be slower than you would like.

Campaign

A campaign consists of one or more ad groups. The ads in a given campaign share the same daily budget, language and location targeting, end dates, and distribution options.

Cascading Style Sheet (CSS)

A technology used to control the presentation and layout of a Web page.

Client-side

Applications or software that are downloaded and run by the user's Web browser rather than on the Web server.

Click

A visitor interaction with an advertisement.

Click rate

The click rate is the percentage of ad views that resulted in click-throughs. Although there is visibility and branding value in ad views that do not result in a click-through, this value is difficult to measure.

Click stream

A recorded path of the pages a user requested in going through one or more websites. Click stream information can help website owners understand how visitors are using their site and which pages are getting the most use. It can help advertisers understand how users get to the client's pages, what pages they look at, and how they go about ordering a product.

Click-through

A click-through is what is counted by the sponsoring site as a result of an ad click. In practice, click and click-through tend to be used interchangeably. A click-through, however, seems to imply that the user actually received the page. A few advertisers are willing to pay only for click-throughs rather than for ad impressions.

Click-through rate (CTR)
The percentage of how many times users click on an ad divided by how many times your ad has been shown.

Co-branding
Co-branding on the Web often means two websites, website sections, or website features displaying their logos, and thus their brands, together so that the viewer considers the site or feature to be a joint enterprise.

Common Gateway Interface (CGI)
Technology that allows a Web browser to communicate with a program on the Web server.

Content Management System (CMS)
A collection of tools designed to allow the creation, modification, organization, and removal of information from a website.

Conversion rate
The percentage of site visitors who respond to the desired goal of an ad campaign compared with the total number of people who see the ad campaign. The goal may be, for example, convincing readers to become subscribers, encouraging customers to buy something, or enticing prospective customers from another site with an ad.

Cookie
A small text file downloaded to a user's computer that can be used to track user activity on a website or store user information about a visitor.

Cost-per-action (CPA)
What an advertiser pays for each visitor that takes some specifically defined action in response to an ad beyond simply clicking on it. For example, a visitor might visit an advertiser's site and request to be subscribed to their newsletter.

Cost-per-click (CPC)
The amount of money an advertiser will pay to a site each time a user clicks on an ad or link.

Cost-per-lead (CPL)
This is a more specific form of cost-per-action in which a visitor provides enough information at the advertiser's site — or in interaction with a rich media ad — to be used as a sales lead. Note that you can estimate cost-per-lead regardless of how you pay for the ad; in other words, buying on a pay-per-lead basis is not required to calculate the cost-per-lead.

Cost-per-sale (CPS)
Pricing based on the number of sales transactions an ad generates.

Cost-per-thousand (CPM)
Cost per thousand ad impressions; an industry standard measure for selling ads on websites. This measure is taken from print advertising. The "M" is taken from the Roman numeral for "thousand."

Creative
Ad agencies and buyers often refer to ad banners and other forms of created advertising as "the creative."

Since the creative requires creative inspiration and skills that may come from a third party, it often does not arrive until late in the preparation for a new campaign launch.

Demographics
Data about the size and characteristics of a population or audience; for example, gender, age group, income group, purchasing history, and personal preferences.

Domain name
A unique name that identifies one or more IP addresses.

Double opt-in
A message is automatically sent to the person who has been signed up for a mailing list, asking whether they want to be added to the list. Unless they actively reply positively, their name is wiped from the list, and they never get another message.

Download
The transfer of files from a remote machine — or Web server — to a user's machine.

E-commerce
The process of buying, selling, and transferring money through the Internet.

Expression Web
A Web page authoring application from Microsoft.

Filtering
The immediate analysis by a program of a user Web page request in order to determine which ad or ads to return in the requested page. A Web page request can tell a Website or its ad server whether it fits a certain characteristic, such as coming from a particular company's address or that the user is using a particular level of browser. The Web ad server can respond accordingly.

File size
The amount of space that a file takes up when stored on disk measured in bytes, kilobytes (K), megabytes (MB), or gigabytes (GB).

File Transfer Protocol (FTP)
The most common way of transferring the files from one computer to another across a network.

Firewall
Software designed to protect networks from unauthorized access.

Flame
To post a hostile comment or personal attack on a blog.

Flame war
A series of flames going back and forth on a blog.

Flash
A vector-based, multimedia technology that can be embedded in HTML pages, typically in the form of animations. Entire websites may be developed in Flash.

Flickr
A digital photo-sharing website and Web services suite.

Fold
"Above the fold," a term borrowed from print media, refers to an ad that is viewable as soon as the Web page arrives. You do not have to scroll down or sideways to see it. Since screen resolution can affect what is immediately viewable, it is good to know whether the website's audience tends to set its resolution at 640 by 480 pixels or at 800 by 600.

FrontPage
A Web page authoring application from Microsoft.

Google bomb
To intentionally insert words or phrases into as many blogs as possible to increase the ranking on the Google search engine.

Group blog
A blog maintained by two or more bloggers.

GNU Image Manipulation Program (GIMP)
An open source graphics creation and manipulation application.

Graphic Interchange Format (GIF)
A popular image file format.

Harvesting
Using automated scripts known as "bots" to identify the correct syntax of e-mail addresses on Web pages and newsgroup posts and then copy the addresses to a list.

Hit
The sending of a single file, whether an HTML file, an image, an audio file, or another file type.

Home Page
The first page a user sees when visiting a website.

Hypertext Markup Language (HTML)
The language of the Web. Web pages are written in HTML.

Hypertext Transfer Protocol (HTTP)
The protocol used to transfer Web pages on the Internet.

Impression
According to the "Basic Advertising Measures" from FAST, an ad industry group, an impression is "the count of a delivered basic advertising unit from an ad distribution point." Impressions are how most Web advertising is sold, and the cost is quoted in terms of the cost per thousand impressions (CPM).

Insertion order
An insertion order is a formal, printed order to run an ad campaign. Typically, the insertion order identifies the campaign name; the website receiving the order and the planner or buyer giving the order; the individual ads to be run or who will provide them; the ad sizes; the campaign beginning and end dates; the

CPM; the total cost; discounts to be applied; and reporting requirements and possible penalties or stipulations relative to the failure to deliver the impressions.

Internet
A worldwide collection of computers all connected together to form a huge network.

Internet Information Services (IIS)
A Web server created by Microsoft.

Internet Protocol (IP) address
A unique number assigned to each machine connected to the Internet to uniquely identify it.

Internet Service Provider (ISP)
Entity which provides users with connectivity to the Internet.

JavaScript
JavaScript is a client-side scripting language used to create dynamic Web pages. JavaScript should not be confused with Java, the full featured programming language.

Joint Photographic Experts Group (JPG or JPEG)
A popular image file format.

"Junk" e-mail
E-mail messages sent to multiple recipients who did not request it and are not in the right target audience.

Keyword
A word or phrase that a user types into a search engine when looking for specific information.

Keyword matching options
There are four types of keyword matching: broad matching, exact matching, phrase matching, and negative keywords. These options help you refine your ad targeting on Google search pages.

Keyword searches
Searches for specific text that identifies unwanted e-mail.

Link
An object on a Web page that connects the user to another section of the page, the website, or the Internet. Links are normally a different color to stand out from the rest of the text on a page.

Link baiting
Writing good content with the sole purpose of getting it linked from multiple sites.

Linux
An open source operating system.

Lurker
A reader of a blog who never comments.

Macintosh (Mac)
An Apple Macintosh computer.

Markup

The process in which text and other data is converted into Web pages by using HTML tags.

Maximum cost-per-click (max CPC)

With keyword-targeted ad campaigns, you choose the maximum cost-per-click (max CPC) you are willing to pay.

Maximum cost-per-impression (max CPM)

With site-targeted ad campaigns, you choose the maximum cost per thousand impressions (max CPM) you are willing to pay.

Media broker

Since it is often not efficient for an advertiser to select every website it wants to put ads on, media brokers aggregate sites for advertisers and their media planners and buyers, based on demographics and other factors.

Media buyer

A media buyer, usually at an advertising agency, works with a media planner to allocate the money provided for an advertising campaign among specific print or online media — such as magazines, TV, or websites — and then calls and places the advertising orders. On the Web, placing the order often involves requesting proposals and negotiating the final cost.

Meta tags

Hidden HTML directions for Web browsers or search engines. They include important information such as the title of each page, relevant keywords describing site content, and the description of the site that shows up when a search engine returns a search.

MP3

The file extension for MPEG. These files can be embedded into website to provide audio.

Newsgroups

Topic-specific discussion and information exchange forums open to interested parties.

Non-permission based e-mail marketing

An e-mail message which is or appears to be sent to multiple recipients who did not request it, even though they may be in the right target market

Open source

Programs that allow the source code to be distributed, thereby allowing programmers to alter and change the original software.

Opt-in e-mail

E-mail containing information or advertising that users explicitly request — or opt — to receive. Often, a website invites its visitors to fill out forms identifying subject or product categories that interest them and about which they are willing to receive e-mail from anyone who might send it. The website sells the names, with explicit or implicit permission from their visitors, to a company that specializes in collecting mailing lists that represent different interests. Whenever the mailing list company sells its lists to advertisers, the website is paid a small amount for each name that it generated for the list. You can sometimes identify opt-in e-mail because it starts with a statement that tells you that you have previously agreed to receive such messages.

Page impressions

A measure of how many times a Web page has been displayed to visitors. Often used as a crude way of counting the visitors to a site.

Page requests

A measure of the number of pages that visitors have viewed in a day. Often used as a crude way of indicating the popularity of a website.

Paid search

The area of keyword, contextual advertising, often called pay-per-click.

Page view

A common metric for measuring how many times a complete page is visited.

Paint Shop Pro Photo X3

A powerful graphics application.

Pay-per-click (PPC)

In pay-per-click advertising, the advertiser pays a certain amount for each click-through to the advertiser's website. The amount paid per click-through is arranged at the time of the insertion order and varies considerably. Higher pay-per-click rates recognize that there may be some "no-click" branding value as well as click-through value provided.

Pay-per-lead (PPL)

In pay-per-lead advertising, the advertiser pays for each sales lead generated. For example, an advertiser might pay for every visitor that clicked on a site and then filled out a form.

Pay-per-sale (PPS)

Pay-per-sale is not customarily used for ad buys. It is, however, the customary way to pay websites that participate in affiliate programs, such as those of Amazon.com and Beyond.com.

Pay-per-view (PPV)

Since this is the prevalent type of ad buying arrangement at larger websites, this term tends to be used only when comparing this most prevalent method with pay-per-click and other methods.

Permalink

The unique URL of a single post on a blog, used when anyone wants to link specifically to a post rather than to the most recently updated page of a blog.

Photoshop
The industry standard graphics application.

PHP Hypertext Preprocessor (PHP)
A server-side programming language designed for Web programming.

Ping
Used to notify other blog tracking tools of updates, changes, and track-backs.

Portable Networks Graphics (PNG)
A lossless, compressible file format for images on the Web.

Pixel
The smallest point of light that a monitor can produce.

Post
A single unit of content on a blog, usually consisting of at least a title and text. A blog is made up of a collection of posts.

Post scheduling
Using blogging software to write posts and schedule them for publishing in the future.

Practical Extraction and Reporting Language (Perl)
A server-side, interpreted programming language commonly used with CGI.

Proof of performance
Some advertisers may want proof that the ads they have bought have actually run and that click-through

figures are accurate. In print media, tear sheets taken from a publication prove that an ad was run. On the Web, there is no industry-wide practice for proof of performance. Some buyers rely on the integrity of the media broker and the website. The ad buyer often checks the website to determine the ads are actually running. Most buyers require weekly figures during a campaign. A few want to look directly at the figures, viewing the ad server or Website reporting tool.

Relational Database Management System (RDBMS)
A database management system that allows data arranged in a tabular form to be related to data in other tables via common fields.

Reporting template
Although the media have to report data to ad agencies, media planners, and buyers during and at the end of each campaign, no standard report is yet available. FAST, the ad industry coalition, is working on a proposed standard reporting template that would enable reporting to be consistent.

Return on Investment (ROI)
The bottom line on how successful an ad or campaign was in terms of what the returns (often sales revenue) were for the money expended (invested).

Rich media

Rich media is advertising that contains perceptual or interactive elements more elaborate than the usual banner ad. Today, the term is often used for banner ads with popup menus that let the visitor select a particular page to link to on the advertiser's site. Rich media ads are generally more challenging to create and to serve. Some early studies have shown that rich media ads tend to be more effective than ordinary animated banner ads.

RSS

Really Simple Syndication. A method of describing news or other Web content that is available for "feeding" (distribution or syndication) from an online publisher to Web users.

RSS aggregator

Software or service that automatically check a series of RSS feeds for new items on an ongoing basis, making it possible to keep track of changes to multiple websites in real time through one application.

RSS feed

The file that contains the latest updates to an RSS-equipped page.

RSS publisher

A Web server that publishes RSS feeds for retrieval by aggregators and RSS readers.

RSS reader

An application that reads many RSS feeds on behalf of one or more RSS subscriber.

Run-of-network

A run-of-network ad is one that is placed to run on all sites within a given network of sites. Ad sales firms handle run-of-network insertion orders in such a way as to optimize results for the buyer consistent with higher priority ad commitments.

Run-of-site

A run-of-site ad is one that is placed to rotate on all non-featured ad spaces on a site. CPM rates for run-of-site ads are usually less than rates for specially-placed ads or sponsorships.

Screen reader

Software that reads the content of the screen aloud to a user.

Search Engine Marketing (SEM)

Promoting a website through a search engine. This most often refers to targeting prospective customers by buying relevant keywords or phrases.

Search engine

A special site that provides an index of other website addresses listed according to key words and descriptions in the original page.

Search Engine Optimization (SEO)

Making a website more attractive to search engines, resulting in a higher page rank.

Secure Shell (SSH)
A secure way of transferring information between computers on a network.

Server-side
Programs residing on the server that a user can interact with through the CGI or more directly through the Web server.

Spam
An unwanted e-mail message sent in bulk to thousands of addresses to try to advertise something.

Spambot
A program designed to collect, or harvest, e-mail addresses from the Internet in order to build mailing lists for sending unsolicited e-mail.

Spam posts
Messages posted to e-mail discussion groups, chat rooms, or bulletin boards that are off-topic or distinctly promotional.

Splash page
A splash page is a preliminary page that precedes the regular home page of a website and usually promotes a particular site feature or provides advertising.

Sping
A ping sent from a splog to make recipients think content has been updated; a combination of "spam" and "ping."

Splog
A blog composed of spam; a combination of "spam" and "blog."

Sponsor
Depending on the context, a sponsor simply means an advertiser who has sponsored an ad and, by doing so, has also helped sponsor or sustain the website itself.

Syndication
The distribution a news article through an RSS or Atom feed.

Targeting
Purchasing ad space on websites that match audience and campaign objective requirements. TechTarget (www.techtarget.com), with over 20 Websites targeted to special information technology audiences, is an example of an online publishing business built to enable advertising targeting.

Trackback
A protocol that allows a blogger to link to posts, often on other blogs, that relate to a selected subject. Blogging software that supports trackback includes a "Trackback URL" with each post that displays other blogs that have linked to it.

Trackback ping
A ping that signals a blog's server that a post on that blog has been commented upon.

Trackback spam
Sping sent by means of the trackback system.

User session

A user session occurs when someone with a unique address enters or re-enters a website each day, or some other specified period. A user session is sometimes determined by counting only those users that have not re-entered the site within the past 20 minutes, or a similar period. User session figures are sometimes used, somewhat incorrectly, to indicate "visits" or "visitors" per day. User sessions are a better indicator of total site activity than "unique visitors," since they indicate frequency of use.

Universal Resource Locator and Uniform Resource Identifier (URL and URI)

A string of characters used to identify a resource on the Internet. Commonly called the domain name.

Unix

An operating system commonly used for Web servers.

Unique visitor

A unique visitor is someone with a unique address who is entering a website for the first time that day, or some other specified period. Thus, a visitor that returns within the same day is not counted twice. A unique visitors count tells you how many different people there are in your audience during the time period, but not how much they used the site during the period.

Upload

The process of moving files from a local computer to a remote computer.

User session

A user session is someone with a unique address that enters or reenters a website each day, or some other specified period.

View

A view refers to either an ad view or a page view. There can be multiple ad views per page view. View counting should consider that a small percentage of users choose to turn the graphics off and not display the images in their browser.

Visit

A visit is a Web user with a unique address entering a website at some page for the first time that day, or for the first time in a lesser time period. The number of visits is roughly equivalent to the number of different people that visit a site. This term is ambiguous unless the user defines it, since it could mean a user session or it could mean a unique visitor that day.

Web Accessibility Initiative (WAI)

A W3C initiative aimed at improving the accessibility of the Web.

Web Content Accessibility Guidelines (WCAG)

A set of guidelines to make a website accessible.

Web design
The selection and coordination of available components to create the layout and structure of a Web page.

Web designer
A person who designs Web pages.

Web developer
A person who performs programming for a website.

Weblog
Longer, alternative form of blog. An online diary listing thoughts on a specific topic, often in reverse chronological order.

WebPlus X2 Website Maker
A Web page authoring application from Serif.

Web server
The computer — and software — that hosts a website.

Website
A collection of Web pages available on the World Wide Web through a Web server.

White lists
A list of approved e-mail addresses that an e-mail blocking program will allow messages to be received from.

World Wide Web Consortium (W3C)
Developer of specifications and guidelines for the Web.

eXtensible HyperText Markup Language (XHTML)
This next-generation language uses the same expressions and basic code as HTML, but also complies with the XML standard. It will help you to create Websites that contain more features, functionality, and flexibility than ones created using HTML.

Yield
The percentage of clicks versus impressions on an ad within a specific page.

Author

Bruce C. Brown is an award-winning author of more than ten books as well as an active duty Coast Guard officer, where he has served in a variety of assignments for more than 26 years. Bruce is married to Vonda and has three sons: Dalton, Jordan, and Colton. His previous works include:

- *How to Use the Internet to Advertise, Promote and Market Your Business or Website with Little or No Money* — Winner: The National 2007 Indie Excellence Book Awards Business Finalist, 2007 Independent Publisher Book Awards Computer/Internet Bronze, ForeWord Magazine's Book of the Year Awards Finalist, USA Best Books Awards 2007 Business: Marketing & Advertising Finalist, Library Journal: Best Business Book 2006 Marketing/Branding

- *The Ultimate Guide to Search Engine Marketing: Pay Per Click Advertising Secrets Revealed* — Winner: USA Best Books Awards 2007 Business: Marketing & Advertising

- *The Complete Guide to E-mail Marketing: How to Create Successful, Spam-free Campaigns to Reach Your Target Audience and Increase Sales*

- *Complete Guide to Google Advertising: Including Tips, Tricks, & Strategies to Create a Winning Advertising Plan*

- *The Secret Power of Blogging: How to Promote and Market Your Business, Organization, or Cause With Free Blogs* — Winner: Florida Publishers Association 2009 President's Book Award (Silver Medal - Business

- *Returning From the War on Terrorism: What Every Veteran Needs to Know to Receive Your Maximum Benefits*

- *The Complete Guide to Affiliate Marketing on the Web: How to Use and Profit from Affiliate Marketing Programs*

- *Google Income: How Anyone of Any Age, Location, and/or Background Can Build a Highly Profitable Online Business with Google*

- *How to Open and Operate a Financially Successful Web-Based Business*

- *How to Build Your Own Web Site With Little or No Money The Complete Guide for Business and Personal Use*

He holds degrees from Charter Oak State College and the University of Phoenix. He currently splits his time between Land O' Lakes, Florida and Miami, Florida.